DATE DUE

MAR 2 1 1997			
APR 2 6 1999			
APR 1 8 2002			
JNS			
MAR 2 2 2006			
OCT 1 0 2006			
WRS			
JUL 0 2 2007			
APR 0 3 2009			

Demco

MERCEDES-BENZ

by W. Robert Nitske

Motorbooks International
Publishers & Wholesalers Inc.
Minneapolis

Books by W. Robert Nitske

The Complete Mercedes Story (Macmillan, New York, 1955)

The Amazing Porsche and Volkswagen Story (Comet Press, New York, 1958)

Rudolf Diesel, Pioneer of the Age of Power (with Charles Wilson) (University of Oklahoma Press, Norman, 1965)

The Life of Wilhelm Conrad Röntgen, Discoverer of the X Ray (University of Arizona Press, Tucson, 1971)

Travels in North America, 1822-1824 (translation of exploration diary of Duke Paul Wilhelm of Württemberg) (University of Oklahoma Press, Norman, 1973)

Second Printing

*All illustrations, except where indicated,
are from the archives of Daimler-Benz A.G.*

Library of Congress Number: 74-22377
ISBN: 0-87938-021-7

Designed by Ad/Graphics
Printed by Shandling Lithographing Co., Tucson, Arizona

Library of Congress Cataloging in Publication Data
Nitske, W. Robert
Mercedes-Benz 300 SL.
1. Mercedes automobile.   I. Title.
TL215.M4N52   629.22'22   74-22377

World-wide distributors:
MOTORBOOKS INTERNATIONAL
Minneapolis, Minnesota, U.S.A.

Contents

The Daimler-Benz Museum is a rich depository of magnificent automobiles and exciting engines built by the company. It offers a fascinating insight into the imposing heritage of our subject car.

Das Daimler-Benz Museum ist ein reiches Lager von prachtvollen Automobilen und Motoren der Gesellschaft. Es bietet einen bezauberten Einblick dar in die grossartige Erbschaft unseres Subjekt Wagen.

An Illustrious Heritage

Ever since automobiles have been built, a truly outstanding model has appeared periodically to startle and to capture the imagination of enthusiasts the world over.

Smaller manufacturers have been generally the developers of such exotic cars. However, over the years, the large company which had more than its share of such unusual automobiles is also the oldest one in existence, and none has ever even approached the eminence of Daimler-Benz.

The unorthodox construction of his original three-wheeled steel carriage in 1885 had earned Karl Benz the admiration of inventors, but not the needed economic support of the general public. The equally advanced two-cylinder steel vehicle of Gottlieb Daimler of 1889 did not fare much better. The public preferred the orthodox and long familiar style of the cumbersome horse carriage.

When in 1901 the first sparkling white Mercedes automobile replaced the former Daimler models, the pioneer automotive engineer Wilhelm Maybach had created what is considered the archtype design of automobile for other manufacturers to follow. Ever since then the name Mercedes meant mechanically advanced automobiles of exceptional excellence.

Victorious racing cars had been built during 1900 to 1910 not only by Benz in Mannheim but also by Daimler in Stuttgart. These ponderous (1900, 1903, 1907, 1908, and 1909) Benz racers were consistently successful machines, winning races and setting world speed records, but the Mercedes cars (of 1901, 1903, 1906, and 1908) were even better. They established new records more frequently in the early years of the century. The 1908 Mercedes won the prestigious French Grand Prix with Benz in second place. In

 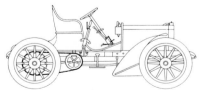 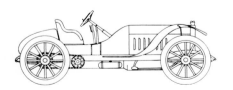 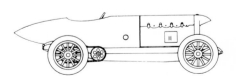

1914 Mercedes startled the automotive world by winning a triple victory at Lyons.

In 1911, the imaginative designer and engineer Hans Nibel created the fabulous Blitzen Benz, the record-breaking racing car with the huge 21.5-liter engine. And ten years later, the unique Benz aerodynamically rear-engined racing car, the Tropfenwagen, designed by Edmund Rumpler and Max Wagner, caused a sensation.

As a consequence of the merger of the two companies, Daimler and Benz, the engineering department came under the direction of Max Wagner and Ferdinand Porsche, two amazingly ingenious and innovative automotive engineers. The solid S model of 1927 was the first of a remarkable series of singularly successful automobiles which earned the highest praise of automobile experts anywhere. Further developments were the legendary SS, SSK, and finally SSKL models.

The Golden Era of automobile racing in 1934 saw the 750-kilogram Formula 4-liter, 453-horsepower Mercedes M 25, designed by Hans Nibel and Max Wagner, pitted against the formidable P-Wagen of Ferdinand Porsche. Then followed in 1936 the incredible 6-liter, 645-horsepower M 125, for which Dr. Rohr was partly responsible after the death of Nibel.

When in 1938 a new formula, allowing a displacement of only three liters, became effective, Rudolf Uhlenhaut joined the engineering directorate, under the leadership of Max Wagner, to develop the M 163. The twelve-cylinder engine had a supercharger and developed an amazing 485 horsepower, giving the racing car a maximum speed of 164 miles per hour. When in late 1938 the 1.5-liter, 278-horsepower M 165 was created, Uhlenhaut headed this engineering group. In the years 1938 and 1939, Mercedes cars won 12 out of 16 international Grand Prix races against strong Auto-Union competition.

This, then, was the marvelous Mercedes-Benz heritage of the 300 SL.

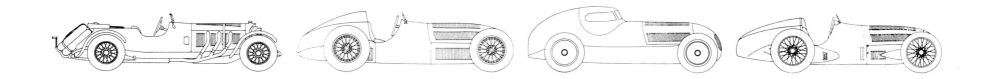

Our Personal Involvement

It was a memorable trip, our first trip to Europe in the spring of 1956. From Antwerp we took a train to Stuttgart where at the Daimler-Benz factory we were received most cordially by Prince Albrecht von Urach, chief of the foreign press section.

A year or two before, we had had considerable correspondence with him regarding much detailed information on a thousand and one items for our book, *The Complete Mercedes Story,* which was first published in 1955. Now we met personally for the first time. Soon we became good friends.

We were given the Small Red Carpet treatment, as Prince von Urach called it, at that and subsequent visits. This included meals in the elegant dining rooms for company officials and their special guests, at least one gala dinner at some extra fine restaurant with the general manager and top officials, especially escorted tours of all factory facilities, and so on. It did not include a special line-up exhibiting the entire production from trucks, buses, to all models of passenger vehicles. That was the Big Red Carpet treatment, given only to really important persons.

On our visit we dined with Fritz Könecke, the general director, Fritz Nallinger, the chief engineer, and Dr. Wills, the production chief, at our table. Other notables present were Artur Keser, chief of the Press section, and Prince Albrecht von Urach, also Alfred Neubauer, racing director, and Rudolf Uhlenhaut, engineer in charge of passenger car development, and several others.

The tour of the manufacturing plant at Untertürkheim with von Urach was of great interest to us, but the special testing room where an engine for a 300 SL was on the stand with flaming exhaust being run at 6,000 revolutions per minute, at least for some of the six hours, proved the noisiest and most fascinating area. The next day von Urach took us to Sindelfingen, where after a thorough visit of the assembly plant we took delivery of our new car.

As he handed the keys and necessary papers over to us and we took official possession of our silver grey coupe with red leather interior, I could not help but clearly see in my mind the youngster of many years before who so admired a white SS sports car and considered ownership of such a car an absolutely unattainable dream.

That afternoon we drove to our hotel after having practiced driving a bit on the spacious factory grounds. We knew all of the essential buttons and switches and were well aware of the awesome power of the engine.

The next day — it was a fine Sunday — we drove to the nearby historic university town of Tübingen, parked the car on the main

Prince von Urach handing us the papers for our car
Fürst von Urach gibt uns die Papiere für unseren Wagen

street, and went to eat dinner close by. After the meal, we walked to the area where our 300 SL was parked and saw some hundred students surrounding it. We wondered if we had left something on and blown up the car, or what could be wrong. Getting closer, however, we found the young people just crowding around it to look the car over closely. At that time there were only twelve such cars in all of Germany, and eight of them were in Stuttgart, driven mainly by factory executives, nearly all of whom are sports car-minded and try to emulate Caracciola, under the guise of testing their product.

After enjoying our spectators' enthusiasm for a while we got through the crowd to the car and having opened the doors we were confronted with the delicate maneuver of having my wife Betty get into her seat without embarassment. We succeeded fairly well that early time.

I got into the driver's seat and after diligently trying to recall just what buttons to push in what sequence without appearing to be a foolish novice, started the car successfully on the first try. I blipped the engine several times briefly, then put my foot down to let it really roar, to the great delight of the students, and then managed to get it under way in a fairly reasonable manner. I felt like Caracciola myself. He could not have had a more interested and fervent audience after winning a race on the Nürburgring.

That year we covered the Grand Prix races for *Motoracing* and thus attended nearly all of them on the continent. The Monaco Grand Prix, always a gay affair, was the opening event. Practicing in the streets begins usually at six o'clock in the morning, and therefore sleep is severely curtailed during those days. But the excitement and glamor is as great, if indeed not greater, than at any of the other races.

At the Nürburgring we tested our skill and the power of our new car, when after the actual race the circuit was open to us. We failed quite miserably in setting any records. In fact, it took us about twice the time to lap the course as it took Juan Manuel Fangio and his Mercedes-Benz racing sports car a year or two later. However, I was proud to have hit the groove of the carrousel exactly right, a not-too-easy maneuver for a novice driver.

At the fast Francorchamps course we did not even time our laps, being afraid that the then victorious Ferrari cars would have looked even better in comparison than they actually were. We stayed at the hotel where most of the drivers were and got to know most of them quite well. We took our meals with the Maserati contingent. And so it went that season with the Grand Prix circus.

Often our 300 SL so stunned the appointed guards that they freely allowed us to park it with the private vehicles of the drivers in the especially reserved sections. We did not at all mind being taken for a participant.

When visiting Modena, the Maserati factory test driver Guerrino Bertocchi tried to convince me that their new three-liter model was superior to the Mercedes, but he succeeded only in scaring me almost to death when I rode with him to Maranello. He proved that he was a better driver than I was, by a wide margin.

Enzio Ferrari was kind enough not only to grant me an interview, a concession he did not often make to members of the press, but offered me a berlinetta to drive and showed me around his factory.

In Scotland we barely missed showing our car to the Duke of Edinburgh, who surely would have been an enthusiastic observer of it, although understandably he drove then an Aston-Martin sports car.

Our 300 SL had immensely assisted us in granting many entrees of generally closed areas, besides being terrific fun to drive. Open roads were its millieu, but we also managed all right getting through the badly battered remains of the Maginot Line where roads were almost nonexistent.

Then we put the car on the *Liberté* and sailed for New York. From there we drove across the country to our home in Santa Barbara, California. But it was not a thrilling experience. The restrictive speed laws did not allow us to really drive the car in the manner it should have deserved.

photo by the author

Author's wife Betty with car at home in Santa Barbara
Des Verfasser's Frau Betty mit dem Wagen zu Hause in Santa Barbara

photo by the author

Author sitting on entry panel of car with door open
Der Verfasser auf dem Einsteigesitz mit der offenen Tür

9

Especially pleasing was the memory of some really wonderful driving experiences in Europe. Not only on the closed racing circuits but on public roads in many countries we could test our skill and the excellent roadability of the 300 SL. On a drive from Frankfurt to Hamburg we averaged a bit over ninety miles an hour. When we finally stopped, the surrounding solid ground kept rushing toward us for some time. Still, it was a genuine thrill to drive a superb car at good speed for a sustained period. The only hairy episodes we encountered were when on an appreciable incline we passed a slow-traveling truck spewing black exhaust onto the inside passing lane where a slightly faster cabin roller might be attempting to pass the truck. That would have been a disaster for us all. But our brakes were excellent, and slower traffic rapidly moved out of our way when we blinked our lights. In fact, it often seemed that those drivers smiled at our faster car, perhaps most enviously. Generally it was perfectly safe and greatly enjoyable, even exhilarating, to drive fast on the still fairly good autobahns.

Ever since European cars were brought into the United States, soon after World War II, we have written about them, for periodicals and newspapers. And since the Mercedes-Benz Club of America was founded in 1955, we have contributed stories, historical articles, and a regular page on the European Auto Scene for the club's publication.

The first edition of the book, *The Complete Mercedes Story,* and others, were before that time. Prior to the expansion of activities of Mercedes-Benz of North America — and when Count Marcus Clary helped us so graciously in these matters — we have relied for material on the factory people.

And so, over the years, we have visited Stuttgart and Daimler-Benz repeatedly and have maintained most friendly relations with all of the fine persons with whom we have had contacts over there.

Once director of Archives and Museum, Friedrich Schildberger now writes company and automobile history, as did Alfred Neubauer — but of a more personal nature. The new Archives and Museum head, Klaus Huegel, has also been helpful to us in securing material for this book. The new Press Chief who followed Artur Keser, an old acquaintance from our reporting days, Günther Molter, has given us equally invaluable assistance, as had Dirk H. Strassl, who took the position of our good friend Fürst Albrecht von Urach. Frau Witzel has made literally hundreds of copies of the thousands of photographs in her charge. We thank them all, most gratefully, for their aid in getting this book together.

Our closest friend there, Fürst von Urach has passed on, as has Wolfgang Lambrecht. General Director Fritz Könecke has retired long ago, and so has Chief Engineer Fritz Nallinger, and Karl Kling, who headed the competition department after the retirement of Neubauer. And Rudolf Uhlenhaut now sails his power boat on the Mediterranean, far different from the frenzied activities of the racing and development department in Untertürkheim.

Seemingly, time rushes on, in high gear. And we hurry to set down our own impressions and remembrances along with history in books, just like this one.

The Idea Conceived

Concentrated, massive bombing attacks in 1945 had destroyed nearly three-fourths of the Stuttgart-Untertürkheim factory. And the Sindelfingen plant was almost a complete loss.

The next year, Daimler-Benz built, under supervision of the victorious Allies, their first post-war trucks, the L 3500 model. Utility vehicles were sorely needed to assist in cleaning up of rubble and in the vast rebuilding tasks.

In 1947, a total of 381 passenger vehicles were assembled, but the following year 4,204 automobiles of the old 170 V model were produced. The company was on the road to recovery from the tremendous devastation of the war.

As Alfred Neubauer remembered it, during 1950 General Director Wilhelm Haspel discussed with him the possibility of participation in racing events to let the world know that Daimler-Benz was back in business. Two old racing cars, the M 163 of 1939, were available. No new cars were to be built for that purpose. These cars seemed to the race director really not serious contenders and were certainly not sufficiently competitive, but they promised a beginning. When two similar cars were located in Berlin, the owners insisted on a steep price. They asked for brand new 170 sedans, exceedingly costly when automobiles were sold at a high premium, the canny Neubauer felt. But he needed the cars and paid.

Plans were formulated to participate in the Argentine Grand Prix in February 1951. But the victorious Mercedes racing team of former years could not be fully recreated.

Rudolf Caracciola, who lived at Lake Lugano, Switzerland, and Hermann Lang, who had spent years in a prisoner of war camp in Russia, came to join Neubauer. Manfred von Brauchitsch had, after many personal difficulties, gone to the Eastern sector to become a prominent sports figure in the government there. A replacement was needed, for the team should consist of at least three good drivers. A former customer service engineer of the company, Karl Kling, was chosen. He had been quite successful in driving two-liter BMW and Veritas racing cars in these earliest post-war years.

Men and machines went to the Nürburgring for practice. Most disappointingly, lap times remained at over ten minutes, highly unpromising indeed.

When Alfred Neubauer suggested that perhaps the drivers had become tired over the years, Caratsch replied that the problem was the tiredness of the cars instead. Still, the decision to go to Argentina stood.

Then Caracciola refused to go because of the apparent hopelessness of their competitive position. Neubauer had to look about for his replacement. The race director remembered having heard of a new driver, just arrived on European circuits, the 39-year-old Juan Manuel Fangio, who had competed in six important races and amazingly won them all against the best Italian seasoned drivers. And Fangio was from Argentina.

But Rudolf Caracciola was correct in his estimate. The Buenos Aires Grand Prix races, run in two separate heats of 97.65 miles each on the 2.17-mile Costanera circuit, were won by Froilan Gonzales, driving his 2-liter Ferrari at 62.45 miles per hour, ahead of Lang and Fangio. The second race, a week later, on February 25, was again won by Gonzales at a speed of 62.21 miles per hour, ahead of Kling and Lang.

Although Fangio had made the fastest lap in 2 minutes, 2.2 sec-

The six-cylinder Mercedes-Benz 300 sedan

Die Sechszylinder Mercedes-Benz Limousine Typ 300

onds, at 72.4 miles per hour, the actual race results were conclusive proof that the old cars were not capable of victory against the more modern racing cars of Ferrari. Still, they beat the Maserati and Alfa Romeo cars.

These 1951 South American races marked the last public appearance of the Mercedes racing cars of 1939. The old 4.5-liter formula remained in effect for two more years, until 1953. Beginning in 1954, a new formula specifying 2.5-liter displacement, or 750 cubic centimeter supercharged engines, would take effect. Thus, Daimler-Benz officials realized that the two remaining years would hardly allow sufficient time for the development, testing, and finally successful competing with a newly-designed racing car. They would have to wait three years before they could again seriously compete with new and modern cars.

To enter a crash program could not be financially justified either. Then, Chief Engineer Fritz Nallinger suggested that a sports car be developed using the existing 300 engine. This car could be entered in sports car races until the new construction of a regular Grand Prix car could be seriously considered.

Neubauer, together with Hermann Lang and Karl Kling, had visited Le Mans to personally investigate the current entrants in that 24-hour classic event. Upon their return, a conference on the proposed sports car was held with Rudolf Uhlenhaut, chief of the testing department and himself a most competent racing driver. Karl Wilfert was chief of the department for body styling and design. Designers Franz Roller, Ludwig Kraus, and Manfred Lorscheidt were also present at that meeting.

Uhlenhaut and Joseph Müller of the construction department got busy with plans for such a vehicle. But because of the relatively heavy weight of the available engine and drive components, the chassis and body would have to be of unusually light construction. Uhlenhaut had previously designed a small rear-engined competition car when soon after the war he worked briefly with an engineering section of the British occupation army. He had then used tubes of varying sizes, and now suggested that tubes again be utilized for the frame construction.

Designing the light metal tubular chassis, they ran into difficulties in fitting doors to this revolutionary construction without adversely affecting its stability. Eventually, it was decided to cut part of the roof open to provide adequate doors.

"There is no comparable solid frame," Rudolf Uhlenhaut said later in an interview, "to that of the lattice-type tubular frame of the 300 SL, not even in the passenger cars where weight does not play such a significant role as in sports cars. Naturally we need certain experiences in the dimensions of the tubular pipes and in the best connection of the various tubes to one another. But the idea of developing a frame whose tubular units are dependent only on pressure and pull stresses has been well carried out in practice.

"The weight of the frame for the car is about 70 kilograms (154 pounds), more than enticing for the designer. And the cost of construction is not high, either, because simple steel tubes are utilized. More problematic is the insulation of the chassis against heat and dust. With regular frames, this is a rather simple matter. The height dimension of the tubular frame is also a factor and the use of regular doors is impossible," Uhlenhaut concluded.

At a New Year's celebration of company officials, General Director Wilhelm Haspel announced that the Mercedes Star would again be represented at international racing events with the newly-conceived 300 SL sports car. The announcement was received with jubilation by all present, Neubauer happily observed.

Sadly, soon thereafter, on January 6, 1952, Haspel suffered a fatal heart attack. Nevertheless, the decision was made to go ahead with the plans for the new sports car, despite the untimely death of its originator. For it was he who had wanted to enter racing again.

Years later when commenting on that decision to build the 300 SL sports cars and to enter competition with them, Fritz Nallinger said, "We wanted to open a small window and look at the international sports scene. With the 300 SL we could, under the then existing conditions, do that best and easiest."

Developing further the existing three-liter engine proved not too difficult a task. This engine was originally used in the prestigious 300 model, a limousine shown first at the Frankfurt Auto Show in

The author's elegant 300 S Coupe at home in Tucson

Das elegante 300 S Coupe des Verfassers zu Hause in Tucson

April 1951 and put into regular production in November of that year. That 3-liter six-cylinder engine, equipped with two Solex downdraft carburetors, developed 115 DIN horsepower at 4,600 revolutions per minute and had a compression ratio of 6.4 to 1. A further refinement of that engine was the type installed in the luxury 300 S model. This elegant and sporty vehicle, either as a coupe, open roadster, or convertible coupe, was presented to the public at the Paris Salon in October 1951 and was manufactured first in the early summer of 1952. The engine had three Solex carburetors, and with a compression ratio of 7.8 to 1, developed 150 DIN horsepower at 5,000 revolutions per minute. (This author was fortunate to purchase a similar wonderful show car — a beige gray coupe with green leather upholstery — and enjoyed driving it for over ten years and well over a hundred thousand miles.)

Uhlenhaut, Nallinger, and Scherenberg. Neubauer in rear
Die Herren Uhlenhaut, Nallinger, und Scherenberg. Neubauer dahinter

The earliest style — doors only in windows and roof
Die erste Ausführung — Türen nur im Fenster und Dach

16

Specifications of the First 300 SL

Soon there was talk of a new car being built and tested, but none of these rumored competition sports cars were ever observed by eager automobile reporters on the roads. Usually passenger vehicles were tested on the streets, and even in their customary disguises with faked grilles were recognized as soon-to-be-revealed new models, but the 300 SL was not seen by others than the involved construction engineers at Daimler-Benz.

Eventually, a finished car was driven and speed-tested on the autobahn between Stuttgart and Karlsruhe. But by then, a photographer had been alerted to take the authorized pictures, although the car had been brought to the freeway in a closed transporter.

The American magazine, *Road and Track,* carried an article on these cars in its May-June 1952 issue, giving a short description, basic specifications, and illustrated by four factory pictures from the Daimler-Benz company.

Several months before, however, the German automobile magazine, *Auto, Motor, und Sport*, had carried a short article. In its January 19, 1952, issue, this periodical stated that engineers at the Daimler-Benz factory had been working on the development of a new sports car. Already in December, Karl Kling had undertaken tests on the nearby Hockenheim Ring, reaching such fantastic lap speeds of 190 kilometers (about 118 miles) per hour, and a maximum speed of 240 kilometers (about 150 miles) per hour. The body style of the car — referred to as the 300 SS — was that of an enlarged Porsche. The six-cylinder engine was estimated to develop 170 DIN horsepower. It was equipped with two Weber carburetors and had a newly designed half-domed combustion chamber, the article stated.

On March 13, 1952, a model of the 300 SL was first shown to the press. On the autobahn, it was compared with a 300 S model. Overall height of the new sports car was only 1,265 millimeters (49.8 inches), lower than the Porsche models, despite the fifteen-inch wheels. The engine was exactly as speculated earlier. The interior was rather sparse, as befitting a true competition sports car. Instrumentation was well arranged and easily observed. Speedometer, tachometer, oil pressure gauge, and fuel gauge were augmented by some half dozen knobs on the dash board. The long, bent gear shift handle appeared awkward. There was a thin, four-spoked steering wheel. The body was smooth and well streamlined, and the entry was through the window space and portions of the roof, a most unorthodox arrangement indeed, the automotive writers found. The trunk was filled with two spare tires, and the fuel tank held a maximum of 170 liters (44.88 gallons).

The factory released some detailed technical information on the car. The single overhead camshaft six-cylinder engine with overhead valves had a bore of 85 millimeters and a stroke of 88 millimeters, displacing 2,996 cubic centimeters. At 5,200 revolutions per minute, the engine developed 173.25 DIN horsepower. Maximum torque was 188 pounds-feet at 4,200 revolutions per minute. (Some of the engines developed as much as 175 horsepower, while others came up to only 172.) This power output was considered quite satisfactory since the paramount goal was to achieve utmost reliability and durability, so necessary for the long-distance races such as the Mille Miglia, Le Mans, and the Carrera Panamericana. (However, Neubauer believed that a 200-horsepower engine was needed to be competitive.)

Compression ratio was 8 to 1. A higher ratio was not deemed

Rear view of earliest style competition model

Die erste Ausführung, von hinten gesehen

The second model — doors are cut into side of body
Der zweite Typ — Türen nehmen schon teilweise die Seite ein

19

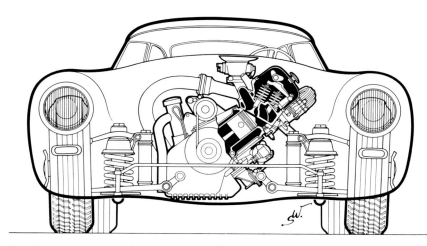

Drawing clearly showing slanting engine position
Draufsichtszeichnung des schrägliegenden Motors

practicable since the regulations specified the use of only super gasoline in sports car competition, and that was generally only 90 octane at that time.

Three Solex downdraft carburetors, model 40 PBJC, with twin electric fuel pumps were used. (The fuel injection engines were not built until 1953 and 1954. They developed 215 to 225 horsepower.)

The gear ratios were 3.16 to 1 in first gear; 1.89 to 1 in second; 1.325 to 1 in third; and 1 to 1 in fourth gear. Optional ratios were 3.33 to 1 in first gear; 2.12 to 1 in second; 1.45 to 1 in third; and 1 to 1 in fourth gear.

To achieve a lower hood line, the engine was tilted 45 degrees to the left. A new sump was designed, and the inlet and exhaust manifolds were modified to fit the altered position of the engine. The carburetors were mounted vertically, and the large air chamber

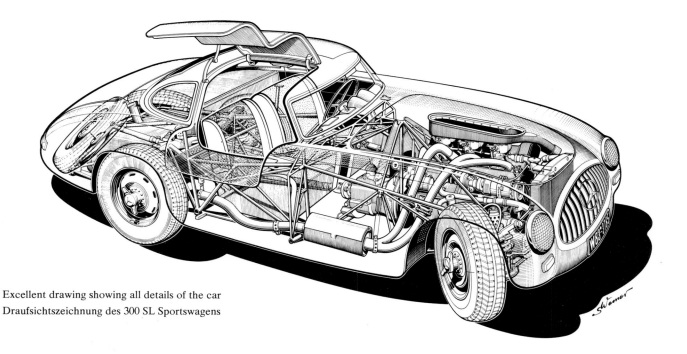

Excellent drawing showing all details of the car
Draufsichtszeichnung des 300 SL Sportswagens

fitted tightly against the hood cover. A thick rubber molding acted as sealant.

The aerodynamic coupe with an extremely low frontal area was of the envelope body type and less than fifty inches (49-3/4) high. The seamless body, of extra thin aluminum, was exceedingly light. The doors were of an unorthodox airplane type, consisting of the framed windows and a portion of the top, and swung upward. This revolutionary door design made possible a lighter and also a stronger body construction.

Since the door space conformed to the regulation square foot area, Neubauer believed that the FIA would consider them acceptable in competitive events.

The oval grille with the large-circled three-pointed star was reminiscent of the Mercedes-Benz 1939 Grand Prix racing machines.

This streamlined body form had been tested in the wind tunnel of the Stuttgart Technical High School, well-known through the tests conducted there before World War II by Professor Winnibald Kamm. The maximum speed of 240 kilometers per hour indicated that the air resistance of the 300 SL was less than 0.38.

With the aluminum body, the car weighed but 840 kilograms (1,850 pounds), giving the 3-liter coupe an advantageous 4.7 kilogram per horsepower ratio and an excellent acceleration of under seven seconds for the 0 to 100 kilometers. The official figures were not as generous. They gave 7.8 seconds. Gear ratios used were 1:4.11, 1:3.89, 1:3.64, 1:3.42, 1:3.25, while the regular model ratio was 1:3.64.

A small flap in the rear of the roof, regulated by a lever, was used for ventilation and narrow side window wings were installed. The windows themselves could not be lowered.

The light-weight, thin steel tubular X-frame had individual front-wheel suspension with parallel arms and frictionless coil springs with additional rubber springs and wheel springs. The oscillating rear axle had coil springs. Since the speed potential of this sports car was 150 miles per hour, equal to that of a true Grand Prix car, it is interesting to note that the old style swing axle, first used on their

1922 rear-engined racing car and later replaced with the de Dion axle from 1937 on, was again used. Hydraulic telescope type shock absorbers were used on front and rear. The large oil-pressure four-wheel brakes had two forward shoes in the front drums and one forward and one reverse shoe in the rear drums. They had a diameter of 260 millimeters and a width of 90 millimeters, an increase over the former type. The Ferodo linings were cemented to the cast aluminum brake shoes and small holes around the drum face allowed the lining dust to escape and the finning of the outer surface was designed to act as centrifugal blower with the shrouding of the wheel. Total brake area was 258 square inches. An additional mechanical hand brake acted on the rear wheels.

Still, Neubauer felt that the brakes would prove inadequate for such long-distance events as the Mille Miglia and Le Mans. He wanted 16-inch wheels and larger brake drums. But 15-inch disk wheels with cooling slots were provided, and special 6.70 by 15 tires were mounted on the 15-inch rims.

Tires used in competition were generally Continental, either the Monza or Nürburg types, of 6.50 and 6.70 size. Occasionally, Engelbert tires were used.

The official figures quoted for the weight was not generous either. It usually was given as 870 kilograms (1,918 pounds).

The wheelbase of the 300 SL was 94.5 inches, and the overall length was 166 inches. Tread was 58.2 inches in front and 60 inches in the rear. Fuel tanks were installed according to the circuits and generally held between 150 and 220 liters of gasoline.

A large tachometer, redlined at 5,800 revolutions per minute, and an equally large speedometer, calibrated to 270 kilometers per hour, was advantageously placed almost at the eye level of the driver. Smaller instruments were an oil pressure gauge, water temperature gauge, oil temperature gauge, and a fuel gauge, which indicated the precise amount of fuel in liters. Later this was changed to show merely full, half, and reserve.

The steering wheel was removable for allowing entry and exit of the driver into the deep bucket seat. Each man had his individually measured seat installed for maximum comfort, but they were all of one and the same color and a plaid texture.

The long floor shift lever was easy to reach and to operate the four synchronized gears. An air circulating system was installed for the Daimler-Benz officials were always fully convinced that driver comfort was a most important factor in every race.

Three body styles were actually constructed in 1952 — the coupe, the open roadster for such twisty courses as the Nürburgring, and a newer style coupe with a lowered door. The high door of the first body style was 88 centimeters from the ground; and in races where the drivers had to change, the lower door models (56 centimeters) were used. The first of these altered coupes was actually driven by Fritz Riess at Bern. From the Le Mans event on, all competition coupes had the lower doors.

Altogether ten such cars were built in 1952. Several of these were to be used in practicing for the various competitive races, but only after the drivers had thoroughly familiarized themselves with the respective circuits. (Later, two or three of these cars were sold to private individuals.)

The second model, with doors wide open
Der zweite Typ, mit den Flügeltüren ganz geöffnet

Mille Miglia XIX

The first international sports car race in which the new 300 SL cars were to be entered was the Mille Miglia XIX, on May 3-4, 1952.

Twenty-one years before, Rudolf Caracciola, with Sebastian as navigator, had won the thousand-mile race, driving a SSKL at an average speed of 62.85 miles per hour, against formidable French and Italian competitors, generally with lighter cars.

This time, a large number of highly competitive Ferrari cars were participating, either the tested 3-liter machines or the new 4.5-liter sports cars with Grand Prix engines. Piero Taruffi was to drive one of these powerful cars. However, the Ferrari factory team was without their champion driver, Alberto Ascari, who was at Indianapolis. And Luigi Villoresi was still recovering from a serious accident. Giovanni Bracco was the stellar driver, with Rolfo, with a 3-liter Ferrari. A strong team of special Ferrari cars was also entered by Marzotto. And Lancia was well represented with Luigi Fagioli as leading driver of the large factory contingent.

The Mercedes team had gone to Brescia early, and every driver had driven the entire course at least ten times to familiarize himself thoroughly with every characteristic of road surface and to memorize turns and curves of the road to be traveled. Every night, films of the route were shown to again impress the drivers and their navigators with all the minute details of the 971.8-mile-long course. Refueling and tire changing were undefatigably rehearsed.

The two 300 SLs which were used for practice could also be used as back-up cars in the race, should the need arise.

The classic route of the Mille Miglia, starting at Brescia, led to the Adriatic Sea through Verona, Vicenza, Padova, and Ravenna, then along the coast to Rimini, Ancona, and Pescara, and then inland to Popoli, Terni, Narmi, and Rome. From here the course turned north to Bolsena, Lorenzo, Siena, Firenze, Bologna, Modena, Parma, Placenza, Cremona, and finally Brescia again. Control points were set up at Ravenna, Aquila, Rome, Siena, Firenze, and Bologna.

The appearance of the new Mercedes-Benz cars overshadowed all other entrants, but a problem of eligibility arose when race officials objected to the unorthodox arrangement of the doors. Having caused some consternation among the judges, the peculiar doors were finally ruled acceptable by Count Maggi, sports president at Brescia.

Of the 605 participating cars, the 3 Mercedes-Benz 300 SLs, driven by Rudolf Caracciola with Knurrle, Hermann Lang with Erwin Grupp, and Karl Kling with Hans Klenk, were almost the last ones to leave the starting ramp. Rain, thunder, and lightning accompanied their baptism of international competition.

Their first race was under way. At Ravenna, Bracco was in the lead with his fast Ferrari. Kling was in second place, five minutes behind the leader, having averaged an amazing ninety miles per hour during nearly constant rain on wet and treacherously slick roads.

Caracciola was among the others, a bit behind, but Lang was out of the race. The 42-year-old veteran Grand Prix driver, perhaps a bit nervous and over-anxious, had crashed some twenty-five miles from the start. Hitting a kilometer stone on the side of the narrow road, he had damaged his steering system beyond quick repair. Lang and his companion were not hurt, but his hoped-for comeback in international competition seemed definitely shattered.

After Ravenna, Bracco had tire troubles and lost thirteen minutes, allowing Kling to lead. At Terni, Kling was ahead of Taruffi, and

In foul weather at a Mille Miglia check point
In schlechtem Wetter bei dem Mille Miglia Rennen

Caracciola had pushed ahead into fifth place.

But in Rome, Karl Kling was the leader. Although he won the Camperi Prize, this appeared less than a joyous occasion, despite much enthusiastic shouting by the spectators, for the proverb was that "he who leads into Rome never leads into Brescia" (and therefore does not win the Mille Miglia).

Kling was 6 minutes 30 seconds ahead of Taruffi, and 11 minutes 40 seconds ahead of the third-place Bracco.

Still, Kling kept his lead into Firenze (Florence). Perhaps the old Rome saying would not hold true this time. But then, news came that Bracco had a lead of twenty-five seconds into Modena, the historic city of Ferrari and Maserati. At Parma, Kling was two full minutes behind the leader, and Caracciola had gained another position. However, his car did not appear to run at its maximum performance.

Fagioli, the old rival and who had once attacked him with a copper hammer in a short burst of rage, was just ahead of Caracciola. Both men had, of course, aged considerably, but were still fierce competitors in any race. Soon, the car of Caratsch lost cooling water and he had to stop four times to refill the radiator.

Back at the starting place in Brescia, Giovanni Bracco was the first man across the finish line. Karl Kling followed 4 minutes 32 seconds later, having driven 12 hours and 14.17 minutes and averaging 77.363 miles per hour. The Italian driver had known the route better than Kling, and when it rained toward the end of the long race again, the open Ferrari was a definite advantage over the enclosed Mercedes-Benz coupe. Besides better visibility, the Italian's tires were perhaps a bit better suited for the wet surface. Anyway, Bracco had gained appreciable time at the Futa and the Raticosa passes.

Fagioli placed third with his Lancia, and eight minutes behind him came Caracciola. At the age of 51 he had driven for almost thirteen hours (12.40.25) without relief. Despite the severe leg injury bothering him, he still averaged 76 miles per hour. (The crash at Indianapolis in 1946 had seriously affected his performance later.)

The new 300 SL cars had not won the important Italian race, but they had placed quite well in this their first competitive appearance.

Preis von Bern

Two weeks later, on May 18, the 300 SLs competed in the 81-mile Grand Prix of Bern. Eleven cars participated in this event for sports cars of over 1.5-liter displacement, scheduled as a special attraction to the regular Swiss Grand Prix, a formula I race.

To the regular Mercedes-Benz drivers (Caracciola, Lang, and Kling), newcomer Fritz Riess was added as driver of the fourth entry. The cars to be driven at Bern by the regular drivers were those they had driven in the Mille Miglia. The Riess car, however, had a lower cut door. Experience at the Italian road race had shown that the climbing in or out of the driver's seat of the 300 SL was too time-consuming. For the coming race at Le Mans, with its repeated changing of drivers, an easier and less cumbersome manner of getting into and out of the car had to be devised. It was hoped that this lower door would be the solution to that problem.

Race director Alfred Neubauer firmly believed that at least three cars should be entered in any race to ensure a fair chance of victory. This had been his practice during the glorious pre-war years when the mighty Auto-Union racing cars were the prime antagonists of the Mercedes-Benz silver arrows.

The four 300 SLs were pitted against seven other entries, among them Ferrari, Aston-Martin, Lancia, and Jaguar sports cars, driven by Felice Bonetti, Luigi Fagioli, Geoffrey Duke, and Reginald Parnell. But of special interest was the appearance of the Swiss champion driver Willy Daetwyler, who had a brand-new twelve-cylinder 4.1-liter Ferrari. And Geoffrey Duke, a former motorcycle champion, drove a 2.6-liter Aston-Martin in this his first race on the continent.

In practice, Daetwyler had made the fastest time. At 2:55.6 his Ferrari was nearly five seconds faster than the best Mercedes-Benz. Kling drove 3:00.1, with Caracciola doing 3:00.5. Then came Lang; Riess was considerably slower.

Neubauer had ordered the gear ratios of the 300 SLs changed during the night to add three to four seconds to their lap times in the actual race. Unfortunately, the Ferrari of Daetwyler broke the drive shaft and barely rolled across the starting line. The Mercedes cars were the first away, with Caracciola in the lead.

The beginning of the race seemed like old times for the veteran race manager. Alfred Neubauer was quite correct in his judgment that Rudolf Caracciola was the best driver ever. He rated him ahead of Rosemeyer, Nuvolari, and later Moss and even Fangio.

On the second lap around the 4.5-mile Bremgarten circuit, the four 300 SLs closed rank and traveled together in the lead. In the third lap, Lang passed Caracciola, and Kling passed him in the fifth time around the wooded race course. During the eighth lap, Kling took the lead. During the eleventh lap, Lang set a new lap record at 93 miles per hour. Caracciola was then the last of the group, about thirty seconds behind the leader. Still, the Mercedes cars rounded the circuit in record time with the other competitors completely outclassed and left way behind.

Then, during the thirteenth lap, when Caracciola tried to catch Lang, his car appeared momentarily unsteady in the slippery Forsthaus curve and slipped off the road, hitting a large tree. Caracciola was badly injured, breaking his good leg and suffering a concussion.

His driving career seemed definitely ended now. Rudolf Caracciola was to remain in a wheelchair for the next two years.

The 300 SLs won a triple victory, with Kling, Lang, and Riess finishing in that order. The winner Karl Kling had averaged 89.9 miles per hour. And Hermann Lang had driven the fastest lap, a respectable 2:56.1, almost as fast as Daetwyler and his 4.1-liter Ferrari during practice.

What would have been a wonderful and most successful triumph was saddened by the realization that the beloved Caratsch had driven his last race.

In fine weather at the Prize of Bern event

In schönem Wetter in einer Kurve bei Bern

Les 24 Heures du Mans

By now the new Mercedes-Benz 300 SL sports cars had demonstrated their ability to successfully compete with cars of other manufacturers, and the entire sporting world eyed expectantly the silvery coupes at the important Le Mans 24-hour endurance race.

It was at Le Mans where in 1873 Amédé Bollée, Père, had built and operated his steam omnibus, the L'Obeissante. Now, on June 13, 1952, at the famed 8.68-mile Sarthe circuit, the best sports cars of the world would compete in this tortuous endurance test of men and machines.

Rumors of fantastic speeds of the 300 SLs had preceded the cars, and all competitors awaited them anxiously. When, almost at the last possible practice time, the cars appeared and the one equipped with an air brake made its first lap around the circuit, spectators were astonished by the demonstration. A large flap ran the width of the roof, behind the doors. A lever brought the brake into action, and when, coming down the Mulsanne straight at about 150 miles per hour, the driver pulled the lever to activate the brake, the car suddenly slowed to about 75 miles per hour, within split seconds. However, the air brake was not used in the race. Speculation was that the ingenious Neubauer had used this device merely to demoralize the stronger competitors. However, he had actually suggested such an expedient contrivance to assist in slowing down the cars from top speeds to 25 miles per hour, which they had to do about every two minutes during the race. He feared that the regular brakes would prove inadequate to that tremendous task.

Three new cars were used. The teams were Karl Kling with Hans Klenk, Hermann Lang with Fritz Riess, and Theo Helfrich with Norbert Niedermayer. The last three drivers had proven their ability to drive fast in Veritas racing cars and were known as reliable men who were easy on their cars, yet were able long-distance drivers.

The cars had been slightly altered from their earlier appearance. A huge fuel tank filler extended out of the rear window, and the head lights had screens guarding them. Sturdy leather straps had been made to hold the hood down securely. The engines were detuned to develop 166 horsepower at 5,100 revolutions per minute and 184

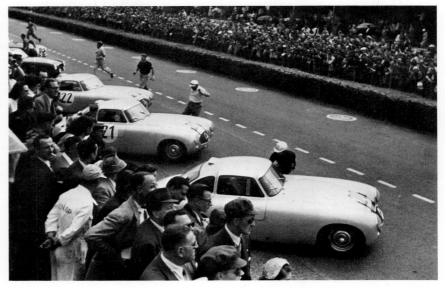

The start of the 24-hour Le Mans Endurance Race
Der Start für das Le Mans 24 Stunden Rennen

27

Taking one of the fast Esses on the
Sarthe circuit

In einer schnellen S-Kurve auf der
Sarthe Bahn

pound-feet of torque at 4,200 by lowering the compression ratio to perform properly with the relatively low octane gasoline provided for the race. During practice, tire wear proved quite excessive and the cars were forced to change tires every 440 miles, approximately 50 to 53 laps of the circuit. These changes would add precious minutes to the pit stops. Fuel consumption was figured at 11.7 miles to the gallon.

When promptly at four o'clock Charles Faroux lowered the flag to start the race, the drivers sped across the track, jumped into their cars, started their engines, and roared away. The unorthodox Mercedes-Benz cars were not among the first of the fifty-seven participants. The drivers had to adjust their removable steering wheels when they climbed in, before starting out to catch the others. The faster cars were quickly away.

Rounding the Tetre Rouge corner at the first lap, Phil Walters led in a 5.4-liter Cunningham coupe, followed by Stirling Moss' 3.4-liter Jaguar, Andre Simon's 4.1-liter Ferrari, Alberto Ascari's 2.9-liter Ferrari, Rolt's Jaguar, Stewart's Jaguar, Pierre Levegh's 4.8-liter Talbot, and others.

Competition was very keen, and the leaders set a furious pace. Records fell. During the first hour of racing, Simon broke the lap record with 105.862 miles per hour, then Ascari with 107.499. Both Ferrari cars widened the gap between their cars and the rest of the field.

When Ascari had to stop because of clutch trouble, the leaders at the end of the first hour were Simon (Ferrari), Manzon (Gordini), Rosier (Ferrari), Walters (Cunningham), Helfrich (Mercedes-Benz), Kling (Mercedes-Benz), Levegh (Talbot), Fitch (Talbot). The Lang-driven 300 SL was in tenth place.

The Mercedes cars drove at their carefully calculated and planned speeds, letting the leaders run away. The Gordini of Robert Manzon actually passed Simon's Ferrari, to the tumultuous enthusiasm of the partisan spectators, and Levegh's Talbot went into second place. By midnight, both French cars were ahead and seventeen had retired.

And then, the Mercedes of Kling-Klenk came into the pits with poor lights. Faulty wiring did not supply sufficient current for the lights to function properly. Neubauer berated the Bosch representative unmercifully, but the car was out of the race for good.

At dawn, after twelve hours of racing, Levegh was in the lead with the Helfrich-Niedermayer car in second place and the Lang-Riess car in third place.

Twelve hours were still left to race. And now, most of the really serious contenders retired from the course. Generator failures, broken drive shafts, and other malfunctions were taking their toll. The two remaining 300 SLs were running steadily and reliably, like clockwork. The leading Mercedes-Benz lost valuable time in the pits to have a damaged wheel repaired.

Then, an hour and fourteen minutes before the finish, while two full laps ahead, the engine of the leading Talbot melted a connecting rod and the courageous Pierre Levegh had to give up, having driven practically all the way.

The Lang-Riess Mercedes-Benz placed first, the Helfrich-Niedermayer Mercedes-Benz second (a lap behind), the Johnson-Wisdom Nash-Healy third, the Cunningham-Spear Cunningham fourth, and the Simon-Vincent Ferrari fifth.

Forty-one of the starting participants had dropped out during the long race. The two Mercedes-Benz cars made an indelible impression upon the 400,000 enthusiastic spectators by their steady, almost monotonous regularity with which they rounded the fast circuit.

The winners Lang and Riess set a new distance record, having covered 2,320.07 miles in 24 hours at an average speed of 96.67 miles per hour. The second place car averaged 96.32 miles per hour. The previous year, a Jaguar XK120C, driven by Peter Walker and Graham Whitehead, had covered 2,243 miles at an average of 93.498 miles per hour to win the Le Mans classic race.

The two victorious 300 SLs were driven the 525 miles back to the factory where an examination of the large turbo brakes revealed that they would have lasted effectively another thousand miles.

The close formation of 300 SLs at the Jubilee Prize
Die enge Gruppe der 300 SLs auf dem Nürburgring

Grosser Jubiläums Preis

The fifteenth running of the German Grand Prix on August 3, 1952, was also the twenty-fifth anniversary of the Nürburgring. This superb racing circuit had been built in the impoverished Eifel mountain area to aid the distressed inhabitants by providing work during the post-war depression.

To properly celebrate these events, the organizing body added a race for sports cars, the Grand Jubilee Prize of the Nürburgring, to the regular formula I Grand Prix. Canceling the 1,100 cubic centimeter class, one was substituted to include cars from 3 to 8 liters displacement. This would allow the 3-liter Mercedes-Benz 300 SL cars, even with superchargers, to participate.

Actually, the cars had never appeared on race circuits in Germany, and this race provided the first opportunity for the many enthusiasts to see them perform.

To provide better visibility for the drivers on this twisty circuit than the closed coupes could, open roadsters were built. Neubauer also insisted on lighter cars, anticipating really strong competition. One of the coupes was turned into a roadster simply by cutting off the top. The driver's side was covered with an aluminum cover, and such unnecessary instruments as the speedometer were removed. This car was given to Helfrich for the race. Kling's car was new, as were the two others, to be driven by Lang and Riess. To ensure success on the home circuit, Neubauer thought it prudent to have again four entries instead of the customary three. Failure to score heavily would never do.

Earlier, during practice a supercharged car actually beat the lap times made by formula II cars and the four-cylinder Ferrari sports car. However, cooling and other problems appeared too difficult to overcome by race time, and the four 300 SL roadsters used were powered by their regular engine types. The car Kling drove had a slightly shorter wheelbase than the others, 86.7 inches instead of 94.5 inches (2,400 millimeters), and a somewhat smaller grille opening.

Start of the Grand Jubilee Prize on the Nürburgring
Der Grosse Jubiläumspreis für Sportwagen (Nürburgring)

Winner Hermann Lang in his 300 SL roadster

Der Sieger Hermann Lang im 300 SL Roadster

Serious competition was expected from Stirling Moss driving a Jaguar, Geoffrey Duke an Aston-Martin, and Consalva Sanesi the new Disco Volante of Alfa Romeo. And the 2.3-liter Gordini driven by Robert Manzon was a very fast car and promised to be a real competitor, as it had at Le Mans.

During the initial lap, Manzon passed the cars of Riess, Helfrich, and Lang, and ran behind the leader, Kling. But before passing Kling in the fourth lap, the gear box of the Gordini failed him and forced him out of the race.

Now the Mercedes-Benz cars ran in close-order formation around the tricky 14.25-mile Eifel circuit which has 172 turns and curves and a difference in elevation of 1,250 feet.

Lang passed the leading Kling, whose car developed an oil leak, on the next to the last lap to win the race at an average speed of 79.98 miles per hour, only a few miles less than made by the Grand Prix cars. His fastest lap was run in 10:26.3 minutes, at 81.662 miles per hour. The other Mercedes-Benz 300 SLs followed closely, Kling, Riess, and Helfrich, to make a splendid quadruple victory on home grounds.

The competitors, Jaguars, Allards, Healeys, and a 4.1-liter Ferfari, were never a real threat to the Mercedes, and the close battle which most of the near half a million spectators who crowded around the mountainous circuit expected, never materialized.

In the formula I race, Alberto Ascari won again. He shared the honor, with Caracciola, of having won three German Grands Prix on the Nürburgring.

As suggested, it had been planned to enter the 300 SL cars equipped with superchargers, and many observers fully expected such vehicles there. The vast experience with superchargers in the twenties and thirties promised a considerable increase in power from the relatively low output of the 3-liter engine of the cars. Their former M 194 type became the M 197 with a supercharger, a one-stage Roots blower with two three-vaned pressure chambers, placed between the carburetor and cylinder. The unblown engines had used three Solex carburetors, but these supercharged engines were now equipped with three Weber 45 DOM carburetors. The housing of the supercharger was of poured magnesium. Driven by the camshaft, the unit was placed above the tilted engine on the right side. The hood had to be altered, and a slight bulge allowed for the added space.

The supercharge ratio was between 1:1.13 and 1:1.68, depending upon which size gear wheel was used. The compression of the engine was lowered from 8.1:1 to 7.2:1 to allow for use of regular, 90-plus octane, fuel as the racing competition regulations specified.

On the test bench, the supercharged engine developed at 5,800 revolutions per minute about 230 DIN horsepower against the normal output of between 170 and 175. At 3,000 rpm, it was 115 against the normal 95, and at 4,000 rpm the figures were 165 and 143 respectively.

Kling tested the supercharged car on the Ring, and, of course, Uhlenhaut also drove it to satisfy himself of the improvement. Kling lapped the circuit in 10 minutes 24.8 seconds with the supercharged engine against 10:25.1 with the regular one. This three-tenths of a second advantage was minimal considering the extra work involved to create the more complicated, and perhaps less reliable, power plant.

Apparently the swing axle did not allow the added available power to be properly transferred to the wheels on the ground. The many turns of the circuit could not be negotiated as rapidly or as smoothly with this car as with the non-supercharged one, and thus valuable time was lost. The straights were not long enough to overcome the loss and regain it during the race. Uhlenhaut explained "that the power of the atmospheric induction engine appears to be on the edge of the ability to transmit it to the ground."

At the same time these tests with the supercharger were made, the new fuel injection system was also thoroughly tested. It promised to be a preferred manner of increasing power and better suited for a regular production model of the sports car. Racing participation by the factory for the next year was not anticipated. The new W 106 Formula I 2.5-liter engine had already been designed, and development work on that project took precedence over everything else.

The clean, smooth winning car — but before the race
Der saubere, glatte Siegerwagen — aber vor dem Rennen

Carrera Panamericana Mexico III

The third Carrera Panamericana Mexico was first discussed by the Mercedes racing officials a year before when Piero Taruffi and Alberto Ascari won the second of this series of long-distance races of 1,934 miles — nearly the entire length of Mexico.

The long, difficult road itself made this Mexican race one of the world's greatest road races and a greedy reaper of highly-tuned, expensive machines. The steaming jungle atmosphere at Tuxtla Gutiérrez near the Guatemalan border was a tremendous contrast to the 10,482-foot elevation between Puebla and Mexico City, and the desertlike plains of Chihuahua and Ciudad Juárez on the United States border.

Although Daimler-Benz officials had tentatively decided not to enter any more competitive events with the 300 SL cars, upon the strong urging of the Mexican importer and with an eye on the fast-developing market in the United States for Mercedes automobiles, the management considered it advisable, and profitable, to participate in the important road race. In fact, to ensure superior press coverage of the event in such a fascinatingly enchanting country which would excite the imagination of Europeans especially, the excellent motor journalist Günther Molter was engaged to handle the publicity. He was also put hard to work by Neubauer assisting in the various service depots along the road where he commuted to with a spare 300 SL, the car with which Lang had won at the Nürburgring. Thus, the fifth appearance of the Mercedes-Benz 300 SL sports cars was to be at this race in November 1952.

The racing contingent left Germany by KLM airplane on October 21. The Atlantic flight actually began at Amsterdam, after a short hop, in a DC 6 and took 37 hours. After a brief landing at Shannon, Ireland, the ocean crossing was made to Gander, Newfoundland, then to Montreal, Canada, and at some 18,000 foot altitude across the United States to Monterrey, Mexico, and from there to Mexico City.

The racing cars had been loaded on the M.S. Anita, but that vessel was delayed by a hurricane for several days, after having run for shelter in Cuba, and arrived in Mexico on November 3. After considerable red tape, Alfred Neubauer was able to get the four cars (two coupes and two roadsters) unloaded from the HAPAG seven-ton freighter, but the lackadaisical officials at Vera Cruz taxed the patience of the impatient Rennleiter to its very limit.

In the meantime, Karl Kling and his co-driver Hans Klenk, and Hermann Lang and his companion, Erwin Grupp, used the 300 sedan to learn the route. Another sedan, a 220 model, was also made available to the drivers.

Karl Kling, echoing Neubauer, always insisted that 99 percent of any racing victory is due to preparation and 1 percent to luck. Thus, it was but natural that the participants studied the route diligently. After noting the features carefully, Kling and Lang and navigators would discuss them, decide just how a certain curve should be taken during the race, and Klenk and Grupp would make notes on a pad. These locations were identified by the odometer reading. The drivers noted that the highways were generally constructed in a most advanced style, with curves well banked to allow high-speed driving. The surface, especially in the southern areas, consisted of volcanic materials which were unusually hard and terribly demanding on tires.

With Neubauer and the other drivers in the large sedan, the group drove down to Tuxtla Gutiérrez. The entire route was gone over several times, and every part of the course was covered at least ten times. Nothing was left to chance. The race was too important for that.

In places, the road was in poor condition with deep chuckholes and only a thin surface layer of asphalt. Here, especially great care would have to be taken by the drivers.

The change in altitude from sea level to 3,196 meters above also presented problems in tuning the engines of the 300 SLs for maximum performance. With four gears they were at a decided disadvantage to the 4.1 Ferraris with five gears.

Proper fuel also caused great concern. The low-octane fuel proved unsatisfactory, and a new mixture of fuel with higher octane rating had to be secured to keep the engines from knocking and to assure their projected performance.

With their race cars, the entire contingent ran into a torrential rain storm at the highest altitude of the whole course. John Fitch, who had by then joined the factory team, and Hans Klenk, driving the open roadsters, were completely drenched and found it almost impossible to drive their cars.

(At the time of the German event on the Nürburgring, the popular American sports car driver John Fitch had been invited by Neubauer to drive some test laps with the 300 SL. It was the lanky, capable driver's thirty-fifth birthday. Fitch was immensely impressed with the car and found the engine superbly balanced, more like an electric motor, and "winding it up to 5,800 revolutions per minute through the gears was a delight.")

On the return to Mexico City, the group found that the rain had caused some damage to the streets running under water. With nearly no drainage, that city always suffered during such heavy downpours.

Final carburetor adjustments were made to the 300 SLs on the fast Mexico City to Puebla road.

The Neubauer race strategy was focused principally in beating the powerful Ferrari team. The factory drivers, Taruffi, Ascari, and Villoresi, had flown into Mexico City on November 5, and their cars arrived at Vera Cruz on the 8th.

The large Ferrari sports cars were reputed to have engines of 280 horsepower against the SLs' 180. And while the top speed of the Italian cars was about 167 miles per hour, that of the German cars was about 155. And, of course, Ferrari had the experience of the last race and the exhilaration of its victory when Piero Taruffi with Luigi Chinetti won the Carrera and Alberto Ascari with Luigi Villoresi placed second.

Besides the three 4.1-liter Ferrari Mexico models, the very light Gordini cars of Robert Manzon and Jean Behra with 2.3-liter engines were also powerful contenders. These cars had less weight and power than the 300 SLs, but their performance was about equal to them. And the 2-liter supercharged Lancia Aurelia Gran Turismo driven by Felice Bonetto was to be feared.

In addition to these strong factory entries, the winning new 3-liter Ferrari of the Mille Miglia was driven by Giovanni Bracco, who had carefully marked particularly difficult road sections with yellow paint. And several private entries, such as the excellent American drivers, Phil Hill and Jack McAfee, also driving Ferrari sports cars, had to be considered capable of victory. However, other contenders than those backed by strong factory participation were really not given much of a chance to win the event, except by some miracle.

Alfred Neubauer outlined the race strategy to the contingent when they met for the last instruction before the race. The twelve mechanics were to man the nine depots arranged along the route.

The first depot for tires was located about 220 miles from the start, near a primitive Indian settlement. Besides the two sedans available to the small organization, one truck and two airplanes were also to be used. Neubauer himself would travel from point to point in a DC 3, so as to be at the finish line at the end of the day's racing. The top mechanics would do likewise, and the rest of the personnel would follow with their unused equipment by truck and cars.

It was believed that the Ferrari and Gordini team would drive as fast as possible during the first legs of the race so that they would build up an early decisive lead to ensure victory. Neubauer planned for his drivers to be careful as far as Mexico City, and then, on the wide open stretches, drive all out to win.

The participants had practiced changing tires repeatedly. It took just one minute for the two men to change three tires. All material and equipment were neatly placed for rapid, unobstructed use, because no pit crews were allowed to work on the cars in these depots.

Hermann Lang had drawn starting number 3. Karl Kling had number 4. Both were to drive the coupes. John Fitch had number 6 and drove the open roadster. His was the car used by Riess on the Ring. The car for Lang was new, with some parts used from the wrecked car of Caracciola at Bern. Kling had his old Le Mans 300 SL.

All cars had been slightly altered. The engines were bored out to 3.1 liters because no restrictions were imposed on displacement limitations. They developed a maximum of 177 horsepower at 5,200 revolutions per minute, and torque of 193 pounds-feet at 4,200 revolutions per minute. The exhaust system was improved and realigned on the right side. New window moldings with chrome strips were provided. And the cars were all gaily painted. The large Mercedes emblem on the hood, white car number on top, blue on the fenders and a red official entry shield, all made a colorful car.

The first of the 27 sports cars was sent on its way at 7:00, November 19. Lang was third away at 7:03, Kling fourth at 7:04, and Fitch sixth at 7:06 that early morning. The Third Carrera Panamericana was under way with the first leg, Tuxtla to Oaxaca, a distance of 329.3 miles from this town some 165 miles from the Guatemalan border. The route went through equatorial jungle areas, and the roads were in poor condition. Phil Hill referred to them as donkey trails.

After but a few miles, and after rounding a wide curve at some 50 miles per hour and accelerating to about 85, a large dog ran onto the road from the right side in front of Lang's car. A dull thud indicated that the canine was hit. Slowing down to test the steering and front wheel alignment, Kling passed them. Then, later on, when Kling had to stop because of tire trouble, Lang passed him in turn. However, the hole in the thin body made by the dog affected the progress adversely, acting as a brake at high speeds.

Others had worse luck. Robert Munzon, driving one of the very fast, but also very light, Gordini sports cars with 2.3-liter engines, broke an axle. Now Jean Behra, driving the other Gordini, seemed only more anxious to stay ahead of the other competitors. Through this difficult jungle and mountainous terrain, Alberto Ascari missed a sharp turn and rolled his Ferrari, but was unhurt. And Bonetto's Lancia failed him.

Kling had still more bad luck. After two tire failures on the road, and thus losing valuable minutes, the car hit a zopilote (buzzard) at high speed. Klenk was hit by the broken windshield and Kling stopped to bandage his navigator's head to stop the flow of blood. The air pressure through the large front windshield-less opening caused the rear window to fall out when Kling reached his speed.

At Oaxaca, Kling was third, Fitch seventh, and Lang eighth. All of the 300 SLs had to change their tires three times along the route.

Continental furnished the tires. They shipped some 300 tires for the race, the thick-tread Nürburg type for the more abrasive surfaces encountered early in the event, and the Avus-type, a thinner tire for the high speed sections for the later stages and smoother roads.

The elapsed times were:

1. Behra, Gordini	3:41.44	(Average speed: 89.11 mph)
2. Bracco, Ferrari	3:47.21	
3. Kling, Mercedes-Benz	3:49.45	
4. Maglioli, Lancia	3:54.10	
5. McAfee, Ferrari	3:57.55	
6. Chinetti, Ferrari	3:58.47	
7. Fitch, Mercedes-Benz	4:00.23	
8. Lang, Mercedes-Benz	4:03.00	

Every evening, after a lap was completed, the cars were gone over most carefully by the factory mechanics to get them into the best possible condition for the coming next leg of the tough race. Fitch observed that Neubauer was never openly concerned with the cars of the leading competitors, but concentrated his attention on their own problems. He directed, of course, the preparation of their cars, anticipated the need for extra tires and parts for the depots along the route, and arranged all details to make the team's effort a success. Fitch also felt that the race manager would rather have brought all of the three entered cars to the finish line than to win the

At a tire depot along the Mexican route
Bei einem Reifendepot an der mexikanischen Strecke

After the quick stop, the men make ready to go
Nach einem schnellen Aufenthalt, bald fertig zum fahren

Away again, after installation of protective grill

Wieder weg, nachdem man schützende Rohre angemacht hatte

race. "Neubauer was nothing short of brilliant from a driver's point of view."

The next morning the winners had the best starting positions for this second leg to Puebla, 256 miles away. The road surface was now somewhat better, but the turns even trickier in the mountains.

Through the small village of Acatlan, all of the cars slid against the curb in the square, the loose dirt of the unpaved street affording no traction whatever. McAfee dented the rear end of his Ferrari, and Hill lost much time in replacing a wheel.

Gusty winds added to the already difficult driving conditions, but brakes suffered the most. Behra drove superbly and, after reaching the 7,000-foot crest of the pass, he just ran away from all competitors. But, at the crown of a hill almost toward the end of the leg, the following Villoresi noticed long, black tire marks. Apparently, the brakes on the Gordini had locked and the car skidded to catapult off the road, down a steep embankment. The car was badly damaged, but the French champion driver, who drove without a navigator, suffered only a slight brain concussion.

Villoresi finished first in 3 hours, 3 minutes, and 17 seconds, and averaged 83.83 miles per hour. Fitch, after a splendid drive, followed two minutes later, with Kling a minute and a half behind. Lang was in fifth place. However, Bracco was still the overall leader.

After only a 30-minute rest period, the race was resumed. The distance from Puebla to Mexico City was only 80.7 miles, but the route led over the mountains in a steep climb to over 10,000 feet, only to drop some 2,500 feet in a little over 45 miles into the capital.

Lang referred to this stretch, between San Martin and Rio Frio, as a long-distance hill-climb never seen in Europe. The highway there has about 20 kilometers of sharp turns, tight hairpin bends and curves, and drops of over a hundred feet down the side. Kling made excellent time, slipstreaming the leading Villoresi for a good distance of the way.

About 10,000 eager spectators lined the road, watching the fast cars speed by. Crowds were generally well-behaved. Villoresi led that leg, driving the distance in 48.09 minutes, with Bracco using

55 seconds more. Kling was in third position, with 50.10 minutes, then came Lang with 50.12, and Fitch with 51.21 minutes elapsed time.

Neubauer was well pleased with the drivers' efforts. The Mercedes-Benz group had advanced from their third, seventh, and eighth places to second, third, and fourth places into Mexico City. Total standings now were:
1. Bracco   7:44.31
2. Kling   7:47.24
3. Fitch   7:56.29
4. Lang   8:04.33
5. Villoresi   8:21.31

Neubauer seems pleased with the efforts of Fitch
Neubauer scheint mit dem Fahrer Fitch zufrieden zu sein

The Mercedes contingent ready for another leg
Die Mercedesgruppe ist fertig für die nächste Etappe

Bracco was still 2.53 minutes ahead of Kling. Villoresi was 34.7 minutes behind Kling, and 16.58 minutes behind Lang. Fourteen of the 28 starters remained in the race. And all of the 300 SLs had broken the existing distance records so far.

In Mexico City the gear ratios were changed in the coupes to allow faster maximum speeds on the flat stretches ahead. The lone roadster had had a lower rear end ratio from the start. By then the "cars looked disreputable with the paint literally sandblasted off to the base metal. The bodies were pockmarked by stones, dented by birds, and torn by flying treads which acted as giant whips at high speed," Fitch wrote.

From Mexico City to Léon the road climbed into Toluca and heavy fog, then dropped into a plain where high speeds became attainable. Brakes had caused considerable problems so far. Jaguar cars had cut away the rear fenders for better cooling, and the Mercedes-Benz had louvers installed to get more cooling air to their brakes. Loose rocks and bad road surfaces had caused much damage to the cars, as had the several tire failures, when flying treads scarred the light metal. In fact, McAfee found that at a steady 130 miles per hour he blew his tires with some regularity, and the suggestion was made that the use of magnesium wheels caused this malfunction. Others had also a multitude of tire changes to make, and the Ferrari team feared that the 200 spares which the Pirelli people had brought would prove to be insufficient. The Mercedes-Benz cars were even more handicapped, for their wheels were 15 inches, while the Ferraris used 16-inch wheels. Hill, while making excellent time, and after having just passed McAfee, had his last tire blow out, and thus was forced to drop back.

Villoresi, after winning two legs, again made splendid time, and gained 4 minutes on Bracco, who, although second into Léon, still held the overall lead. The third best time went to Chinetti. The three Ferrari cars were in the lead there, with the three Mercedes-Benz cars following behind. For the 267.2-mile leg, Villoresi averaged 112.8 miles per hour.

The fifth leg, from Léon to Durango, a distance of 333.7 miles, was the longest drive yet. There was much speculation on the eventual outcome of the Carrera. The Ferrari team had the leader in Bracco, but Villoresi and Chinetti were still in contention. The Mercedes team was well placed but still not victorious. It seemed another Mille Miglia situation. Mechanics had worked hard during the night in Mexico City to get the machines in top condition for the day's run.

But at Durango, Villoresi failed to appear, having been eliminated by gearbox failure of his Ferrari. Kling finished first in 2 hours, 58 minutes, and 7 seconds. Bracco was one minute behind him. Lang arrived in Durango four minutes later and Chinetti moved up somewhat in the overall standings.

The fast lap had been tremendously demanding on the cars, and they all showed it. Hill had trouble with the fuel available to him, and the entire fuel lines had to be cleaned out. The Jaguar of Ehlinger had a fouled-up carburetor which could not be tuned to operate at over 4,500 revolutions per minute.

But repairs were hastily made by the expert mechanics of the Ferrari factory team and the fine mechanics carried by the private entries. The small airplane carrying three Mercedes mechanics to Durango also ran into fuel problems and was forced to land before reaching its destination. The mechanics were able to fix the malfunction, caused by poor quality fuel, but they had lost so much time that Kling was forced to make the necessary repairs to his car himself, with assistance from his navigator Klenk. The few garages in Durango were busy places during that night.

Kling's average had now increased to over 125 miles per hour. Pressed by this aggressive driving, Bracco had overstressed his car and broken the rear axle drive. The official average of Kling was 179.784 kilometers per hour. (Ascari's last year record was 157.672.)

Elapsed times for the Léon to Durango leg were:

Kling	2:58.07
Bracco	2:59.13
Lang	3:03.13
Chinetti	3:10.26
Maglioli	3:20.10

From Durango the 251-mile road to Parral was in fairly good condition, except for a section of about 40 miles right out of town. Phil Hill described it as a goat trail, but actually it was part of the highway. From then on, however, nearly all of the level road could be covered at high speeds.

Lang said that the road generally was uneven and that visibility was limited and curves could not be seen from far enough away to properly judge them. No doubt this was true, and it was precisely why Neubauer had so strongly insisted that his drivers practice and remember the route intimately.

When Kling arrived first at Parral, he had averaged 106 miles per hour despite the miserable, slow stretch and several slower crossings. Lang came in second, and Chinetti placed third. Bracco, who was fourth, had believed that his seven-minute lead would be sufficient to maintain the coveted first overall position, but the Mercedes-Benz cars had bested him. McAfee and Hill, both private entries, had excellent positions behind the factory team drivers.

With the race still wide-open and the chances of winning favorable for several participants, the Italian drivers now believed it necessary to make their moves. Leaving Parral for Chihuahua, 186.4 miles away, Chinetti pushed his Ferrari to pass Lang, as did Maglioli his Lancia.

The Lang-Grupp car, after an overnight stop
Der Lang/Grupp Wagen, vor einer Uebernachtungsgarage

Fitch had a windshield extension installed on his car
Fitch hatte ein höhere Windschutzscheibe an seinem Wagen

However, Kling won the leg, averaging 126 miles per hour — a truly fantastic speed for the distance. Bracco, in a last powerful effort to win the race, had been forced to retire when his transmission failed him completely.

When Neubauer observed from above that Bracco had trouble and was forced to quit the race, he tried to signal to Kling below to slow down. Maximum speed was now unnecessary, but the number 4 car outsped the airplane flying overhead, and there was simply no way to communicate to the driver the favorable happening. For that turn of events secured a victory for Kling, unless bad luck would again strike their 300 SL.

Fitch had problems with the front wheel alignment again. Into Durango his car had developed 1½ inch front wheel toe-out, which apparently had been corrected. Now it plagued him once more, causing three tire failures and costing valuable time he could not afford to waste. When leaving Parral, the sponginess in his steering returned, and rather than go on with the troubling malady, he went back to the starting line, after having driven about 250 yards. Others reported that Fitch had never reached the actual starting line when he drove backward to have the mechanics correct the trouble.

The rules stated, however, that once under way, the driver could not return to the starting line. Moreover, after having started, no person except the driver and his co-driver were allowed to work on the car to repair whatever was needed to keep the car in the race. Consequently, after the mechanics had fixed the front wheel alignment, Fitch was disqualified.

Still, he went on with the race and arrived in Chihuahua in fourth position.

The last leg of the Carrera, from Chihuahua to Juárez on the United States border, but actually to the airport some ten miles south of town, was a distance of 230 miles. A huge crowd had gathered to witness this historic finish of the long-distance race.

Alfred Neubauer had left the last starting place right after his 300 SL drivers were on their way, and his twin-engined airplane had a difficult time keeping up with the leader of the race below.

Surprisingly, John Fitch and his navigator Erwin Geiger arrived first in Juárez with the roadster. Although Fitch was disqualified, he had driven faster than the record of Kling, which was adjudged official and was entered in the record book. That time was a fabulous 135.7 miles per hour, or 213.2 kilometers per hour, against Fitch's 213.7 — a difference of about a third of a mile. Chinetti was second, and Lang third.

When stopping at the last tire depot, and after the tire change had been made, Lang apparently did not close one of the doors of his 300 SL properly, for suddenly at high speed the door flew open and the strong wind tore the light door right off. The icy blast hampered the driving, but even more so, the loss of the door affected the aerodynamic balance of the car and robbed it of considerable speed. Otherwise, Lang felt, he would have come into Juárez in second place.

The official totals of the Third Carrera Panamericana were:

1. *Karl Kling*
   Mercedes-Benz 300 SL   18:51.19 hours (102.5906 mph)
2. *Hermann Lang*
   Mercedes-Benz 300 SL   19:26.30 hours (99.50 mph)
3. *Luigi Chinetti*
   Ferrari 4.1   19:32.45 hours (98.96 mph)
4. *Umberto Maglioli*
   Lancia S   20:11.20 hours (96.90 mph)
5. *Jack McAfee*
   Ferrari 4.1   20:21.15 hours (95.10 mph)
6. *Phil Hill*
   Ferrari 2.6   20:33.46 hours (94.00 mph)

Confidence in the race and the eventual victory must have been great, for but a few hours after the double victory Daimler-Benz air mailed appropriate posters, printed in eleven languages, to dealers throughout the world.

In comparison, the totals of Taruffi in the Second Carrera were 21:57.50 elapsed time, or 88.04 miles (141.729 kilometers) per hour. Kling's average speed was 165.011 kilometers per hour in this Third

The victorious Kling car, crossing the finish line

Der Siegerwagen, von Kling gefahren, geht durch das entgültige Ziel

Carrera. Even Lang bettered the old record. (The Mille Miglia average speed of the winner was 75.52 miles per hour, a considerably slower race.)

Participation in this Third Carrera Panamericana by Daimler-Benz was, by far, the most ambitious undertaking with the new 300 SL sports cars, but the painstaking preparations and close attention to all details had paid off handsomely. Neubauer was well pleased with the results, although he fully expected a triple victory, after seeing his cars in such excellent positions the last days.

The Mexican Road Race had been a spectacular affair, quite different from the circuit races, such as Le Mans or the Nürburgring. Even the historic Mille Miglia was not nearly as impressive and tough. It was estimated that some eight million people watched while the cars sped through the greatly diversified Mexican country. Indian sheep herders in ageless, colorful dress on the hills, and peons in the fields behind their burro-pulled wooden plows, watched as the cars raced past them. Gay señoritas, men and women with proud weather-beaten, wrinkled faces, and joyful barefoot boys milled around the cars and drivers at all overnight stopping places. The ultramodern glass and steel buildings of Mexico City were a great contrast to the many ornate, historic churches and plain adobe huts in the fields or villages. It seemed that all the two million inhabitants of the capital were on the festively-decorated streets when the participating cars arrived in the metropolis. In other cities the congestion caused by the spectators taxed the abilities of the authorities to the extreme limit. Crowds gathered at many choice spots along the highway, and their interest in the race was amazing.

Interest in this country in the Third Carrera Panamericana was enhanced by the participation of 64 sedans of several American manufacturers. Of the cars entered in this class, 28 finished, slightly better than the percentage of the 11 sports cars out of 27 entries.

Four Lincolns, excellently prepared by Bill Stroppe, finished ahead of two Chryslers. Others included nearly all makes. Last of the finishers was a Henry J, which took 27:58.01 hours against the winning Lincoln of Chuck Stevenson which took 21:15.38 hours to cover the distance.

Racing Activities

The 1952 season was over. Participation in international competition with the 300 SL cars had been most gratifying to the Daimler-Benz officials. At the initial appearance of the sports cars at the hotly contested Mille Miglia, where the Italian drivers were very much at home and thoroughly familiar with the route to be driven, the second place finisher Karl Kling, with Klenk, had done extremely well. Hermann Lang had dropped out, almost before he was even in the race, and Rudolf Caracciola had placed fourth. These results were not too good but constituted a start which gave pause to the established competitors and made them work even more diligently to maintain their superiority on the racing circuits.

The 300 SL sports car, developed from the regular passenger sedan, or perhaps better, based on components of that and the luxury 300 S model, was in great contrast and an exactly opposite approach to the development of the competitive sports cars of the other manufacturers. These were developed from actual racing machines, often using the very same Grand Prix units, or at least a tuned-down version of these powerful racing engines. That Daimler-Benz engineers were able to accomplish what they did with basically an engine of a regular production passenger automobile was certainly a herculean task and a mark of their brilliant engineering ability. Their ultimate goal, however, was to eventually produce an unbeatable, highly competitive sports car which was based on the formula racing cars, but that would not be for another year or two.

The second appearance of the 300 SLs was at the sports car race at Bern. That was an all-Mercedes affair. The few competitors were not too seriously contesting the race, and thus the 300 SLs could win the first three places.

Le Mans was a different situation. This important long-distance race was without doubt the prestige race of any season and a victory in it had tremendous consequences. The winning car in this 24-hour contest was the undisputed king of the sports cars, at least until the next year when either a repeat victory would strengthen that position enormously, or another make would rise victoriously and take over the coveted spot. The Daimler-Benz racing department had made an immense effort to win this prestigious race and was handsomely rewarded. The malfunction of the electrical system robbed them of certain triple victory when Kling's car was forced out of contention.

Then, the special sports car race at the Nürburgring was a rather mild racing contest. It was a splendid opportunity to parade the 300 SLs before a German audience, but the competition was badly outclassed and really never challenged the highly disciplined Mercedes-Benz team of drivers and their meticulously prepared cars.

The Third Carrera Panamericana was, even more than the Le Mans participation, a precarious gamble for Daimler-Benz. The Italian cars were theoretically superior to the 300 SLs, but unflagging effort and diligent preparation by the entire racing organization of Daimler-Benz paid off. The racing strategy of Alfred Neubauer was faultless, despite some misgivings during the first days of the five-day affair when the competitors were well ahead of the Mercedes-Benz team. Had it not been for the unfortunate wheel alignment problem on the car of John Fitch and his consequent disqualification, again a triple victory would have been a certainty.

The year 1952 had ended and so had the racing activity of the company. At least, for the time being. This suspension was but a temporary expedient, so as to gain time and all possible manpower

Fangio (8) and Moss (10) in the Nürburg-type Formula I car
Fangio und Moss auf dem Nürburg-Typ Formula I Wagen

to construct the Formula I racing car. Mercedes-Benz would again be represented on the Grand Prix circuits of Europe, and such a representation against strong international competition would take all of the ingenuity and total efforts of the personnel of Fritz Nallinger's department in order to be successful in the best tradition of the company.

Three secretly developed 2.5-liter Formula I Mercedes-Benz racing cars, Model W 196, started on July 4, 1954, at Rheims-Gueux for the running of the forty-first French Grand Prix. During practice the Argentine master driver Juan Manuel Fangio, who had been world champion in 1951, lapped the 5.18-mile, extremely fast circuit in an amazing performance at more than the magic 200 kilometers (more than 124 miles) per hour. Next to him, in the first starting row, was Karl Kling. And Hans Herrmann started in the third row.

As the starting tricolor fell, the two leading silvery Mercedes-Benz racers sped away with tremendous acceleration, ahead of the field of 21 fast Ferrari, Maserati, and Gordoni machines. In the very first lap the fastest Maserati, driven by Ascari, was forced to retire. In the second, Gonzales pushed his Ferrari briefly into second place but soon fell behind the Mercedes-Benz driven by Kling. Herrmann drove his car hard, set a new lap record for the course, and was in third place after the twelfth lap. The Ferrari contingent with such outstanding drivers as Gonzales, Hawthorn, Trintignant, and Manzon, and the Maserati works cars with Villoresi, Marimon, Bira, and Ascari, who eventually used up several cars, did their excellent best to fight off the Mercedes-Benz threat, but to no avail.

When the halfway mark was reached, two Mercedes-Benz racers were well ahead of the remaining eight cars. The other cars had been unable to stand up to the terrific speed set by the leaders. The Mercedes-Benz of Herrmann had retired in the seventeenth lap. The average speed was over 118 miles per hour, but now the leading cars, changing positions frequently, slowed the brutal pace somewhat.

Fangio crossed the finish line first, with Kling a few feet behind. Manzon, driving a Ferrari, placed third. The average speed of the winning Mercedes-Benz car was 115.98 miles per hour for the 307-mile distance. In 1938 von Brauchitsch had driven his winning 485-horsepower supercharged, 3-liter Mercedes-Benz an average of 101.3 miles per hour over a similar distance.

Generally, the builders of a new racing car do not expect their creation to be victorious at the very first competitive appearance, but consider the initial debut as a dress rehearsal. But the first showing of the new, streamlined Mercedes-Benz Formula I racing cars resulted in an astonishingly impressive victory over the well-proved, successful Italian Grand Prix machines. It was reminiscent of the French Grand Prix of 1914 at Lyons, when the new Mercedes racers swept all opposition aside and won the first three places decisively. Or of the 1939 Tripoli when the 1.5-liter Mercedes-Benz racing cars bested the large field of strong opposition. The impossible had been done at that time by Daimler-Benz just as it was achieved now, fifteen years later.

The second appearance of the Mercedes-Benz racing cars was two weeks later at the British Grand Prix, run during extremely foul weather on the slow 2.93-mile Silverstone airport course. But their monoposto bodies were not ready for the cars. Rather than cancel their anxiously-awaited appearance in the British Isles, the Mercedes-Benz cars started in their fully streamlined version, most unsuitable for the short circuit, which was entirely devoid of fast straightaways. Fangio started at the pole position, having incredibly made the fastest practice lap at an average of 100.35 miles per hour, the fastest time ever recorded at Silverstone. Kling was in the second row. Among the other 28 starters were Ferrari, Maserati, and Gordini racing cars.

Until the fifty-fifth lap, the Mercedes-Benz of Fangio was in second place, although both front fenders were badly crumpled by numerous encounters with hay bales and pylons. Even an experienced Grand Prix driver has to see his front wheels when rounding the tricky turns of the course. With considerably impaired visibility, Fangio was unable to take full advantage of the course and skirt the corners by a razor's-edge width.

After 90 laps, the end of the 274-mile race, Gonzales and Hawthorn, driving Ferrari cars, were first and second; and Marimon was third, driving a Maserati. Fangio placed fourth, and Kling seventh. The winner's average speed was 89.69 miles per hour.

When, again two weeks later, the European Grand Prix was held on the mountainous Nürburgring in Germany, the new-type bodies were ready for three of the four Mercedes-Benz cars entered. Ferrari and Maserati cars were well represented among the 19 starters. Fangio had again made the fastest practice time. He bettered the lap record made by Lang in a supercharged 3-liter Mercedes-Benz. This remarkable achievement suggested a tremendous development in usability of available engine power, immensely improved suspension, brakes, and other mechanical parts of the car, as well as excellent driving ability.

After five laps around the twisty 14.17-mile Eifel Mountain circuit, the three Mercedes-Benz cars of Fangio, Lang, and Kling were in the lead, breaking lap records repeatedly as they roared around the 174 curves and turns of the punishing course. But Herrmann, who drove the streamlined Rheims-type Mercedes-Benz, went out of the race during the seventh lap.

It looked as if the Mercedes-Benz cars would make the most of their opportunities on their home course. The cars, with some technical improvements quickly made, but not fully tested, but well prepared by the Daimler-Benz racing department in Stuttgart, directed advantageously by the able race manager Alfred Neubauer, and expertly driven by the masters Juan Manuel Fangio, Hermann Lang, and Karl Kling, appeared invincible.

At the halfway mark the average speed was 84.2 miles per hour. Then Kling made the fastest lap of the race at 85.75 miles per hour, and Lang spun his car at a tricky turn and was unable to start it again. When Kling was forced to make an unscheduled pit stop in the nineteenth lap, the Ferraris of Hawthorn and Trintignant passed him. What had looked like another certain one, two, three win for Mercedes-Benz now became but a single victory. Fangio won the European Grand Prix at the Nürburgring at an average speed of 82.77

Moss driving with fine precision at the British Grand Prix
Moss fährt mit schöner Genauigkeit beim Grossen Preis von England

Fangio in the tricky Carrousel at the Nürburgring
Fangio in der tückischen Karussell des Nürburgrings

miles per hour for the 312 miles. Kling placed fourth.

The Swiss Grand Prix was run on the Bremgarten circuit near Bern. Three of the open Nürburg-type Mercedes-Benz cars with Fangio, Kling, and Herrmann started. Fangio led the field of fifteen cars after the first lap. At the halfway mark the Mercedes-Benz racers were in first, fourth, and fifth places. Fangio drove the fastest lap of the race with an average of 101.9 miles per hour. Kling retired his car at the thirty-ninth lap.

Fangio won, driving his Mercedes-Benz at an average speed of 99.2 miles per hour for the 288 miles. Gonzales, driving a Ferrari, placed second; and Herrmann in his Mercedes-Benz placed third. With this victory, the 38-year-old Juan Manuel Fangio of Buenos Aires secured the 1954 World Champion automobile racing title.

In the Italian Grand Prix at the fast Autodrome track at Monza, three Mercedes-Benz racers participated against seventeen other Grand Prix cars. Here, the Italian competition was especially fierce. Ascari was allowed by Lancia to drive the more competitive Ferrari, to strengthen that team and offer the strongest possible competition to the invading Mercedes-Benz team, consisting of two Rheims-type, enclosed racing cars driven by Fangio and Kling, and an open Nürburg-type model driven by Herrmann. By virtue of the fastest practice time, Fangio had the pole position. Kling started in the second row, and Herrmann in the third. Fangio was first away, with Kling close behind him.

The lead changed several times during the fast race. Kling retired his Mercedes-Benz during the thirty-seventh lap. Fangio won the race, driving his Mercedes-Benz at an average speed of 111.99 miles per hour for the 80-lap, 313-mile event. Hawthorn and Maglioli, driving Ferraris, placed second and third, respectively. Herrmann in his unstreamlined Mercedes-Benz finished fourth.

The Berlin Grand Prix was run on the extremely fast Avus track with its steeply-banked high-speed turns. The only other works team entered was that of the French Gordini, although Ferrari and Maserati cars were among the ten starters.

The fully streamlined Mercedes-Benz racers finished in the first three places, after traveling well in the lead, and with great regularity, around the course for sixty laps. Kling won with an average speed of 133 miles per hour for the 312-mile distance. Fangio placed half a second behind the winner, and Herrmann was third.

Three Nürburg-type Mercedes-Benz cars participated in the Spanish Grand Prix at the 3.93-mile Pedralbes circuit at Barcelona. Fangio again started in the first row; but Ascari, driving a new Lancia, had made the fastest practice time by one second. In the front row were also a Ferrari and a Maserati. The Mercedes-Benz of Herrmann

was in the third row, that of Kling in the fourth. There were 21 cars.

As early as the second lap one of the new Lancia cars retired. In the next lap a Ferrari gave up. The fast Lancia of Ascari quit after nine laps. The terrific pace took its early toll.

At the halfway mark, Hawthorn, driving a Squalo Ferrari, was in the lead with Fangio in second place. When a nasty whirlwind blew papers and debris onto the racing cars and clogged their cooling systems, several retired promptly because of overheating.

Herrmann went out on the fiftieth lap. Hawthorn won the 80-lap

Three streamlined Formula I cars on the Avus track

Herrmann, Kling, und Fangio in der Südkehre der Avusbahn

Stars and Stripes over the Avus curve in Berlin

Die amerikanische Flagge über der Avus Curve in Berlin

race at an average speed of 97.99 miles per hour for the 314 miles. Musso, driving a Maserati, placed second, and Fangio third. Kling placed fifth.

Because the newly-adopted Grand Prix Formula I had limited supercharged engines to 0.75-liter displacement, the Daimler-Benz engineers decided to abandon their historic tradition and construct an unsupercharged engine of 2.5-liter capacity for their racing cars.

The remarkably successful Mercedes-Benz racing car was powered by a straight 8-cylinder engine, placed at an angle to achieve a lower frontal area. The bore was 76 millimeters, and the stroke 68.8 millimeters (2.99 by 2.71 inches), giving it a total displacement of 2,496 cubic centimeters. Compression ratio was believed to be around 13 to 1, and output to be around 280 brake horsepower.

The engine had a central crankshaft drive which provided a power take-off from the center of the 8-cylinder engine. This minimized torsional vibration greatly and placed the strain of only four cylinders upon the crankshaft. The direct Mercedes-Benz fuel injection, with pump and nozzles of Bosch manufacture, was designed especially for racing purposes and took more than a year to develop. It ensured a better mixture distribution between the cylinders at all speeds and improved low-speed performance considerably. The throttling effect of a normal carburetor venturi was eliminated by the direct fuel injection, thus increasing peak engine performance. The improved distribution of the mixture made also for more economy in fuel, because the fuel quantity injected into each cylinder was exactly the amount used. A large fuel tank was placed behind and on the left side of the driver. Refueling stops for races of the regular Grand Prix distances of 500 kilometers (310.7 miles) were completely eliminated.

The clutch was a single dry plate and the five-speed transmission was mounted directly on the rear axle, behind the wheels. Independent wheel suspension was used with a genuine swing axle with lowered pivot point in the rear. In this type, the joint center of motion of the swing arms lay in the middle of the vehicle below the rear axle housing. The swing arms were longer, and the center of motion was lower, giving greatly-improved driving qualities over the former double-joint axle.

Torsion bars were provided. The huge four-wheel brakes, with light metal alloy brake drums, were turbo-cooled and were mounted inside. Fresh air, for the comfort of the driver and to cool the rear brakes, entered through the grilled opening in the cowl in front of the windshield. Sixteen-inch wire-spoke wheels were used with tires of various dimensions, best suited to the different racing circuits; and the tires were so much improved that, under ordinary racing conditions, the entire Grand Prix distance could be traveled without a change.

Two body styles were available in the Mercedes-Benz 2.5-liter Formula I racing car. The fully-enclosed and highly streamlined Rheims-type for long and fast courses, and the open monoposto Nürburg style for short and twisty circuits where visibility of front wheels and maximum maneuverability of the powerful racing machines were of prime consideration.

The formidable Mercedes-Benz Grand Prix racing cars had won five of the seven events in which they were entered in 1954. One of these was a double triumph, one was first and third place, two of them were first and fourth places, one was only third and another was merely fourth, while the minor Berlin race gave the Formula I cars a triple victory. And Juan Manuel Fangio again won the World's Driving Championship with 42 points. The long-dominant, red Italian racing cars were now decisively beaten on the Grand Prix circuits of Europe by the Mercedes-Benz silver arrows. The winning combination of extensive Diamler-Benz engineering experience and superb workmanship, indefatigable race preparation, and excellent team management, as well as faultless championship driving, was again nearly impossible to beat. It seemed as if another era, similar to that one of twenty years before, might once more be repeated.

The Daimler-Benz racing program for 1955 was even more extensive than that of the previous season. A racing sports car model was now developed and ready to be entered in such races. Actually, participation with the 300 SLR had been announced in 1954 for the Le Mans Endurance Trial, the Italian Mille Miglia, and the Carrera Panamericana, but this had been cancelled.

The 300 SLR was developed from the Grand Prix racing car, with the same technical features but an enlarged engine of three liters displacement. The body was, of course, built to conform to the exact specifications of the FIA for sports cars, but many features of the 300 SL, such as the air scoops to cool the brakes, were also used — as they had been in the Formula I car.

While in the Formula I competition the Italians were the only real adversaries, in the sports category a much larger number of opponents existed. Besides the Italian makers, several British manufacturers were also constructors of competitive sports cars.

The 1955 racing season started in South America. At the Autodrome at Buenos Aires in January, the Mercedes-Benz team experienced a difficult problem, that of adjusting after a 36-hour flight from the bitter cold wintry climate in Europe to the over 100 degrees Fahrenheit heat of Argentina. Consequently, the full capabilities of their racing cars could not be achieved on the circuit, and thus the less powerful and less skilled competitors were quite successful.

Juan Manuel Fangio, however, made the fastest practice lap at 80.75 miles per hour, and despite the terrific heat, won the Grand Prix at an average speed of 74.79 miles per hour. The extraordinary accomplishment of Fangio's driving to victory becomes clear only when one considers that the other cars needed three drivers to finish the race. The second place Ferrari was driven by Gonzales,

The successful Mercedes team at the end
of the season
Die erfolgreiche Mercedes-Mannschaft am Ende
der Saison

53

The clean lines of the 300 SLR roadster

Die sauberen Linien des 300 SLR Rennsportswagen

Farina, and Trintignant, the third place Ferrari by Farina, Maglioli, and also Trintignant, and the fourth place Mercedes-Benz by Herrmann, Kling, and Moss.

Two weeks later, a Formula Libre race, the Grand Prix of Buenos Aires, was held, to be run in two separate heats. The Mercedes-Benz cars had the 3-liter SLR engines installed for that contest. With the weather also more favorable than at the running of the Argentine Grand Prix before, Fangio was able to win the combined race, with Stirling Moss second, and Karl Kling placing fourth.

On May first, the 300 SLR sports racing cars made their first appearance at the Mille Miglia. The entire racing department at Daimler-Benz hoped that these cars would be more successful than the 300 SL sports cars were at their initial outing in the same competitive event three years before.

The engines had been road-tested in Argentina, but the demands of this 1,000-mile road race were quite different from those of the circuit race at Buenos Aires where they had been victorious. The Mille Miglia was definitely a race belonging to the Italian drivers, and their cars as well, because many of them were as familiar with the route to be traveled as was Piero Taruffi, who drove a large portion of it every week. And, of course, national honor demanded the car manufacturers to do their very best to win the race in their home country. Only once did a foreigner win the overall category of the Mille Miglia: Rudolf Caracciola won the event in 1931. The 300 SLR cars seemed to have a good chance this year to be victorious. A total of 533 appeared at the starting line, although 648 cars were entered in the race, which was divided into thirteen categories.

Stirling Moss, with the journalist Denis Jenkinson as navigator, drove a truly brilliant race and won the tortuous event at an average speed of 97.93 miles per hour. Fangio, driving alone, placed second. It was indeed an auspicious beginning for the new 3-liter racing sports car. The Ferraris had engines of 3.75 and 4.4-liter displacement but could do no better than place third, with Maglioli driving a 3.75-liter car.

In the Gran Turismo category over 1,300 cubic centimeters, the fuel-injection production 300 SL sports cars also achieved splendid victories. John Fitch, with Gessel as navigator, won at 86.62 miles per hour; Olivier Gendebien, with Wascher, placed second; and Casalla was third. The three 300 SL cars were really the fifth, seventh, and tenth overall winners as well, a truly superb showing for these cars. Fitch's elapsed time was actually only three minutes more than that of Ascari when he won the overall victory the year before. In 1952, Kling had, under poorer weather conditions, needed 45 minutes more with his racing version 300 SL. Even the special class for diesel-engined sedans was a triple Mercedes-Benz victory for their 180 D models.

Retter, with Larcher, placed first; Reinhard, with Wiesnewski was second; and Masern, with Cardiner was in third place. However, Retter's automobile took 16 hours 52.25 minutes to complete the 992 miles, while the 300 SLR of Stirling Moss needed 10 hours 07.48 minutes, and the 300 SL with John Fitch driving used 11 hours 29.21 minutes to travel the distance.

Three weeks later, at the Monte Carlo race, also the Grand Prix of Europe that year, the three Mercedes-Benz Formula I entries failed to finish. The cars were plagued with a minor mechanical problem when a small safety screw malfunctioned, although Fangio had been able to drive the fastest lap at 68.54 miles per hour during practice. As so often, the defect did not show up at the short distance but materialized later, during the 100-lap race around the houses of the gambling spa.

It was only a week later when the 300 SLR sports cars were at the difficult Nürburgring, competing in the Eifelrennen. They were a great success. Fangio won the event at an average speed of 80.98 miles per hour, with Moss placing second, and Kling fourth.

The Belgian Grand Prix was held on June 5 at the fine Francorchamps-Spa circuit in the Ardennes Forest area. Here, the Mercedes-Benz racing cars were not hampered by flying debris nor by any mechanical problems. Again, Fangio was able to drive the fastest practice lap, averaging 121.10 miles per hour. The magnificent Argentine driver also won the race, but his speed for the distance

Above, the 300 SLR with experimental air brake in place. Below, the Mille Miglia 300 SLR in its competitive trim.

Oben, der 300 SLR Rennwagen mit der eingesetzten Luftbremse. Unten, der 300 SLR in der entgültigen Ausführung für die Mille Miglia.

67169

was 118.75 miles per hour, still nearly 4 miles per hour faster than the previous year. Moss placed second in this Belgian Grand Prix.

The hotly contested Le Mans Endurance Race ended in a horrible disaster. Through a series of unfortunate events, not of his own making, the courageous Pierre Levegh, driving a 300 SLR, crashed into the crowd of spectators on the straightaway. Eighty-two persons lost their lives. The participating Mercedes-Benz cars were withdrawn from the race in respect to the dead team member and the many enthusiasts of the sport. (Fangio was two full laps ahead of the rest of the contenders at the time.)

The Dutch Grand Prix, run on the Zandvoort circuit in the sand dunes, was won by Fangio, but he did not achieve the fastest practice time. His winning average speed was 89.59 miles per hour, and Moss placed his Mercedes-Benz in second position, close behind the winner.

As expected, the British Grand Prix was a Stirling Moss affair. The best practice time was made by him, at an average speed of 89.62 miles per hour. The Daimler-Benz racing organization did its very best to ensure an overwhelming victory, remembering the disasterous participation of the previous event at Silverstone where Fangio could do no better than place fourth. Now, at the new Aintree circuit near Liverpool, with the stands filled to capacity, the Mercedes-Benz team fully expected to be victorious. Fangio had already ensured himself of winning the World Championship, and that may well have been the deciding factor, but nevertheless Moss won the event at an average speed of 86.52 miles per hour. Fangio was close behind the Britain, with the Mercedes-Benz of Kling and that of Taruffi next in order. Hans Herrmann had been sidelined after his accident at Monte Carlo and Piero Taruffi had taken his place on the factory team.

The Swedish Grand Prix was a sports car event, held at the circuit at Kristianstad on August 7. Fangio, driving the 300 SLR, won at a speed of 99.98 miles per hour, with Moss in second place. The Gran Turismo class over 2,000 cubic centimeters was a triple victory for the 300 SLs of Kling at 89.42 miles per hour, ahead of Erik Lundgren's and followed by Perrson's car.

At the fast Monza course for the Italian Grand Prix, Moss made the fastest practice time at 133.95 miles per hour, the fastest practice time on any of the Grand Prix circuits. However, Fangio won the Grand Prix, driving his Mercedes-Benz at an average of 128.42 miles per hour, more than five miles per hour slower than the best time posted by Moss. However, Moss's car failed to finish the race, while Taruffi brought his Mercedes-Benz across the line in second place, ahead of a Ferrari and two Maseratis.

The Tourist Trophy Race was held on September 17 at Dundrod in Northern Ireland. Three Mercedes-Benz 300 SLR cars were entered with Fangio and Kling, Moss and Fitch, and von Trips and Simon driving. Count Wolfgang von Trips was new to the team, but the French driver Simon had driven a Mercedes Formula I car at Monte Carlo. Competition was exceedingly keen at this 84-lap event on a narrow and twisty circuit, and the outcome of the 623-mile race

Moss and the 300 SLR at the Swedish Grand Prix
Moss auf 300 SLR bei dem Grossen Preis von Schweden

Neubauer, Fangio and wife, quite informal
Rennleiter Neubauer, mit Champion Fangio und Frau

was constantly in doubt. Finally, all opposition was successfully overcome and the Mercedes-Benz cars achieved a triple victory. Moss and Fitch won at an average speed of 81.32 miles per hour, with Fangio and Kling second, and von Trips and Simon in third place.

The historic Targa Florio came a month later. Again three 300 SLRs were entered with Fangio and Kling, Moss and Peter Collins, and Desmond Titterington and Fitch driving. The tortuous 45-mile Madrone circuit is a most difficult one to remember and the 1955 race had been increased to thirteen laps, totaling 582 miles. But a Mercedes victory was needed for the championship points. After several minor mishaps, Moss and Collins won the fiercely-contested race at an average speed of 59.8 miles per hour, with Fangio and Kling in second place. This fine victory gave Mercedes-Benz the sports car championship for the year.

The year 1955 was an excellent one for the Mercedes-Benz racing team. Juan Manuel Fangio won again the World's Driving Championship, amassing 41 points, actually one less than last year.

Schock-Moll in the wintry Sestriere Rallye
Schock/Moll auf der schneebedeckten Sestriere Rallye Strecke

More snow for Schock-Moll on the Sestriere Rallye
Mehr Schnee für die Fahrer Schock/Moll auf der Sestriere Rallye

Stirling Moss was second with 23 points, and Piero Taruffi earned 9 points for sixth place in the standings.

In six Grand Prix events, the Mercedes-Benz Formula I racing cars had won 5 firsts, 4 seconds, 1 third, and 2 fourth places. Of the five victories achieved, 1 was a quadruple, 3 were double, and 1 was a single triumph. And on five Grand Prix circuits, Mercedes-Benz cars also had been able to make the fastest lap times.

In four of the five sports car races, the Millie Miglia, the Eifel Race, the Swedish Grand Prix, and the Targa Florio, the Mercedes-Benz 300 SLR sports cars had won double victories, and in the Tourist Trophy a triple victory. It gave the factory the Sports Car Championship.

To demonstrate the possibility of a wide range of application, but perhaps more of an engineering exercise, the M 196 engine was installed into an especially-designed racing car transporter. This truly unique truck was capable of traveling at a speed in excess of 100 miles per hour on a fast road to deliver a racing car or quickly-needed spare parts to a racing event. This streamlined conveyance created tremendous interest whenever it appeared in the car parks of a racing circuit and also proved a most extraordinary publicity-getting object with reporters covering the race itself.

The 300 SL sports cars were also successful in several other events than the Mille Miglia and the Swedish race that year. W. J. J. Tak and Niemöller were victorious in the Tulip Rallye in April-May, when the Mille Miglia was held.

Olivier Gendebien won the 189-mile Dolomite Gold Cup Race in July, won with Stasse the 3,150-mile-long Liege-Rome-Liege Rallye, where Engel with Straub placed fourth, and won with Thirion the Stella Alpina, the Mountain Reliability Run over 693 miles, in August, while Fabregas with Bas placed second, all driving the Mercedes 300 SL.

The amateur driver Werner Engel of Hamburg won the European Touring Car Championship of 1955. He won a class victory with the 220 sedan in the Tulip Rallye and the ADAC Rallye, then changed to the 300 SL and placed third in the Wiesbaden Rallye in June, won the Adria Rallye in July and placed fourth in the Liege-Rome-Liege Rallye that August. With his sixth place in the Tour de Belgique in

Lippmann-Zirion, winners in the Guatamala Race
Lippmann/Zirion, Sieger im Grossen Automobilrennen von Guatamala

Two 300 SLs leading in the Swedish Grand Prix
Zwei 300 SL Spitzenfahrer im Grossen Preis von Schweden

Pollet-Moss driving in the Tour de France

Pollet/Moss fahren in der Rouen-Les Essarts Tour de France

A 300 SL leading two Ferraris in the Tour de France

Ein 300 SL führt zwei Ferrari Wagen in der Tour de France

Moss ahead of Fangio at Aintree in the British Grand Prix

Moss vor Fangio bei dem Grossen Preis von England (Aintree)

Kling in the 300 SL at the Swedish Grand Prix

Kling in einem 300 SL im Grossen Preis von Schweden

October, Engel became also the long-distance champion of Germany. And Armando Zampiero won the Italian Sports Car Championship.

In 1956, the team of Walter Schock and Rolf Moll were able to win the Acropolis Rallye and the Sestriere Rallye and place tenth in the Geneva event with their 300 SL sports car. That year, Willy Mairesse with Genin, driving a 300 SL, won the Liege-Rome-Liege Rallye, the classic European 3,145-mile country race.

In 1957, the Fifth Rallye Around Spain was won by Andres with Portoles and their 300 SL, and the great National Auto Race Caracas-Cumana-Caracas, a 992-mile distance event, was won by the team of Dos Santos and Huertas.

The following year, among the Mercedes-Benz victories were that of Cotton and Simon with their 300 SL of the French Snow and Ice Rallye.

In the United States, several drivers entered their 300 SL coupes in amateur racing events. The all-aluminum bodied cars, equipped with the optional racing cams, were especially successful, and were seen frequently in club events throughout the country.

Some of the more persistent and often victorious drivers were Rudy Cleye, Lance Reventlow, Bruce Kessler, Tony Settember, Charles Wilson, and Arthur Simmons. But the most successful, by far, was Paul O'Shea, who won the national sports car championship three years in succession.

Speculation as to actually how fast the 300 SL would go intrigued not only the factory engineers but also private owners of the car. Traveling to the famed Bonneville salt flats, William Scace in 1955 reached a maximum speed of 136 miles per hour, and the following year Albert Schmidt achieved 152.095 miles per hour with his 300 SL. Then, in 1959, J. A. Stallings drove his car to clock an average of 143.769 miles per hour. The next year, Stallings again returned to the salt flats and bettered his former speed to reach 144.839 miles per hour, while at the same time Gordon Worthington was timed at 148.209 miles per hour, the best yet.

Years earlier, in Germany, the car driven by John Fitch in 1955 at the Mille Miglia, was taken to the autobahn, north of Munich, and driven by Mischke, one of the Uhlenhaut assistants. He reached 155.5 miles per hour with a 3.09 to 1 axle ratio installed.

Near Zagreb, in the Liege-Rome-Liege Rallye
In der Nähe von Zagreb, während dem Liege-Rome-Liege Rallye

Fangio jubilant after a strenuous drive in the Argentine Grand Prix

Fangio ahead of Moss winning the Dutch Grand Prix at Zandvoort

Der siegreiche Fangio beendet die anstrengende Fahrt im Grossen Preis von Argentinien

Fangio gewinnt den Grossen Preis von Holland vor Moss (Zandvoort)

The Production Coupe

The 1952 racing activities of Daimler-Benz in Europe had once again brought the Mercedes-Benz name before the American automobile racing enthusiasts, but participation in the merciless Mexican Road Race brought an enormous amount of additional publicity.

Here then was a million dollars worth of free advertising for the Mercedes-Benz automobiles, but taking advantage of it proved a difficult task for the company. Sales of cars increased appreciably.

The distributor for the United States, the Hoffman Motors Corporation of New York, was naturally concerned with this problem, because it was not always an easy matter to transfer the success of a specially built sports car to the line of regular passenger sedans. Even if the engines were practically the same and basic construction features were almost identical to the 300 models, the two cars were certainly not alike in appearance and performance.

From 1949 to June 30, 1952, Daimler-Benz produced a total of 4,432 cars of the 300 and 300 S models, and the entire world export business of the company had increased from 156 million marks in 1951 to 225 million marks in 1952.

Max Hoffman had been a sports car racing enthusiast. During his earlier years, in 1922 to 1924 in Europe, he had competed with an Amilcar and Grofi in Austria, then drove a Bugatti and Lancia in other races on the continent. As importer of the Porsche cars into the United States, he competed in some races, naturally driving the early Porsche coupe, and no doubt thus calling objective attention to the agile competitiveness of this small imported sports car.

In fact, Hoffman was responsible for bringing many European makes of automobiles into this country, introducing besides the Mercedes-Benz and Porsche, also the Volkswagen, Alfa Romeo, Fiat, Lancia, Maserati, BMW, and others.

At a Daimler-Benz director's meeting at Stuttgart-Untertürkheim, the astute Max Hoffman suggested that a sports car identical to the competition 300 SL be built and sold to the general public, perhaps at first to selected sportsmen who would participate in racing events. (Sports car clubs were just coming into their own at that time and club racing was a popular activity all over the country.)

During the discussion of this suggestion, Chief Engineer Fritz Nallinger expressed opposition, but the new General Director Fritz Könecke favored the proposal. The whole question was settled, at least to the complete satisfaction of the board of directors of Daimler-Benz when the courageous Hoffman placed a firm order for 1,000 such sports cars. This was, of course, an immensely daring commitment to make, but obviously the importer had the conviction that he could sell such a car to the American public. Had it not been for the visionary Max Hoffman, the 300 SL would never have gotten into production at all, for the officials of Daimler-Benz did not believe that a sufficiently large market for such a sports car existed.

Almost the identical situation was repeated when, upon the suggestion of Hoffman, Daimler-Benz agreed to build the 190 SL, but not before he again made a firm commitment to take 1,000 such cars.

More than a year after the successful participation of the 300 SL factory cars, the new prototype model, available to the public, was shown at the International Motor Sports Show in the Seventh Regiment Armory in New York on February 6 to 14, 1954. However, actual production of the slightly changed cars did not get under way in Untertürkheim until that early fall.

The engine as well as the body were considerably altered. Although the engines of the competition cars were equipped with carburetors, comprehensive tests had been made on fuel injection

The pre-production model of the 300 SL coupe

Der Vorserienwagen des Typ 300 SL

engines, and when final plans for the production of sports cars were made, it was decided to use the gasoline-injected engines.

Daimler-Benz had, of course, considerable experience in building fuel injection engines for aircraft, having delivered a total of 70,485 units of their famed DB 601, 603, and 605 types during the years 1936 to 1945. (By the end of 1960 a total of 2,830 fuel-injected 300 SLs were produced, according to Hans Scherenberg.) Scherenberg was responsible for the development of direct fuel injection for diesel engines and had been able, with Heinz Hoffmann, to effect the fantastic output of 2,770 horsepower for the DB 601 twelve-cylinder aero engines which powered the Heinkel He 100 planes and gave them a speed of 746 kilometers (about 463.54 miles) per hour and the Me 209 V 1 of 755 kilometers (about 469.13 miles) per hour. (Thirty years later, the Grumman F8F-2 Bearcat reached 776 kilometers per hour, when Greenmeyer developed a suitable engine for that aircraft.) In 1952, Hans Scherenberg was made director of passenger car construction and various central development sections.

The direct fuel injection system for the 300 SL, developed in conjunction with Bosch engineers, was similar to that used in diesel engines. A new cylinder head had the necessary smaller combustion chamber, larger valves, and ports.

The six-cylinder gasoline injection engine was designated as the M 198 type, but was the same size as the old one. It had a bore of 85 millimeters (11/32 inches) and a stroke of 88 millimeters (15/32 inches), for a total displacement of 2,996 cubic centimeters (183 cubic inches). The compression ratio was raised to 8.55 to 1.

Maximum horsepower output of the engine was 240 SAE horsepower and the top revolutions allowed were 6,400. Maximum power output, however, was at 5,800 revolutions per minute.

The single overhead camshaft engine with seven main bearings showed a remarkable flexibility from idling speed to 6,000 revolutions per minute (red-lined). In high gear, one could drive smoothly in city traffic at 25 miles per hour and drive satisfactorily at the maximum speed of about 140 miles per hour. (After taking delivery of my car at Sindelfingen, I once drove off from a standing start in third gear. It was quite sluggish, but the car responded to the mistake.)

The four-speed syncromesh gearbox was similar to that of the 300 model sedan, but considerably modified to accommodate the greater engine power. The ratios were 3.34:1, 1.97:1, 1.385:1, and 1:1. Reverse was 2.73:1.

Attention was also paid to the problem of starting a very cold engine or restarting a hot one after a hard drive. By means of the choke, a good fuel mixture was provided to the cold engine. And the electric fuel pump, located in the tank, assisted the starting of the engine also at high temperature. It acted as a pump to supply the reserve fuel for the engine, of course.

The sufficient supply of clean oil, free of all foreign matter and elimination of oil foam, to all parts was of great importance to high performance engines, and therefore a dry sump was chosen. The engine had an excellent oil circulating system. From the reservoir the oil was brought by the pump through a filter located in the main oil channel of the engine and directed into all parts. The used hot oil was caught in the pan and forced by means of another pump through the oil cooler to be quieted down and then restored at the proper temperature and without turbulence and foam to the engine again.

The new valves had 49-millimeter heads capping ports of 44 millimeters. The exhaust ports remained at the old 36 millimeters, but with new 42-millimeter valve heads. The Bosch injection nozzles sprayed precisely-measured amounts of fuel directly into each of the cylinders through the holes formerly used for the spark plugs.

Early engine tests with this redesigned cylinder head, using Weber carburetors, gave the engine a power output of 186 horsepower at 5,800 revolutions per minute and a torque — up from 175 — at 193 pounds-feet at 4,200 revolutions per minute. With the fuel injection, the same engine showed an improvement to 214 horsepower at 5,700 revolutions per minute and a torque of 206 pounds-feet at 4,500 revolutions per minute. While this represented a noticeable increase in power, it was still considerably less than the output of the supercharged version of the competition car in 1952. That engine developed 230 horsepower.

One of the documents in the archives showed an exhaustive test

The neat fuel-injection unit makes for a clean engine

Die saubere Benzineinspritzungsanlage ist sehr ordentlich

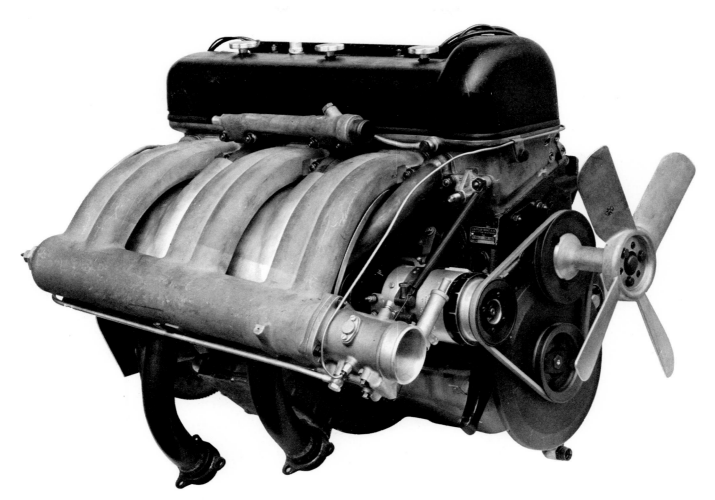

The induction pipes obstruct engine details below
Die Ansaugsrohre verdecken weiteres an dieser Seite des Motors

of one of these engines, which was made periodically, usually on every 35th engine to be installed. That comprehensive test showed not only the engine performance but also fuel consumption and wear of component parts. It was all part of the strict quality control program of the factory. The compression ratio was 8.7 to 1. (The variance of the compression ratio was always within two-tenths of a point of the nominal ratio of 8.55 to 1.) Power output was 219 horsepower at 5,800 revolutions per minute and torque of 207 pounds-feet at 6,400 revolutions per minute. A one-hour-long check was made at 5,750 revolutions per minute, and the output was 217 horsepower.

All of the engines were thoroughly tested. They were run for twenty-four hours on a dynomometer with six hours under full load. We visited the room where an M 198 powerplant underwent such a test, running continuously for these six hours at 6,000 revolutions per minute. The heat was almost unbearable and so was the noise. The exhaust pipe was a fiery red, and the cooling oil ran like water as it circulated to cool the motor through the radiator. Then, after another careful check, these engines were allowed to be installed in the 300 SL.

The light tubular frame structure was similar to the competition

Author and wife watch the testing of an engine for the 300 SL

Der Verfasser and Frau beobachten einen Motor auf dem Prüfstand für den 300 SL

models, consisting of thin, straight tubes, stressed only longitudinally and thus taking no bending stresses. Somewhat strengthened, it had two side rails, built up of braced cross-sections, with the uppermost tubes on about a level with the driver's elbow. In front and in the rear of the cockpit were two pyramidal structures ingeniously placed to support the weight of the engine and the suspension systems. The wheelbase remained the same, but the track was slightly changed to 54.6 inches in front and 56.5 inches in the rear.

The complete frame with attachment plates and blocks for the engine, axles, and such, weighed 82 kilograms (180.4 pounds), according to engineer Karl Müller.

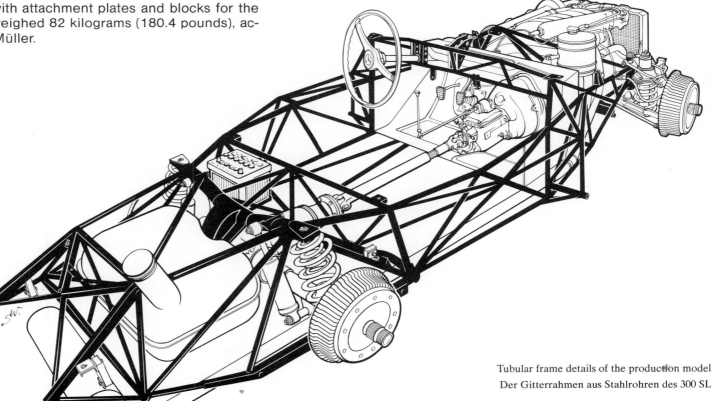

Tubular frame details of the production model
Der Gitterrahmen aus Stahlrohren des 300 SL

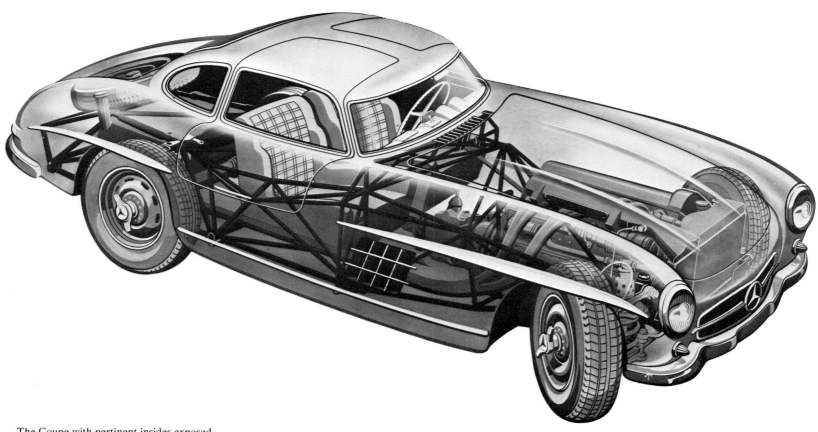

The Coupe with pertinent insides exposed

Durchsichtszeichnung des Sportwagens

But this production model weighed 1,200 kilograms, against the austere competition model's 840 kilograms. With about 20 percent more power available, it meant that the former advantageous 4.7 kilogram per horsepower was now a 5.6 kilogram per horsepower. Still, 0 to 60 miles was less than 9 seconds, and 0 to 100 miles per hour could be achieved in about 18 seconds. Considering that a speed of about 75 miles per hour could be reached in second gear, it was a good performance.

Aerodynamically the production model was not as clean as the simple, unadorned factory cars of 1952. Front and rear solid bumpers, a modernized shape of the frontal area with arrangements of the headlights, the chrome strip and the profile pieces over the wheel wells, all these refinements and decorations had raised the wind resistance factor by 0.397 to 0.7079. But the maximum speed was still a brilliant accomplishment. (With the 3.25 rear axle, the theoretical maximum was 161.5 miles (260 kilometers) per hour.)

The front axle was that of the 300 sedan. The rear axle was also similar to that of the regular passenger sedan model, a two-part swing axle. Independent rear suspension assured a solidly adhesive road contact, lower chassis clearance, and less weight. Coil springs and large shock absorbers were used all around. The car had a slight tendency towards oversteer, a preferable condition in racing events because such a vehicle is easier to handle than one which has understeer characteristics.

(The rear axle arrangement did not always find enthusiastic acceptance of all drivers, according to Richard Frankenberg. The system was adapted from the regular 300 model cars which weighed considerably more and were never driven as vigorously as the 300 SL. At high speeds the oversteer caused the rear of the car to break away frequently and especially in rain presented some serious problems for the fast driver. When applying the brakes hard, the direction of the car would alter, the vehicle would lift out of the rear springs, the wheels collapsed slightly, and the driver had to correct with utmost precision to forestall a break-away. That the arrangement was not the best solution, Frankenberg insisted, was proved when on the later roadster model it was changed.)

In a published paper on the "Technical Review of the Mercedes-Benz Sports Cars," Engineer Karl Müller stated that "racing has often shown that a slightly oversteering car is more easily controlled than one which understeers." He suggested that by the proper utilization of the swing axle and through proportioning of the springing between the front and the rear suspension, as well as the torsion bar at the front, the engineer can markedly influence the tendency toward either oversteer or understeer. The 300 SL had, like the Mercedes racing cars, in its cornering behavior a slight tendency toward oversteer.

The Al-Fin brake drums had an inside ring of silumin covering and the finned ribs of light metal acted as air pumps. The heavier front brakes got about 50 percent more pressure than those at the rear wheels through a Treadle-Vac servo booster which also reduced the pedal pressures quite noticeably. (With a total braking area of 1,664 cubic centimeters they were eventually considered inadequate with a full load of fuel and at maximum speed, and on the subsequent roadster were replaced with disc brakes.)

The body of this production coupe was, of course, considerably refined. The door was cut in a curve wider in the front for better entry, and the handle had undergone several changes in design from the hole for a finger-grip, to push-button, to the final handle which came out of a slot by simple pressure of the thumb. Instead of the austere cloth-covered thin seats, more substantial ones with real leather upholstery were shown. The center vent on the side windows had been replaced by opening quarter windows and removable side glass panels. The door opening mechanism was also greatly modified, now using spring-loaded struts.

Forward visibility was excellent. Both front fenders were visible to the driver and, because of the very low hood, the road in front of the car could be seen at only thirteen feet ahead of the car.

The well-placed instruments allowed for a quick reading by the

The production model with knock-off hubs

Der Serienwagen mit den Sonderausrüstung Rudge-Naben

driver. The steering wheel was hinged so that entry into the car and exit was possible for the driver without contortion. The bucket seats were comfortable and the leather upholstery was quite elegant.

Ducts in the cowl sent air through a double dash panel for good ventilation and a small opening at the rear top allowed the air to escape. Wind wings were provided but the side windows could not be lowered. However, they were removable.

Most of the trunk space was occupied by the large spare wheel and tire, the electric fuel pump and the fuel filler cap, with only a minute space for baggage, such as a pair of shoes or a very small grip. The space behind the seats, however, allowed for a generously-sized piece of luggage, and an especially designed and fitted suitcase was made available at extra cost. (The announced price for the 300 SL in Germany was 29,000 marks — from 1954 to 1957.)

The "Verkaufsinformationen," furnished by the Daimler-Benz sales organization to its salesmen in 1955, called "In the Headlight," pointed out the highlights of this, "the fastest German production sports car, the Mercedes-Benz model 300 SL."

The sixteen-page folder went on to call attention to the fact that the extraordinary success of the 300 SL sports car in the 1952 Carrera Panamericana Mexico focused special interest of all motor sports enthusiasts upon this product of the company. Particularly in America, but also in other countries of the world, an active demand for this car had been created. The company followed up this steadily increasing interest and began production of the car, displayed as an available object first at the New York Automobile Salon in 1954 to the public.

Because of its performance of 220, or 240 horsepower with the installation of the special racing camshaft, its high maximum speed, as well as its excellent roadability, the 300 SL is suited to start with promising potentialities in the Grand Turismo Class.

To drive this car is an adventure!

The superb road-holding ability, the powerful and sporty engine, the easy and precise steering, and the effective brakes allow this vehicle to be driven at high and maximum speeds, limited only by the human ability and not by the performance of the engine.

Fully expected surprises which one does not anticipate with this car, and which are not being written about in test reports, can be found only when actually driving in heavy traffic of a large city, in long and tight lines of vehicles, in step-by-step creeping from stopping place to stopping place. The vehicle can be driven equally as cautiously in first or second gear as any other passenger car, but with the advantage that, if necessary, with the powerful engine an incomparable speed can be quickly achieved.

Because of the elasticity of the engine, the third gear is unlimited in range between 30 kilometers (18.6 miles) per hour and 155 kilometers (96.3 miles) per hour, and even at low revolutions the car runs quietly and smoothly; in other words, the vehicle can be driven in city traffic quite easily slow or fast, as for example, the 220 model. In addition, there is the great advantage of maneuverability because of the small size and the superb all-around visibility.

When driving on the open road or on the autobahn it only depends — as with any fast vehicle — "on the head," that is to say, that one is always aware of the brake capabilities, because after but a short distance one can very easily forget the limit of safety and security at speed. (A diagram showed the various stopping distances required in braking.) Allowing a reaction time of one second, it takes exactly twice as long to stop the car on a wet asphalt or macadam surface (3.5 g) as on dry cement of the autobahn (7 g), and again the distance of stopping the car on slick ice (1.5 g) was twice as far as that on a wet asphalt or macadam surface (3.5 g). On dry asphalt or macadam, it was about between the cement and wet asphalt surface (5 g). (With the best brakes and optimum friction values between road and tires at a speed of 100 miles per hour, the car needed a

The regular production version of the 300 SL

Der reguläre Seriensportwagen Typ 300 SL

The spare wheel filled the trunk of the car

Das Ersatzrad füllt bald den ganzen Kofferraum

An early show car had polished air induction pipes

Die ersten Ausstellungswagen hatten polierte Luftansaugsrohre

Earlier version of the dash and gear shift lever

Armaturenbrett und Ganghebel der ersten Typen des Wagens

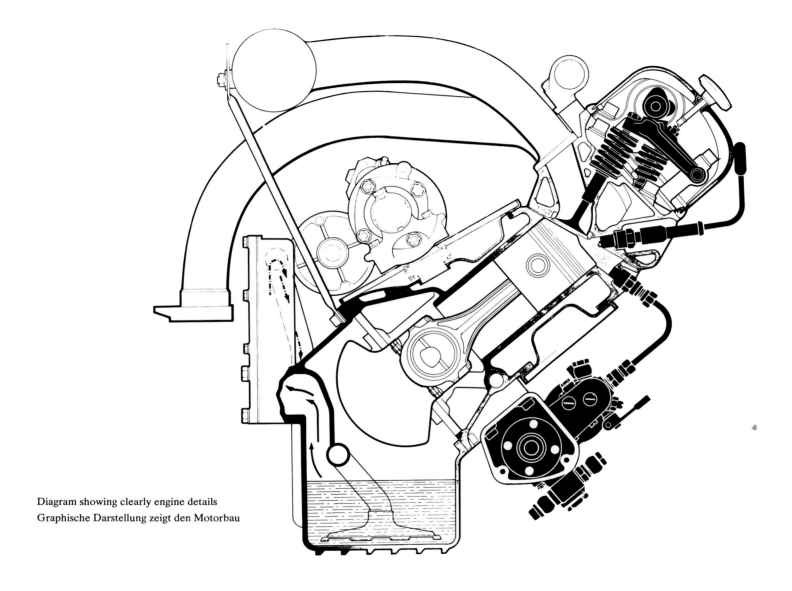

Diagram showing clearly engine details

Graphische Darstellung zeigt den Motorbau

braking distance of over 590 feet (180 meters), after allowance had been made for a reaction time of one second.)

This extraordinary performance is produced by an engine of six cylinders, with a seven main bearings crankshaft in especially sturdy four-metal housing, dry sump lubrication, and large oil radiator, which can hold effortlessly continuous revolutions of 6,000 per minute. With the regular ratio of 3.64 to 1 this equals a speed of over 200 kilometers (124.2 miles) per hour in fourth gear.

The average fuel consumption, depending upon driving practice, is between 12 and 19 liters (3 and 4-3/4 gallons) per 100 kilometers (62.1 miles), while the normal fuel consumption at 80 kilometers (about 50 miles) per hour is only 9.5 liters (2-3/8 gallons) per 100 kilometers (62.1 miles).

A large diameter air suction pipe makes available an almost uninterrupted air supply at top acceleration. High compression and thus improved performance in the entire revolution range are the advantages of fuel injection, which supplies each individual of the six cylinders and thus meters out the precise quantity of fuel necessary over the whole range of engine revolution. It guarantees at the same time the smoothness and elasticity of this six-cylinder engine and its jerk-free acceleration in direct gear from 25 kilometers (about 15 miles) per hour on. A thermostat in connection with an atmospheric device on the injection pump guarantees automatic compensation of air temperature and air pressure in different altitudes.

In the cylinder head is placed an automatically adjusted double roller chain, driving the camshaft and steering the valve mechanism of the 300 SL engine with relatively few moving masses, despite the large diameter of the valves. By this means the quiet and proper working operation, even at highest revolution, is assured.

The normal camshaft gives the engine an especially advantageous turning speed and therefore good acceleration in the lower and medium range.

Beyond that there exists the possibility of installing a special racing camshaft so that the maximum revolutions lay in an even higher turning range. This is, however, suitable only for drives in special competitive motor sport events for an average continuous turning of 4,000 to 6,000 revolutions.

The engine compartment is covered by a hood which opens in the driving direction, therefore cannot fly open during travel, and allows for easy access to the engine placed at an angle. Two fins, extending toward the rear, on the sides of the fenders, are interrupted by air exhaust vents which facilitate cooling of the engine compartment. The four forward speeds are fully syncronized.

Instead of the regular 3.64 to 1 rear axle ratio which is meant particularly for fast acceleration, on special order a ratio of 3.42 to 1 which allows still greater maximum speeds, can be installed. Beyond that, a third ratio of 3.25 to 1 is available which allows the greatest maximum speed, but offers considerably less acceleration and is not at all suited for driving the car in city traffic. The choice of ratios must, in every case, be made at the time of placing the order because a later alteration is very expensive.

The stress-free, third-dimensional tubular frame of this full swing axle car — the individual tubes are influenced only by pressure and pull factors — at light weight makes a considerable contribution to the unusual roadability of the Mercedes-Benz 300 SL, which is not lessened by maximum speed or poor roads.

The especially rugged body is bolted together with the frame as one unit. In its lines it appears elegant and racy and gives the vehicle an ideal aerodynamic form, not interrupted by the built-in headlights and combined blink-, rear-, and brake-lights.

The driver's compartment is provided with the well-known warm air exchange, air and heat, individually controlled for each side. An additional, quite effective fresh air system can be activated by a pull lever below the dash. This can be augmented by the use of the windows for greater air circulation. A double wall with air space protects the inside effectively against the high temperature as well as noise from the engine.

Two wide doors are opened upward and are held open by a telescope spring. Through this unique means of entry, Daimler-Benz has performed pioneer work on low sports cars. This allows for easy

Hinged steering wheel for easier entry and exit
Umgeklapptes Lenkrad macht Ein- und Aussteigen einfacher

Showing that the gull-wing doors are easily reached
Die Dame zeigt wie man einfach die Türen erreichen kann

and comfortable entry into the car. The outside door grips, set into the panel, can be swung up by a light pressure. Each door has an outside locking mechanism.

Two sprung and well-upholstered seats (gabardine combined with tex-leather), developed from racing seats, give the feeling of absolute safety when driving fast and in sharp curves. Both seats are divided and are adjustable lengthwise, and so offer even especially tall persons adequate room. For persons with a short upper body, a special cushion is provided.

Naturally, the 300 SL also has the tested hydraulic dampened Daimler-Benz ball point steering system, again returned to its straight construction. If so desired, a shorter or longer steering column can be installed.

The front axle is equipped with parallel cross bars which with the rear swing axle give the vehicle a solid hold on curves and provide completely safe roadability. These qualities are elevated and augmented by four unobstructed coil springs and four large-diameter shock absorbers. If desired, heavier shock absorbers which are, however, suited only for purely competitive driving, can be installed. Here too, later installation or change in construction is very expensive.

The automatically adjustable, hydraulically-operated brakes, with servo booster, allow hardest braking without physical exertion. These especially powerful turbo brakes, because of the highest heat conductive factors of the aluminum brake drums, allow the brake heat to escape into the surrounding air and therefore retain an extremely high braking action. Because of the strong air stream of the radial scoops, the brake drums are being cooled effectively even at continuous, strong usage. At the application of the brake pedal the pressure booster is activated which reduces the pedal pressure considerably.

One suitcase of real leather with strap or one set of suitcases consisting of two pieces of tex-leather with strap, can be tied on a metal rod in the large luggage space located behind the seats.

In the rear trunk space, easily accessible through the deck lid

which can be locked, small pieces of luggage can be accommodated. It contains, besides, the handily-arranged spare wheel and the filler top for the 130-liter (34.3-gallon) capacity fuel tank, which gives the car a driving range of 650 to 1,000 kilometers (404 to 621 miles).

Although the vehicle is a typical sports car, we have not neglected to outfit it with great driving comfort which can even be wider augmented according to the taste of the customer.

(A sketch showing the various items in the cockpit, as seen from the driver's seat — Fahrersitz-Type 300 SL — and identifying 22 items, followed. A similar view is reproduced in the Appendix section.)

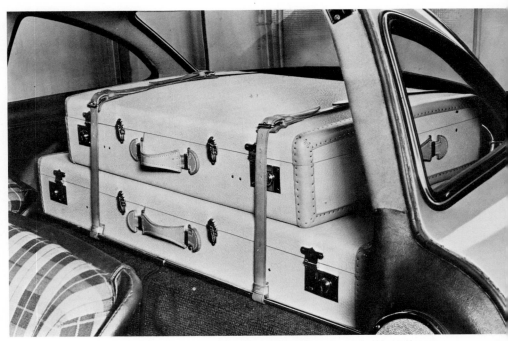

Fitted luggage rests neatly on shelf behind seats
Zwei Leder Koffer in der Gepäckablage hinter den Sitzen

Clean and easy to see dash board of the 300 SL

Sauberes und gut übersehliches Armaturenbrett

Two windshield wipers with two speed-steps guarantee even in bad weather an excellent view through the large, slightly curved windshield which can, like the side windows, of course, be defrosted.

The instrument panel is softly upholstered on its lower edge with a foam material. The instruments are positioned in an advantageous view of the driver. (Then follows a sketch showing the instrument panel and detailing 27 items. A similar reproduction is found in the Appendix.)

An auxiliary signal horn can also be used by the co-pilot, or the passenger.

The possible desire of the following special accessories supplements the already comprehensive outfitting:

A radio; upholstery with real leather; horns for front and rear bumpers; knock-off racing hubs, which, however, increase the weight of the vehicle by 12 kilograms (26.4 pounds); the very highly recommended distance blink-light signal installation; and the various possibilities of the previously-mentioned luggage.

The production paint work of the 300 SL sports car, equipped with five special tires, is the general metallic silver gray (nitro) DB 180.

Choice of upholstery:
1. Gabardine, blue-checkered, L I
   combined with blue tex-leather, L I
   (Inside decor: gray cloth. Carpet: Bouclé blue)
2. Gabardine, red-checkered, L II
   combined with creme tex-leather, L II
   (Inside decor: light beige cloth. Carpet: Bouclé creme)
3. Gabardine, green-checkered, L III
   combined with green tex-leather, L III
   (Inside decor: green-gray cloth. Carpet: Bouclé green)

Also available are several special colors with corresponding special upholstery, at additional cost.

(The next three pages list technical details of the engine, chassis, vehicle data, and fuel consumption. These, similar, figures are found in the Appendix, and listing them here would only be repetitious.)

The last item on this folder for the salesmen was: Naturally, our factory announced the 300 SL model at the FIA for international participation in sports car events. According to the international division, the vehicle competes in Group 2, middle section, also called Gran Turismo Class (Grosse PKW Klasse).

Thus, the factory was greatly interested to have the production version of the 300 SL used in competitive events, not only through direct factory participation but also by individual competitors elsewhere. The cars were accepted by the FIA for international competition in the sports car category Group 2, Gran Turismo Class.

Consequently, as a competition version, the production 300 SL was available with an all-aluminum body. The regular model had the main body panels made of steel, while the hood, trunk lid and doors were of aluminum. Twenty-nine such light competition models were produced over the years, and their weight was reduced by 176 pounds over the regular version.

A competition camshaft was also furnished. The coil springs were of a higher rate, and more stiffly adjusted shock absorbers were supplied with that lighter body style. Dunlop racing tires were generally fitted. But Continental had developed a new tire by 1954, which was exhaustively tested on the autobahn and proven satisfactory to the factory engineers. The tires were 6.70 x 15 on 5½K rims. Standard size was 6.50 x 15 on 5K rims.

To assist the cooling of the brakes, six large vent holes were bored on the front drums, covered by scoops facing outward. Rudge knock-off hubs were available, but they added some extra weight.

The 130-liter (34.3-gallon) capacity fuel tank was deemed to be adequate for long-distance competition and was not changed from that of the regular model.

During the autumn of 1953, Hans Herrmann had tested a new, and considerably lighter, 300 SL coupe on the Solitude Rennstrecke, near Stuttgart. The more powerful engine developed about 214 horsepower, and the driver was able to better the then existing motorcycle record for that circuit. Plans included to give the car an even lighter body of magnesium, lighter fuel tanks, and using cast alumi-

Drawing showing engine position and front end

Durchsichtszeichnung des Motors und der Vorderräder

num instead of cast iron for the cylinder block and transmission casing. For improved transmission of power to the rear wheels, the wheelbase was to be shortened to 90.6 inches, and the battery and oil tank were to be relocated at the rear for added weight, with the transmission mounted in the back and attaching it by a light magnesium adapter to the front end of the differential. A lowered pivot center was to be provided for the swing axle. But when later that year, Juan Manuel Fangio took the car Herrmann had driven, to the Monza circuit, he lapped that fast circuit at 110.61 miles per hour, still somewhat slower than the speed of the 3-liter Ferrari and Lancia cars of the previous June.

The work on the Formula I car and the 300 SLR sports racing car, however, took precedence and the refinements for the old 300 SL models were never carried out.

Asked if any great problems were encountered when changing from carburation to fuel injection, Rudolf Uhlenhaut in an interview stated that "with the 300 engines we have experienced no difficulties with the exception of a very few instances where the fault was with the proper functioning of the injection pump. Considering the total results, these few malfunctions are insignificant and not worth mentioning. For example, the electric pressure pump was originally planned and the very first cars built were fitted with all of the necessary connections for it. But delivery problems caused these early

vehicles to be produced without these fuel pumps. Installations were made after delivery of the cars to the customers, however.

"Actually, the injection mechanism is in reality not as complicated as it is generally believed to be by the public. Any problems of regulation at idle and at part-throttle were solved in our testing laboratories. The customer experiences no such problems. The only possibly-needed adjustment for proper idling is made by the turning of a screw, similar as with the regulation of a carburetor. It is a simple task, but it is, in my opinion, incorrect not to suggest to the purchaser of a car that the servicing of the fuel injection system is much simpler than that of a carburetor installation.

"The manufacture of certain parts of the fuel injection system is more complicated. The valve supports are, as in the carburetor, a solidly-poured piece with but few movable parts which give hardly ever any trouble. And, in large quantities, these units can be made quite reasonably in cost. We certainly envision," Uhlenhaut added, "this system as that of the near future."

Some minor changes were made in the production of the cars. My Santa Barbara mechanic, Hank Carnow, insisted that he had not seen two of the 300 SLs alike, but that was probably only an exag-

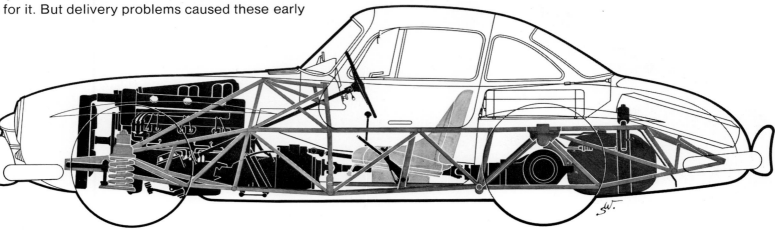

Transparent drawing
of engine and
drive components
Durchsichtszeichnung
des Sportwagens

From any side, the 300 SL looked powerful and competitive

Von jeder Seite, der 300 SL sieht mächtig und kampffähig aus

geration. He worked on the "competition version" owned by Hastings Harcourt, then a fairly successful amateur participant in club races on the West coast, and also serviced my car which was of the standard kind.

The prototype and the first 55 production cars had the rather awkward, long gear shift levers, angling back from the transmission, but easily handled. The shorter, vertical lever, used from 1955 on, had a remote linkage installed, and was preferred to the first type installation. The steering system also was eventually changed (after the first 150 cars) from the ZF worm and nut system to the proven recirculating ball steering gear of the 300 sedan type. The earlier Treadle-Vac vacuum booster was replaced, after some 350 cars were built, by the Ate T50 assist mechanism. And there were naturally other changes, too. The 300 SL was under constant surveillance by factory executives, most of whom drove such a car. And fast. For recreation they would drive out to the nearby Solitude or the farther Nürburgring in the Eifel Mountains. No doubt that each one of the directors had his personal suggestion to make to the technical director Nallinger for improvement.

Production figures, as officially released by Daimler-Benz, were as follows:

300 SL coupe, in 1954	146 cars
1955	867 cars
1956	311 cars
1957	76 cars
total number 1,400 units	

300 SL roadster, in 1957	554 cars
1958	324 cars
1959	211 cars
1960	249 cars
1961	250 cars
1962	244 cars
1963	26 cars
total number 1,858 units	

The nine-digit Baumuster (model) number on the identification plate showed the model (2), engine type (3), series (2), and the vehicle numbers (2). Later, another digit, the Reinbestell (order) number was added to show if the vehicle was meant for export or domestic sale. On cars where another engine replaced the originally installed one, another plate showed the replacement engine number as well as that of the original one.

Although *Road & Track* magazine had published a detailed announcement of the 300 SL coupe in its April 1954 pages, an actual road test of the car was not published until a full year later.

The long delay in getting to drive such a car for a comprehensive test had not lessened the anticipation of the testing editors, and the sometimes anticlimactic or even disillusioning reaction after extended waiting periods did not occur. In fact, the editors stated unequivocally that in their opinion the 300 SL coupe "is the ultimate in an all-around sports car. It combines more desirable features in one streamlined package than we ever imagined or hoped would be possible."

(H. U. Wieselmann, a well-known writer for the prestigious German automobile periodical, *Auto, Motor und Sport* had said, "Among the sports cars of our time the 300 SL is the most cultivated and most fascinating — a dream car.")

Asking some pertinent questions about performance, top speed, dual purpose, comfort, first cost, and depreciation, the editors gave some startlingly enthusiastic answers. Of course, anyone familiar with the car and with the excellence of the enthusiast's magazine, would have expected nothing less. Long before we became closer acquainted with the engineering knowledge of John Bond, we were greatly impressed with the judgment of his staff and their evaluation of the various cars tested over the years. That impression has been heightened, if anything, and the success of *Road & Track* as leader in its field is probably the best indication of its appraisal.

Performance was stated as acceleration from a dead stop to 100 miles per hour in just over 17 seconds. With the standard axle ratio the car can "approach an honest 140 miles per hour in less than 2 miles from a standing start. As a dual purpose car, the coupe can make a very acceptable showing in any type of sports car competition, yet it is extremely tractable and easy to drive in traffic."

The 300 SL coupe "is the most comfortable and safe high-speed cross-country car built today," was the judgment of the testers.

After examining the car carefully and in detail and considering the performance data, the question was "how can they do it for less than $8,000." The quoted list price was $7,463, although when first announced, a year before, the price was given as under $7,000. (The original price was $6,820, but eventually rose to $8,905 when pro-

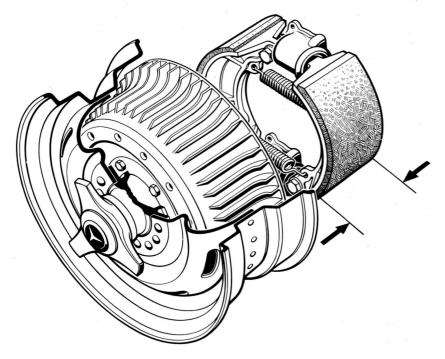

Powerful brake drums and lining detail
Bremstrommeln und Bremsmaterial Zeichnung

duction ceased.) With the Daimler-Benz reputation for quality and durability, plus the law of supply and demand, the editors predicted that it "may be three years before one could pick up a used one for less than five grand." (Twenty years later, one could not buy one for twice that much.)

Since no demonstrator cars were available from any of the authorized dealers in the United States, the magazine was fortunate in securing the personal car of a Santa Anita owner for their testing program. The car had 1,732 miles on the odometer.

On the way to the desert area testing location, the driver noted that the car was easy and comfortable to handle in traffic. The clutch action was just a little heavier than average and the off-idle throttle response had a slight lag, believed to be a typical characteristic of the unusual fuel injection system of the engine.

The seating position was high enough to be comfortable, but the knees of a five-foot-ten driver would tend to hit the underside of the steering wheel. The all-around visibility was excellent and the feeling of driving a relatively wide (70.5 inches) car was soon overcome.

The long cranked gear control lever left something to be desired and the action appeared a trifle stiff, the tester observed, but added that later models had a typical sports car remote control type shift lever. However, a surprising amount of gear noise from an otherwise very quiet automobile was noted.

The steering also was found to be unusual. It felt light and positive with only two turns, lock to lock, but took extra pressure to make any appreciable change in the steering angle. The feeling seemed to be exactly opposite to that of power steering. But after driving the car some hundred miles, the driver never noticed this anymore and at very high speeds the steering effort was quite light, yet remarkably enough it did not feel oversensitive or too quick for a sports car owner. For a former owner of a huge domestic car, however, the testing editor advised considerable caution at first when driving a 300 SL.

Instantaneous acceleration was found when stomping on the accelerator pedal in any gear and at any speed. Two aspects were detailed in the report. With first or second gear engaged at about

1,000 revolutions per minute and full throttle, the acceleration literally forced the driver back into the seat. And as the tachometer swept toward 4,000 revolutions per minute, the driver thought, "Man, what acceleration!" This experience was described as all hell breaking loose, for at the 4,000 mark things really began to happen. The Tapley meter swung way off scale in first, and nearly in second. The instrument had a top graduation of 600 lb./ton. The engine took on a hard note and began to scream, and in third gear, the driver was up to an indicated 100 miles per hour almost before he had time to think. Tremendous acceleration indeed.

When trying the brakes, carefully at first, the tester found that a pressure of only 25 pounds sufficed for a normal, comfortable rate of deceleration, because they are power-boosted. There was a good feel, with perfect control. When applying the brakes hard, at about 120 miles per hour, the nose of the car went down slightly and the passenger had trouble with his own rear-end adhesion to the seat. When applying the brakes repeatedly, there was absolutely no indication of brake fade, or loss of control, and in the opinion of the test driver, they were the best brakes ever employed on a production automobile.

The comfortable cruising speed of the car could be anything the driver liked. Once the tester held it at 120 miles per hour for a few miles, and he found that aside from the dangers of traffic there was no reason to worry at that velocity. In an aside he mentioned that no one could catch him at that speed. The engine felt smooth, and wind noise was almost nonexistent.

To prove his point, the editor wrote that at a timed speed run, at the first attempt, the owner who drove the car then at an indicated 140 miles per hour, shut off the car when he entered the measured strip. He had heard the two stop-watches start, and not being familiar with the procedure of timing, believed the running of the watches to be a signal to end the run.

While conditions for a high-speed test were not favorable, the magazine article credited the car with a genuine top speed of 140 miles per hour, although the average speed attained was actually 134.2 miles per hour. On both runs the tachometer showed 6,100 revolutions per minute, and the correct spark plugs should have added another 200 revolutions per minute. The plugs used were Bosch 280, but 310s are recommended by the factory for competition work. There was no reason in the mind of the editors to question the claim of the factory of a top speed of 160 miles per hour for the car when the engine is in good tune and when the optional high-speed axle ratio of 3.25 to 1 is installed. In the test car, which was one of the very early deliveries in this country, a 3.64 axle ratio was supplied, a compromise which is an excellent one for the average American enthusiast, the tester observed.

Acceleration figures for the various speed runs were as follows: 0-30 miles per hour in 2.7 seconds, 0-40 miles per hour in 4.0 seconds, 0-50 miles per hour in 5.7 seconds, 0-60 miles per hour in 7.4 seconds, 0-70 miles per hour in 9.2 seconds, 0-80 miles per hour in 11.6 seconds, 0-90 miles per hour in 14.2 seconds, 0-100 miles per hour in 17.2 seconds, and the average speed at the end of one-fourth mile, from a standing start was 15.2 seconds; the fastest run was actually made in 15.1 seconds.

Maximum speeds in gears were made at 6,500 revolutions per minute, with 52 miles per hour in first gear, 72.5 miles per hour in second, and 103 miles per hour in third gear. Shift points were at 6,000 revolutions per minute, at 48 miles per hour in first, at 67 miles per hour in second, and 95 miles per hour in third gear.

All of these acceleration figures were achieved without wheelspin and by using brisk, but not brutal, up-shifts. The solid bite of the clutch as each gear shift was completed was noted. Despite the terrific surge forward, the car was easily controlled and displayed no tendency to yaw under the fiercest acceleration. The driver observed that there the standard axle ratio contributed to the amazing acceleration abilities and at the same time gave flexible and tractable low-speed driving qualities which would appeal to the average owner.

The testing editor reasoned that undoubtedly the use of fuel injection in place of normal carburation had also improved the low-speed flexibility of the car, and he noted that this relatively modest

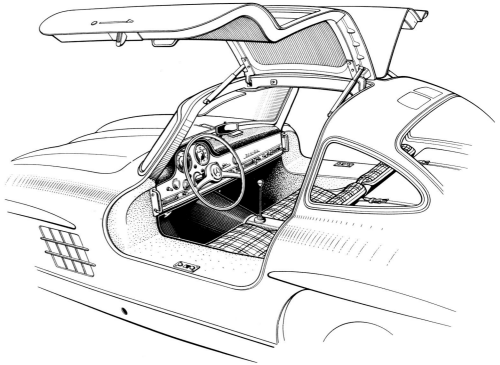

Ink drawing of the interior compartment
Zeichnung der Innenausstattung des Sportwagens

engine which developed over one horsepower per cubic inch at high revolutions had a dual personality. It performed at low speed in a manner nearly comparable to the pre-war American powerplant of the era when the time to accelerate from 5 to 25 miles per hour in high gear was all-important.

On the test car, the tire pressures used were as recommended in the owner's handbook, 43 psi in the front tires and 50 psi in those at the rear. With these rather high pressures the car proved extremely comfortable with a soft suspension that soaked up the bumps without recourse to lower tire pressures.

The editor stated that in his opinion comfort had not been sacrificed in any way on the car. In fact, it was the most luxurious sports car ever road-tested by the magazine. The fully-enclosed coupe had definite advantages over an open car, although one may appreciate

the pleasures of open-air motoring. Even the fact that the windows in the doors did not crank down proved no real drawback thanks to the efficiency of the very elaborate ventilating and heating system designed as an integral part of the car.

In closing, the testing editor stated that "when enclosed comfort is combined with a remarkable ride, uncanny wheel adhesion, quick steering and performance equal to or better than almost any car one can name, the conclusion is inevitable.

"The sports car of the future is here today!"

This honest evaluation reflected correctly the fervent enthusiasm of sports car lovers in this country at the availability of the Mercedes-Benz 300 SL coupe. Many had eagerly awaited such a comprehensive appraisal of the car ever since it was first shown to the public at the New York Automobile Show in February of 1954.

Four versions of the 300 SL: (from right to left): 1952 competition, 1953 pre-production, 1954-57 production, and Special SLR built in 1954

Vier Typen des 300 SL: 1952 Rennwagen, 1953 Vorserienwagen, 1954-57 Serienwagen, und in 1954 gebauter Specialwagen SLR

The 300 SL roadster with removable top in place

Der 300 SL Roadster mit dem abnehmbaren Dach

The Roadster Model

In the summer of 1956 when this writer visited the factory to take delivery of his 300 SL coupe, at a gala dinner with high company officials the conversation naturally turned to this superb sports car. The possible decision to discontinue regular production of the coupe was mentioned. I suggested that this would be a great miscalculation, for while the coupe with the unique Flügeltüren was a most unusual car, a roadster would be just another sports car and a far less exciting one than the original exotic model. Sales were tapering off, the General Director stated, and thus a model change and a further development — if not entire discontinuance of that type — was strongly indicated.

Of course, I was wrong, not in my appraisal of the fascinating style, but in my estimate of sales. The roadster actually outsold the coupe decisively. It was even a vastly better engineered car, was more powerful, superior in handling, and much easier to get into and out of. (But it did hardly deserve the designation L--leicht, or light.)

However, I believe that I was correct in the evaluation that the coupe was uniquely exotic among sports cars. But would it still sell sufficiently well enough to keep it in production? Only 76 coupes were sold in 1957, after the announcement of the decision to cease production. A total of 554 roadsters were sold that year by the company. Still, to sell the entire production of 1,858 roadsters took seven years, while 1,400 gull-wing coupes had been sold in less than four years. Sales of the newer model were quite disappointing to the factory directors, I was told later.

The 300 SL roadster was first shown to the public at the Geneva Automobile Show in March 1957. Production started in May. The price quoted was 32,500 marks, with the extra solid top costing an additional 1,500 marks. As a coupe, the price was 33,250 marks, which did not include a cloth top. (In 1954, the 300 SL coupe had been priced at 29,000 marks.)

The typical line of the 300 SL sports car was maintained, and the air space behind the engine made this car appear even sleeker and more fluent. The entire frontal appearance of the roadster, with headlights, fog lights, and turn indicators, was also considered more stylish than the older model, but had greater air resistance than the coupe. As on the coupe before, the design was created under the direction of Karl Wilfert. The complex tubular frame of the earlier coupe model was redesigned — it was lower and even more compact — to provide the additional stability necessary for the lowered

The 300 SL roadster as fresh-air open road car

Der 300 SL Roadster als Frischer-Luft Wagen

Prince von Urach and roadster at the Brussels World's Fair
Fürst von Urach auf der Weltausstellung in Brüssel

doors, but still maintain its original rigidity. The track was one centimeter wider (55 inches) in the front and 57 inches in the rear. The roadster was also five centimeters longer than the coupe.

Apparently well-aware of the limitations of the swing axle on the 300 SL coupes, first tests with an improved axle had already been conducted in 1951, using the 1939 model W 154 Grand Prix car. Rudolf Uhlenhaut stated that "a swing axle with a low pivot point produces excellent handling characteristics which are at least equal to those of the double-joint axle and are evidently even superior."

The conventional swing axle, the two pivot points outboard of the differential, had been replaced with a low-point swing axle, a single one right in the center. This arrangement resulted in improved wheel geometry — less camber change — and provided better handling, especially in curves. The horizontally placed spring over the rear axle housing had a definite stabilizing effect and gave the roadster a better ride, somewhat softer than that of the coupe. The two main coil springs at the hubs had been softened, and with the addition of a third coil spring the stiffness of the rear suspension was reduced

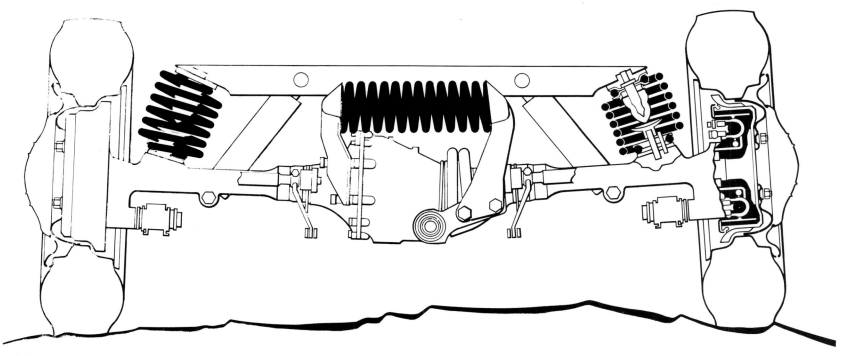

The simple joint swing axle with compensating spring
Die Eingelenk-Pendelachse mit Ausgleichsfeder

without impairing its load-carrying ability. These three springs could be adjusted to produce almost any desired kind of suspension for whatever road or racing circuit condition would be encountered. There was now almost neutral steering, no over- or understeer characteristics. The position of the engine with transmission, as well as the rear and front axle in the tubular frame, was slightly lower to enable the entering into the vehicle from the side. The roadster body also had some trunk space for luggage. (The fuel tank held only 100 liters (22 gallons) instead of the 130 for the coupe, and the spare wheel and tire were placed differently.)

To stimulate interest in the roadster version of the 300 SL in the United States and to demonstrate the car's capability in competitive events, a car was especially prepared by the factory for that purpose. However, the governing body, the Sports Car Club of America, after careful inspection, did not allow it to compete in the regular production class, but ruled that this roadster was a sports racing car and placed it in Class D to run against such 3-liter machines as the Aston Martin DB 3 S, the Maserati 300 S, and the Fer-

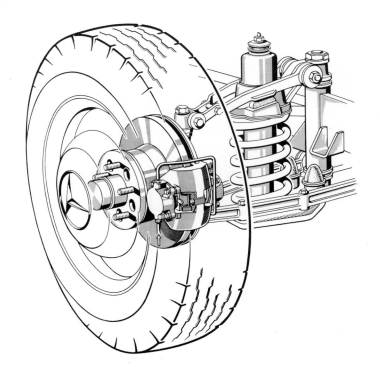 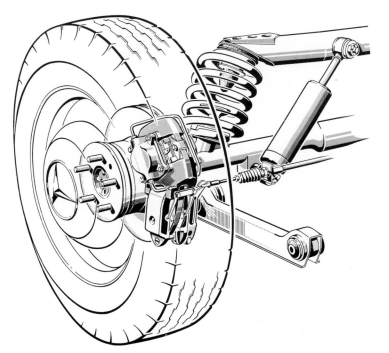

Front (left) and rear suspension (right) with disc brakes
Vorderradaufhängung (links) und Hinterradaufhängung (rechts)

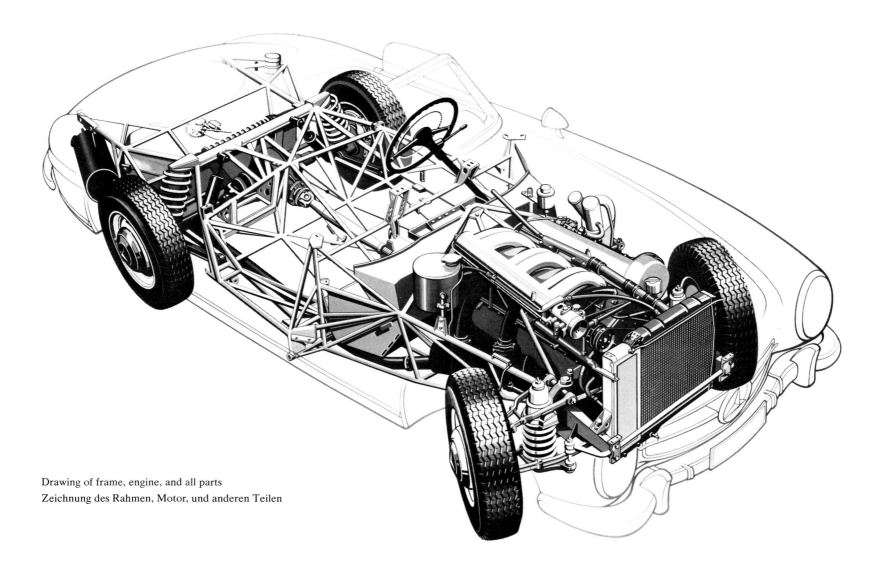

Drawing of frame, engine, and all parts

Zeichnung des Rahmen, Motor, und anderen Teilen

rari Monza models. To be driven by Paul O'Shea, the car was, of course, not standard production.

Holes were drilled in whatever parts could accommodate such weight-saving device, and the entire car was minutely gone over to eliminate any weight anywhere. For instance, the fan was left off. The inlet manifold was fabricated of welded aluminum instead of the usually cast material, the throttle valve assembly was considerably simplified, and proved to be even more substantial. The twin exhaust pipes, below the underhood vent, were arranged to exit from the right-hand-side rocker panel. The seats were also of a vastly lighter construction than the regular types furnished, although solid enough to offer the driver good support. The detachable steering wheel was even a lighter kind than the production cars had, but the cluster of instruments and controls was the standard as found on the regular model. To cover the extra seat, an elaborate tonneau cover was designed which had a scoop for added ventilation of the cockpit and greater comfort for the driver.

Although the competitive Italian sports cars were considered to be faster than this 300 SL roadster, the Mercedes-Benz often proved a more durable car than the formidable competitors. And by participating in practically every event possible, the German car, driven by O'Shea, amassed about three times as many points as did its nearest rival, a Maserati driven by Carroll Shelby, to win the Championship in Class D — Sports Cars in 1957.

When late in 1957 *Road & Track* tested the 300 SL roadster, the authoritative magazine found that merely minor changes had been made in this model from the earlier coupe.

The coupe had the higher compression ratio of the later manufactured coupes (9.5) and the once optional competition camshaft. (However, the earlier roadsters had an 8.55 to 1 compression ratio.) The rear suspension was the low pivot point type, by then adopted to all passenger models. A higher axle ratio was necessary for the heavier car to maintain the performance.

The weight was 2,920 pounds, 210 more than that of the coupe,

and the tested vehicle weighed 3,375 pounds, actually 315 pounds more than the coupe had three years earlier.

The axle ratio of the test car was 3.89, against 3.64 for the coupe and the times for acceleration were: 0-40 miles per hour 4.3 seconds against 4.0; 0-60 was 7.0 against 7.4; 0-80 were even, both 11.6, and 0-100 miles per hour were 18.9 seconds for the roadster against 17.2 for the coupe. All test drives were made with the cloth top up and windows closed, and Paul O'Shea drove these tests.

The engine was in perfect tune and the experienced driver was able to achieve excellent results. The ultimate top speed capability, however, as indicated by the factory, was not tried for. Top speed reached in first gear was 40 miles per hour, in second 68, and in third 96 with shifting points at 6,500 revolutions per minute. The top speed was estimated to exceed 130 miles per hour at 6,200 revolutions per minute, the peaking speed of the 250-horsepower engine. The official factory speeds and axle ratios were: 3.25 ratio and 155 miles per hour maximum speed; 3.42 and 150; 3.64 and 146; 3.89 and 137; and 4.11 ratio and 129 miles per hour. (The Swiss "Automobile Revue" had found their test car with the 225 DIN horsepower to achieve a maximum speed of 147.177 miles per hour.)

The two days of the tests "of this magnificent machine were spent with enjoyment because of the car's combination of qualities," the editors wrote.

The ride of the roadster was adjudged somewhat firm around town but improved considerably when the Michelin X tires were kept inflated at 24 pounds per square inch. At these pressures, the controls felt a little mushy and 31 psi in front and 32 psi in the rear tires was preferred for high-speed cruising. The slower steering of three turns lock to lock felt much safer than before when the ratio was two turns, slightly heavy at low speeds and much too sensitive at high speed for the average driver.

With the low pivot point rear suspension and more adhesive tires, the car was found to handle beautifully under all driving conditions, and the testing editors found a tremendous improvement over the coupe model which, to them, had a tendency to oversteer rather violently if pressed too hard. The roadster appeared to be absolutely neutral in steering, but the observation was made that eventually the rear end would break away rather suddenly.

The 300 SL roadster was considered easy to drive and to control. The seats held the driver firmly in place, but the rear edge of the cushion felt a little harsh after an hour or so of driving. Some drivers would like the very forward position of the steering wheel. The clutch was light and the gearbox control nearly ideal. The servo-ring synchronizers sometimes made the selection of the first gear a little trying and a six-foot driver may well object to hitting his elbow on the seat when pulling the gear shift lever into second gear.

The brakes were judged to be tremendous, as were those previously, with Al-Fin drums, a vacuum booster and 257 square inches of lining area. (In early 1961 the drum brakes were replaced by Dunlop disc brakes.)

The fuel-injection engine idled steadily at 800 revolutions per minute and was believed to be one of the most flexible units ever. Although neither the indirect gears nor the engine were entirely silent when pushed hard, the driver could tootle through town smoothly and quietly at 20 miles per hour in high gear if he so wished.

The price of the car, $10,970, was considered almost astronomical, but there was no doubt in the editors' minds that the 300 SL roadster was a truly great dual purpose sports car, equally at home in traffic and the open road or on the track. (Other sources quoted the original price of the roadster as $11,099 or $11,573 with both tops.)

A road test of the hard-top roadster was made by *Road & Track* in 1961. Some minute refinements had been noted in the car since it was first introduced and tested four years previously. Among the improvements in the outfitting of the car were the perforated leather seats to allow air to circulate and keep the seats cooler than before.

The curb weight of the hard top was 3,050 pounds, against the 3,075 pounds of that of the roadster with the cloth top. All other specifications were practically the same as on the earlier tested car. However, the acceleration times achieved on this later one were ap-

preciably slower than those of the open car, but that was driven by the experienced Paul O'Shea, while the editors tested the hard top themselves.

To reach 40 miles per hour from zero took 5 seconds, while the earlier car took only 4.3 seconds to reach the same speed. Zero to 60 was 7.6 seconds against 7.0; 0-80 was 12.5 against 11.6; and 0-100 miles per hour took 20.5 seconds against the 18.9 which O'Shea had posted.

Theoretically, the hard-top roadster should have been a faster car than the one with a cloth top, since the wind resistance is actually lower on the solid-top model than on the cloth-top one.

This writer had an opportunity to try out the roadster at the Lime Rock, Connecticut, circuit at the 1958 Second National Tri-O-Rama event of the Mercedes-Benz Club of America. We drove a few laps around the hilly track and had a splendid time in comparing the performance of this roadster model with that of our own coupe. However, no detailed scientific test was actually made of comparison figures.

That September, the expert Mercedes competition drivers Paul O'Shea and John Fitch demonstrated the cars to the club members on the SCCA course. In an exhibition five-lap race, the two drivers proved their skill in hurtling the cars around the tight course and, after changing the lead repeatedly, roared across the finish line in a dead heat, side by side — naturally.

John Fitch had been a member of the Mercedes factory team of sports car drivers, having quite successfully competed in the Mexican and several European events.

Paul O'Shea was three times the National Sports Car Champion. In 1955 he won the Cumberland Classic in a 300 SL and went to capture the title, winning fourteen races out of seventeen from coast to coast in the Mercedes sports car. In 1956 O'Shea was again champion. That fall he competed in Europe, driving at Monza, the Nürburgring, and at Solitude. Then he took the championship once more in 1957 for the third time. At Fort Worth, he had a narrow escape when his car was practically demolished, but he was unhurt. When, at the Cuban Grand Prix the Argentinian Juan Manuel Fangio was kidnapped by rebel forces, O'Shea was his teammate. However, he was not harmed. Later, in April that year, Paul O'Shea went out to win at El Salvador.

As he had in previous years with the 300 SL coupe, William Scace took a roadster to the Bonneville salt flats in 1958. Installing a 3.25 rear axle ratio, he averaged 143.191 miles per hour at 5,900 revolutions per minute. The following year, he tried to better that time, but the 3.42 axle ratio proved no help, and neither did the changed tire size. Then, in 1960, Scace installed a supercharger, but that additional implementation caused a piston failure and spoiled any attempt to establish a new record speed for the 300 SL roadster.

And so, over the years, the fascinating 300 SL left its indelible mark upon the auto world.

The spectacular initial successes of the competition version startled the international sports scene and more than opened a small window, as Fritz Nallinger had hoped. The coupe and roadster made a deep and enduring impression upon all who had the good fortune to drive them.

Twenty years after the introduction, the splendid 300 SL was still most desirable and highly valued — a well deserved accolade for a truly magnificent sports car.

The victorious Mercedes team at the
British Grand Prix: Uhlenhaut, Fangio, Taruffi, Moss, Kling, and Neubauer
Die siegreiche Mercedes Mannschaft beim Grossen Preis von England

Above, the 300 SL roadster with matching color top. Below, another view of the 300 SL roadster with top.
Oben, der 300 SL Roadster mit gleichfarbigem Dach. Unten, noch ein Bild des 300 SL Roadster mit Dach.

The elegant roadster model with suitable background
Der elegante Roadster Typ mit passendem Hintergrund

The Daimler-Benz main factory in Stuttgart-Untertürkheim

Das Daimler-Benz Werk Stuttgart-Untertürkheim mit dem Neckar

The Daimler-Benz body and assembly plant at Sindelfingen

Das Daimler-Benz Karosserie- und Montagewerk Sindelfingen

Three versions of the experimental C 111. Newest in center, powered by a four-chamber rotary (Wankel-type) engine. Performance (0-60 in 4.7 sec.) is phenomenal

Drei Modelle des Versuchswagen Typ C 111. Der Neuste in der Mitte mit einem Vierkammer Wankel Motor. Der Wagen hat eine ausserordentliche Leistung

Appendix: Owner's Manuals

I. Type 300 SL Coupe

II. Type 300 SL Roadster

MERCEDES-BENZ
TYPE 300 SL

INSTRUCTION MANUAL

Edition A

DAIMLER-BENZ AKTIENGESELLSCHAFT

STUTTGART-UNTERTÜRKHEIM

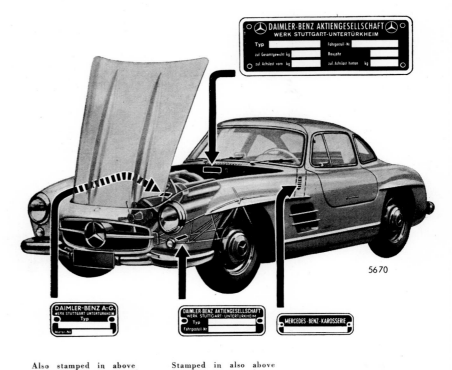

5670

Also stamped in above
the plate in the crankcase

Stamped in also above
the plate on the frame

Carefully note the chassis and engine numbers of your car as well as the complete type designation appearing above the numbers.

Spare parts which may be required – also the ignition key or car key (locking also the rear compartment) – can be supplied quickly and satisfactorily only if your order mentions the chassis and engine numbers as well as the complete type designation.

A Few General Hints

which should be read before the first drive.

Safety first!

Let this be your slogan wherever you go. Make sure your car is in perfect condition, paying special attention to the brakes, the clutch, the steering, the tyres and the entire lighting system. The Mercedes-Benz Model 300 SL is a sports car with an extremely high acceleration and top speed. Owing to its perfect road holding quality and springing, you may easily forget how fast you are actually driving and become careless. Always adapt your driving speed to the traffic and to the road conditions. Wet, snowy or icy roads are treacherous. The braking distance, too, will be increased with rising speed at an even higher ratio than speed itself. The graph on page 22, section "Driving Hints" will give you a clear idea of the respective values. For this reason you will have to decelerate and brake sooner than you would normally do. Do not drive at top speed, unless this is definitely not dangerous. It is you who is responsible for your passenger and for any damage you may cause to other road users.

Always observe the traffic regulations of your country!

Before changing your driving direction always signal with the trafficators. Do not, however, entirely rely on them, nor on the discipline of other people, but look back and into the rear view mirror, especially if you leave the main road to turn into a lane or an entrance.

Before getting out of your car, always look back, especially in city traffic.

Always observe the traffic signs!

Second: Consumption.

Fast, sporty driving will increase consumption to a higher extent than normal road traffic. Smooth driving will, however, obtain favourable consumption figures also with model 300 SL. The graph below shows clearly the relation fuel consumption – driving speed. The values refer to the standard rear axle reduction 3,64 : 1.

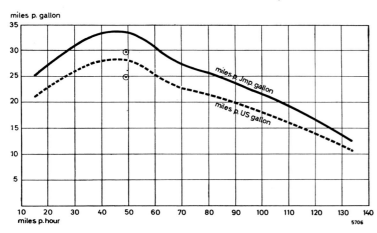

⊙ Standard fuel consumption = the fuel consumption measured in miles/Imp.-US gal. on a smooth uninterrupted 20-km-return-drive (12 miles) on a level highway at ²/₃ top speed – maximum, however, 50 mph (80 km/h) – and with the highest permissible weight minus 10% for unfavourable conditions.

Last but not least: Maintenance!

The best lubricants are just good enough for your car. Make sure the lubricants used are of a viscosity appropriate for the season and conforming to our prescriptions.

Impurities in the oil will damage bearings and cylinder liners. We therefore advise you to regularly clean the oil filter. The oil should be changed within the prescribed periods and, if possible, immediately after returning from a longer drive while it is still hot and thin and will flush away the deposits.

The air filter should always be kept clean and in good condition, as the dust sucked in with the air will grind the bearings and slides and will make the valves untight. On long drives over dusty roads it is advisable to clean the air filter more often than is prescribed in the instruction manual.

Model 300 SL has no central lubrication; at the front axle, the pedals and at the drive shaft there are, however, nipples into which grease should be pressed after the prescribed mileage. Never omit this maintenance work!

The fuel filter should be cleaned, the filter element exchanged, if necessary, and the ignition distributor and the spark plugs checked after the prescribed mileages.

Do not forget to have your battery attended to. A new battery is expensive. The wheels should be interchanged and balanced regularly.

Always keep the tyres at the prescribed pressure; the tyres will thus not be subjected to excessive strain, and steering and springing will remain in good condition. If the tyre pressure is too low, the tyres may, at very high speeds, get too hot so that even the cord will come off.

If you observe these hints

Model 300 SL will always be worthy of your confidence and you will come to appreciate it as a vehicle endowed with all the qualities which make it suitable for intercity and city traffic and which will, moreover, offer its owner the best prospects in the standard sports car and "Grand Tourisme" classes.

Short Description

The following remarkable features contribute to the outstanding achievements of Model 300 SL:

1. The flexible Six-Cylinder-Three-Litre-Engine with fuel injection.

The method of operation of the 300 SL with fuel injection resembles that of the carburettor engine, the only difference is the fuel injection system which replaces the carburettor. The 300 SL-engine only takes in air, the correct amount of vaporized fuel is injected through the injection pump via jets during every intake stroke direct into the combustion chamber of the individual cylinders. Mixture formation in the cylinder must be completed before the compression stroke starts, which follows the intake stroke. Therefore the end of delivery of the injection pump has been set to 60° after UDC in the intake stroke of the engine. The fuel-air mixture which has been formed in the cylinder is compressed during the compression stroke of the engine and at the end of this compression stroke it is ignited as usual by a normal ignition plant (ignition coil, ignition distributor, spark plugs).

The automatic control of the injection system safeguards in the entire speed range, starting with the idle run speed, the injection of the appropriate amount of the fuel-air-mixture for each load, adapting it also to changes in ambient temperature and differences in altitude. It is therefore possible to smoothly accelerate the engine of the 300 SL in direct gear from a speed of 15 mph (25 km/h) up to top speed. It is not necessary to adjust the injection system.

A sturdy transmission with four baulked synchromesh forward gears is mounted to the engine. It can be shifted very quickly. An oil pump will supply all lubrication points with pressure oil.

2. Chassis and Superstructure.

Distortion and consequently damage of the body is successfully prevented even on bad roads by a novel three-dimensioned multi-tubular frame, whose individual members are subject to pulling forces and pressure only and not to bending. The engine-transmission-block is mounted in the frame, the axles are suspended at the frame. The front axle is fitted with trapezoidal wishbones, the rear axle is a swing axle. Front and rear axle have frictionless coil springs and generously dimensioned shock absorbers.

The body is mounted on the chassis as a whole and screwed to the frame in front, in the middle and at the rear.

The entire superstructure is welded together. It comprises the central tunnel with the passenger room, the cowl with the fenders and the air scoops as well as the rear part with rear cover and spare wheel room.

The luggage compartment is in the passenger room immediately behind the seats. The luggage can be fastened by belts to special bars provided for that purpose.

The proper position of the steering wheel and good vision are essential for the driving safety of very fast sports cars. In order to meet these requirements we have provided for steering columns in two different lengths and seat cushions of different thicknesses to be adapted to the height of the customer. **Our salesmen will be pleased to advise you in this respect.** The distance between the driver's head and the roof should be about a hand's width.

Doors:

The passenger entrance which lies somewhat higher than in the common vehicle types, is through folding doors on both sides. The doors are opened from the outside by pressing the grooved cam at the inside of the pivot with the thumb, whereupon the

handle will slip out of its hole far enough to be grasped and pulled out to the stop. The lock is thus opened and the door can be lifted. From the inside the doors are opened by pulling the handle out and lifting the door. The doors are held open by pressure springs in telescopic tubes and secured by a special device. The folding doors are closed from the inside by pulling them down at the vertical handle below the window. To close them from the outside simply push down. A hook lock in the middle of the door will catch as soon as the doors are shut. The doors can be secured from the inside by a clip, from the outside they are locked with a key. The folding doors have large windows, the rear part of which up to the deflector pane can be taken out by opening a spring lock. The panes can be put away in special pockets behind the seats. Thus the car can be driven with open side windows.

To open the engine hood: Pull the lever for the hood fastener (3, p. 8) below the instrument panel, the hook lock is released and the engine hood can be opened towards driving direction. If the hood has been opened completely, a stay will snap in and keep it in place.

To close the engine hood: Push the stay forward and close the hood.

Socket for electrical equipment (12 V).

At the dashboard in the engine room left from the fuse box – as seen in driving direction – there is a socket (12 V) for a hand lamp or any other electrical device.

Driver's Seat

1. Hand brake lever.

2. Tommy screw for hand brake adjustment.

3. Tommy for engine hood fastener, pull handle to open engine hood.

4. Control lever for direction indicators, push upwards to switch on left flashlight and down for right one.

5. Control lever of windscreen rinsing system, it is installed only upon request and against extra charge.

6. Gear shift lever, 4 forward gears, baulked synchromesh, 1 reverse gear.

7. Foot dimmer switch: push down to switch from "dimmed" to "full" again. The blue signal lamp at the instrument panel indicates the distance light is switched on. See p. 10.

8. Clutch pedal.

9. Brake pedal.

10. Accelerator pedal.

11. Tommy for supplementary ventilation.

12. Clock: the clock is set by turning the button at the right.

13. Oil thermometer.

14. Cooling water thermometer.

15. Steering wheel: the steering wheel can be folded down after the securing lever (16) has been released.

16. Securing lever of steering wheel.

17. Button for signal horns.

18. Control lever for distance light signal system, it is installed only upon request and against extra charge.

19. Rear view mirror, it can be folded back to anti-dazzle position to prevent dazzling from vehicles coming from behind.

20. Ash tray: pull out to empty. Lower part can be taken off by pressing at the sides.

21. Sun vizor.

22. Reading lamp, at the same time entrance light. It is switched on or over by turning the light stop.

Light stop closed: lamp switched off.

Light stop half open: entrance light, the lamp is switched on by a door contact switch which is actuated when the driver's door is opened and lights up as long as this door remains open.

Light stop fully opened: reading lamp; the lamp remains lighted.

When getting out of the car, the light stop should always be set to "entrance light".

Instrument panel

1. Revolution counter.

2. Blue distance control light; lights up as long as the distance light is switched on.

3. Speedometer indicating the total and daily mileage covered. The daily mileage meter can be returned to O position by pulling the pull knob (4).

4. Pull knob for returning the daily mileage meter to position O.

5. Signal lamp control light.

6. Ignition timing adjustment.

7. Fuel gauge with "full" and "reserve" marking.

8. Oil pressure gauge; indicates only if the engine is running.

9. White starting control light; lights up as long as the choke is pulled.

10. Charging control light; if the electrical system is in order, then it lights up after the key has been inserted in the ignition lock; it goes out if the engine has exceeded the idle running speed (normal driving).

11. Cooling water temperature gauge. The cooling water temperature should not rise above the red limit mark.

12. Oil temperature gauge.

13. Pull switch for the auxiliary fuel pump; to actuate it, pull out, after which a control light in the switch will light up as long as the pump is in operation. It is necessary to actuate the pump if
(a) the engine should be started in a warm condition;
(b) the fuel is drawing to an end. The pump conveys the remaining contents of the tank to the engine.

14. Lever for the ventilation of the left side of the windscreen. Lever folded back: closed.

15. Lever for the ventilation of the left side of the leg room. Lever folded back: closed.

16. Pull knob "start". Pulling out switches on the starting device of the injection pump; the white control lamp (9) remains lighted for as long as the start button is pulled out.

17. Pull knob for instrument panel lighting: this is switched on if the rotary switch is set in position 1 or 2 and this pull knob is pulled out.

18. Parking light selector switch. The right or left parking lights light up according to whether it is turned right or left (no centre position). The parking lights are switched on by turning the light selector switch (19) to the left.

19. Light selector switch; 4 positions:

Neutral position (control knob vertical):	"Day driving"; if the ignition lock (20) is set on "driving", the following appliances can be operated: starter control lamp, windscreen wiper, signal horns, fuel gauge, auxiliary fuel pump, cigar lighter, brake light, defroster when the car is standing still, blinker and if it is built-in the distance light blinking system.
Turned from neutral until the I. stop on the right (1):	The following appliances are then switched on: licence plate lighting, tail light, parking light, instrument panel lighting, and after engaging the reverse gear, the reverse drive lamp, if one is installed. In addition, the "day-time consumers" as listed above can be set in operation.
Turned until the II. stop on the right (2):	The distance or dimmed light — according to the position of the dimmer switch — is switched on in addition to (1).
Turned from neutral to the I. stop on the left:	Only the parking lights — the right or the left one according to the position of the parking light selector switch (18) are switched on; all other exterior lights are switched off.

The fog lamps, which are only built in upon special request and at a surcharge, are also switched on through the light selector switch, which is then turned to position (1) and pulled out.

20. Ignition lock and starter switch. Turning the key to position 1 switches on the electrical system, flexible continued turning to stop 2 — at the same time, the key should be lightly turned forward — switches on the starter motor.

After the engine starts up, immediately release the key which will then return to stop 1.

21. Two-stage pull knob for the windscreen wiper unit. Pulled out completely: the wiper blades move slowly; half pulled out: the wiper blades move quickly. After switching off, the wiper blades automatically return to their initial position.

22. Control lever for the temperature in the right part of the car. Left position: heating switched off; right position: heating fully opened.

23. Control lever for the temperature in the left part of the car. Position left: heating switched off; position right: heating fully opened.

24. Push button switch for the signal horns.

25. Electrical cigar-lighter: press the button for a few seconds, until the coil glows red.

26. Pull switch for the blowers of the defroster for stationary car. Pulling out switches on the blowers, whereby a control lamp in the pull switch remains lighted for as long as the blowers are in operation.

27. Lever for the ventilation of the right side of the windscreen. Lever folded back: closed.

28. Lever for the ventilation of the right side of the leg room. Lever folded back: closed.

Ventilation and Heating

The ventilation and heating plant consists of two separate, mutually independent systems, of which the right supplies the right side of the car's interior and the left the left side. This arrangement enables both the driver and the passenger to regulate both the amount and the temperature of the incoming fresh air independently of each other and as they please.

The fresh air streams in at the front of the car via two ducts which run right and left of the engine space. A narrow-meshed screen, which can be taken out in order to be cleaned, is placed at the beginning of each duct and prevents insects and other foreign bodies from entering. If it is cold, a large heat exchanger which is installed in each duct and which is connected to the water circuit of the engine serves to heat up the incoming fresh air. The air is conducted on the one hand to the windscreen via a transverse duct, on the other hand to the leg room, through a distributor housing with two flaps which can be regulated independently of each other. Moreover, a fan is built into each duct, so that there a sufficient amount of air is available when the car is parked, or when it is slowly driven, e. g. in city traffic. Both blowers are actuated by pulling the pull knob (26, p. 11), after which a coloured control lamp in the pull knob lights up until the blowers are set out of operation.

The direction of the fresh air is controlled by two regulating levers for each side of the car; these are placed to the right and left of the instrument panel, the right one serving the right side, the left one the left side. The upper levers regulate the flow of air to the windscreen, and the lower that to the leg room; the air supply is opened by pulling the lever in an outward direction.

Lever pushed in: air supply cut off.
Lever pulled completely out: air supply fully open.
Any intermediary position can be adopted as required.

For driving in town traffic and in warm weather, the following ventilation methods are available as need be:

1. Deflector panes at the doors. When closing the deflector panes, the bolts should be securely drawn; should this not be the case, then whistling noises will arise.

2. The supplementary summer ventilation, which allows the fresh air to enter into the interior of the car under the instrument panel through openings in front of the windscreen. This supplementary ventilation is regulated by the tommy (11, p. 9) under the instrument panel. It has 2 stops; half opened and fully opened.

3. The side windows can be taken out and placed in pockets behind the seats. This is especially meant for driving in tropical countries and in very hot weather. However, when driving at high speeds, it is advisable to only remove the window in the driver's door. It is then possible to drive without suffering from draughts and without any distressing whistling noises event at the highest speeds.

The heating is regulated by two temperature regulating levers (22 and 23, p. 11) which are in the middle of the instrument panel. The upper one is for the right side, the lower for the left side. When they are pushed from the left to the right side, the regulating levers allow the engine cooling water to pass through the heat exchanger, so that when the lever is right over on the left, the heating is turned off, and when the lever is **right** over on the right, the heating is completely turned on.

In this case too, it is possible to adopt any intermediary position as required. However, the air regulating levers should not cut off the supply of fresh air.

To ensure fast heating, it is advisable to push the heating levers completely over to the right at first, that is to say to full heating, and then to return them to the roughly required position on the left after 5 to 10 seconds, without waiting for the full heating effect to make itself felt.

In principle, the ventilation and heating in winter should only be set in operation when the cooling water temperature has reached about 158° F (70° C).

In order to defrost frozen windscreens, open the heating levers as well as the upper air regulating levers completely, and, if the weather is very cold indeed, switch on the blowers, until the panes have thawed. Then readjust the levers so as to attain the pleasant temperature required in the car's interior.

Thanks to the various separate regulating possibilities of conveying air to the leg room and to the windscreen, the ventilation and heating of the 300 SL is such as to provide the best possible ventilation and heating for the passengers under all driving conditions. It is possible to adapt it to one's personal wishes. One single point should be carefully adhered to, however:

If one is driving behind a vehicle which leaves dust or exhaust smoke in its trail, then the fresh air supply should be temporarily cut off, i. e. all 4 air regulating levers should be pushed in, so as to prevent the exhaust gases of the front vehicle from entering the interior of the car.

Fuels, Coolants and Lubricants

Fuel

Filling station super fuel with a minimum octane rating of 80 according to the engine method.

Substitute fuels, in particular gasoline with too high a boiling point and poorly-cleaned benzenes, should be used neither in an unadulterated form nor in a mixture.

In particular, we warn you not to use a gasoline benzene mixture which you have made yourself.

The fuel tank contains about 28 Imp. gals. or 34 US gals. (130 liters), of which about 2 Imp. gals. or 2.3 US gals. (9 liters) are a reserve, which suffices for a drive of about 24 to 31 miles (40–50 km), according to the way one drives. The reserve fuel is conveyed to the engine after the supplementary fuel pump has been switched on.

Coolant

The cooling water tank with the filler caps lies separate from the radiator on the right side under the engine hood.

Look out, superpressure cooling system! Open the cover of the water tank only if the cooling water temperature is below 194° F (90° C). Then turn to the I. stop and allow the superpressure to blow off, then turn further and remove the cover. When closing, turn until it stops (II. stop).

Only use covers with the number 80 for the water tank.

The entire cooling system including the water tank and D.B.-heating unit has a capacity of about 27¼ Imp. pints or 32¾ US pints (15½ liters).

Use clean water, with as low a lime content as possible, or well-filtered river water.

The cooling water **should be treated from the very first drive onwards.** If you constantly drive with untreated cooling water, then scale and rust will form, thus gradually lowering the cooling system efficiency. The use of distilled water or rain water does not prevent this either. The following agents can be used in order to treat cooling water:

a) Ferroxan from Messrs. Farbenfabriken Bayer, Leverkusen, 15 tablets for the entire cooling system; when refilling use 1 tablet pro liter (1¾ Imp. pints or 2.11 US pints). For further details consult the separate Ferroxan instructions.

b) Hydrochrome solution from Messrs. Bran & Lübbe. 0.91 cu. in. (15 c. c.) are needed for the entire cooling system; when refilling use 0.06 cu. in. (1 c. c.) pro liter (1¾ Imp. pints or 2.11 US pints). Consult the separate instructions for the hydrochrome treatment for details.

c) Shell Donax C: 1.83 cu. ins. (30 c. c.) for the entire cooling water. Specially suitable for winter operation.

Please note that Shell Donax C can be used with anti-freeze agents, but Ferroxan and Hydrochrome solution may not. If Ferroxan or a Hydrochrome solution are used, then the cooling water should be drained out and the cooling water jackets thoroughly rinsed before an anti-freeze agent is filled in.

Important! When filling in cooling water, proceed as follows:
1. Push both heating levers to the right (completely open).
2. Fill in cooling water slowly until it reaches the filler pipe edge.
3. Allow the engine to run for about 1 minute at an increased idle running speed and with an open filler pipe.
4. Return to normal idle running speed and slowly fill up the cooling system completely, in the following manner:
   a) if the cooling water is cold, fill up to the marking visible in the filler pipe (about 2 ins. – 5 cm below the filler pipe rim),
   b) if the cooling water is warm, right up to the filler pipe rim.

If the engine is hot, only refill with cold water if the engine is running; on the other hand, it is possible to fill in hot water without further ado when the engine is cold.

If the temperature of the cooling water gradually rises above the usual level, then this is a sign that the cooling system is dirty. It should then be degreased and descaled, if possible in a customer service workshop (see p. 47).

Lubricant

In order to ensure safety and economy of operation we must make certain demands concerning the suitability and quality of the lubricants used. These are just as important as the tasks which a structural part is required to fulfil. The special properties of the structural parts and of the lubricants must meet any demands which the engine or vehicle may make on it, and must guarantee a satisfactory functioning.

Lubricants should therefore not be arbitrarily chosen for our units, rather should care be taken to only use suitable brands. Of the many suitable lubricants available on the market, the following have been tested and found satisfactory. Our central customer service department will give you further details upon request.

Ignition distributor:	Engine lube oil for the oiler and for the felt in the cam bore, lubricating grease Bosch Ft 1 v 4 for the grease reserve within the cavity of the commutator's sliding contact.
Injection pump:	Engine lube oil.
Cooling water pump:	Oil as for the rear axle.
Transmission:	2¹/₅ Imp. pints or 2²/₃ US pints (1.25 liters); regardless of the weather: SHELL-Donax T 6; Mobilfluid 200; Veedol transmission fluid type A; Esso ATF 55; Renolin TF 10; Valvomatic type A AQ-ATF 123; ENERGOL TRANS-MISSION FLUID; BV-oil SGF; Nitag Automatic Fluid A; DG 53 type A; Gasoline special transmission oil fluid; Castrol fluid TQ; Texamatic fluid; – for Switzerland only: Canfield Automatic transmission fluid type A ATF 119.
Rear axle:	4.2 Imp. pints or 5 US pints (2,4 liters) regardless of the weather: High pressure transmission oil (hypoid oil) SAE 90; SHELL Spirax 90: Mobilube GX 90; Veedol multigear SAE 90 (hypoid); BV-transmission oil Hyp 90; ENERGOL TRANSMISSION OIL EP (Hypoid) SAE 90; Esso XP 90; Renolin EP 90; Gasoline hypoid transmission oil SAE 90.
Front wheel hubs: normal hub with wheel pin 3 ozs. (80 g) per hub Hub with rudge toothing 4¼ ozs. (120 g) per hub	Roller bearing Mobilgrease No. 5; Esso roller bearing grease; SHELL roller bearing F 4; Renolin F 2 U; Caltex Marfak No. 2 HD; for tropical countries SHELL-Retinax H, Mobilgrease No. 5 or grease of similar quality and of the same consistency.

Steering Gear:

DB-steering:	0.5 Imp. pint or ²/₃ US pint (0.3 liter)⎫ Oil as for
Ross steering:	¹/₃ Imp. pint or 0.4 US pint (0.2 liter)⎭ the rear axle
Hydraulic brake:	0.8 Imp. pint or 0.95 US pint (0.45 liter); ATE blue original brake fluid or Lockheed brake fluid.

Look out! Brake fluid corrodes, damages painting, should not come into contact with brake linings.

Grease nipple at the front axle, at the pedals and at the universal-joint shafts, as well as **for regreasing the door hinges, the hinges of rear compartment cover and of the engine hood:**   SHELL-Retinax C; Mobilgrease No. 4; Esso lubricating grease.

Engine

The engine has dry sump lubrication. The engine lube oil is not filled into the engine itself, but in a separate oil tank, which is under the engine hood at the left side of the engine. The oil dipstick with the upper and lower oil level markings is in the cover of the oil tank. The oil from the oil is fed by a pressure pump to the lubrication points in the engine via the oil filter. The oil which drains off collects at the bottom of the engine, in the "dry sump"; from there, it is immediately drawn off by a second pump, and is then conveyed back into the oil tank through an oil cooler which is on the right side of the water cooler.

When the engine is running, the engine lube oil constantly circulates along the circuit oil tank – oil filter – engine lubrication points – dry sump – oil cooler – oil tank. When the engine is stopped, this process is interrupted. It is therefore necessary to proceed as follows when checking the level of the oil and when refilling:

Before checking the oil level, let the engine run for about a minute at an increased idle running speed, then stop the engine and measure the oil level, which must at least reach up to the lower dipstick mark. If necessary, refill.

When it is cold, it is advisable to cover the oil cooler (see p. 23).

When choosing an engine lube oil, two factors should be considered, the viscosity (degree of fluidity) and the mixture ratio.

The viscosity should be adjusted to the prevailing temperature and your choice should therefore depend on the seasonal outer temperatures. **The following viscosity groups should always be adhered to for the engine of model 300 SL:**

For new and completely overhauled engines:

Summer:	SAE 20 W/20
Winter, spring and autumn:	SAE 10 W

SAE 10 W	corresponds to a viscosity of about 2.6–3.8 Engler degrees at 122° F (50° C); that are 18–28 cSt.
SAE 20 W/20	corresponds to a viscosity of about 4–6.5 Engler degrees at 122° F (50° C); that are 30–50 cSt.

The **quality** of an engine lube oil must n et very high requirements, for the longevity of your engine depends on the engine lube oil used. A good engine lube oil should not only "lubricate", i. e. it should not only ensure the smooth operation of the various parts, but it should also prevent the formation of sludge and dirt in the engine.

As is well-known, every type of engine lube oil can produce sludge if it is exposed to high temperatures. Sludge can also form if the normal operating temperature of the oil is not reached, that is to say, when the engine need only render a very low output, rarely reaches a high speed or is only driven for short distances at long intervals. When this sludge and dirt forms a deposit in the engine, then this can lead to the lube oil ducts and the filter element becoming clogged up, that is to say to a breakdown within the lube oil circulation with all its consequences. To prevent this, one should only use an engine lube oil which successfully counteracts the formation of sludge deposits.

The engine lube oils can be classified into three kinds, depending on how well they fulfil this function and on their mixure ratios. These are:

Regular oil, **premium** oil and **heavy-duty** oil (HD-oil).

The normal mineral oils, which do not contain any chemical admixtures, are classified **among the regular** (normal) oils. This means that they are well suited to perform the task of "lubricating", but are hardly able to counteract the formation of sludge deposits.

Mineral oils to which certain chemicals have been added to avoid corrosion, the formation of sludge and acids, are described as **premium oils**. In particular, chemicals have been added which are necessary to prevent the bearings from corroding. The use of a premium oil does not however preclude all possibility of the formation of cold sludge, which typically occurs when one frequently drives short distances only.

The **heavy-duty oils also contain** detergents in addition to the chemical admixtures of the premium oils. These detergents absorb all impurities in the engine and keep them floating in the oil. Each time the oil is changed they then flow out of the engine together with the oil which is drained out of it. In this way, it is practically impossible for sludge deposits to form in the engine.

The **HD-oils** thus best meet all the demands which an engine lube oil can be expected to fulfil, namely good lubrication and the prevention of corrosion and of the formation of deposits.

We therefore advise you to use the HD engine lube oils tested and recommended by us. Occasionally, the containers of these lubricants bear the inscription "for service MS-DG" abroad; this is a new designation of the "American Petroleum Institute" (API) which has been valid since 1953.

In Germany the API system has not yet been introduced: the abbreviations ML, MM, MS, DG and DS, when used alone, do not therefore afford any guarantee that engine lube oils of **German** production are of the quality which we demand.

When refilling or carrying out customer service work, use the **same** brand, inasmuch as it has been found to cause no operational difficulties. If it should not always be possible to do this, you may either try another well-known HD engine lube oil or **as a temporary expedient** you can also use the engine lube oils with slight admixture of the premium type or the unmixed oils of the regular type. In such cases, we advise you to consult our customer service stations.

In addition to the oil brands listed in our instruction manuals, there will be makes both at home and abroad which also meet our requirements. In principle, we recommend qualities which meet the test conditions Mil-L-2104 A (USA) or DEF 2101 A (England). Until corresponding official tests are introduced in Germany, we are compelled to demand that the engine lube oils comply with the above-mentioned specifications.

(On account of the special conditions which prevail during the running-in period, an unmixed thin engine lube oil is used for the first 300 miles [500 km] driving distance of new or reconditioned engines.)

Through its cleaning action, the heavy-duty oil gradually acquires a dark colour. However, this by no means indicates that a premature change of oil is necessary (see ps. 30 and 31); rather does it show that the residues are floating about in the oil and do not adhere to the engine parts.

Colloidal graphite may not be added to HD and premium oils.

Changing over from normal or premium oil to HD oil.

If an engine has been driven on regular or premium oils for a longer space of time after the first 300 miles (500 km) under unfavourable conditions, then the oil filter should be carefully watched when changing over to HD oil, since the residues, which were loosened by the cleaning effect of the detergents of the HD oil, can in certain circumstances lead to the oil duct and the filter element getting clogged.

When changing over to HD oil, one should therefore proceed as follows:

1. Drain the old engine lube oil whilst the housing is still warm; clean the oil filter carefully.

2. Refill new HD oil until it just covers the lower marking of the oil dipstick and then drive for 5–8 hours at the most. However, during this time, the engine should be driven really hot.

3. Drain off the first HD-filling carefully and carefully clean the oil filter again.

4. Fill in the second HD-filling and drive the engine for 300 miles (500 km) at first. If an unusual coating can be noticed at the oil filter element after this distance has been covered, then the second filling should also be drained of and renewed.

   If the oil filter is still clean after 300 miles (500 km), then one may drive up to 600 or and after checking even 900 miles (1000 or 1500 km) with the second filling.

5. Drain off the second HD oil filling and refill for the third time with HD oil. Drive for about 1250 miles (2000 km) on this filling.

6. After this, one can again go back to the usual oil change periods.

If heavy deposits of carbonic residues can be noticed after the first filling with HD-oils, then this is due to the fact that these decomposition products from fuel and lube oil have settled on the interior walls and drive unit parts to an excessive degree during the previous period of operation.

Supplier	Max. 26.5 Imp. pts./32 US pts. (15 Ltrs.), min. 19.5 Imp. pts./23 US pts. (11 Ltrs.) of oil of an approved brand acc. to our above viscosity prescriptions e. g.		
	Group SAE 10 W	Group SAE 20 W/20	Group SAE 30
BP Benzin- & Petroleum- GmbH.	ENERGOL HD, SAE 10 W	ENERGOL HD, SAE 20 W/20	ENERGOL HD, SAE 30
Foreign designation	Energol Diesel D, SAE 10 W	Energol Diesel D, SAE 20 W	Energol Diesel D, SAE 30
Esso AG.	Esso-Extra-Motoroil Nr. 1	Esso-Extra-Motoroil Nr. 3 (multi purpose oil)	
	Essolub HD 10, SAE 10 W	Essolub HD 20, SAE 20 W/20	Essolub HD 30, SAE 30
Foreign designation	Esso-Extra-Motoroil Nr. 1	Esso-Extra-Motoroil Nr. 3	
	Essolube HD, SAE 10 W	Essolube HD, SAE 20 W/20	Essolube HD, SAE 30
SHELL	SHELL X-100 MOTOROEL (HD), SAE 10 W SHELL Rotella Oel (HD), SAE 10 W	SHELL X-100 MOTOROEL (HD), SAE 20 W/20 SHELL Rotella Oel (HD), SAE 20 W/20	SHELL X-100 MOTOROEL (HD), SAE 30 SHELL Rotella Oel (HD), SAE 30
Foreign designation	SHELL X-100 motoroil SAE 10 W	SHELL X-100 motoroil SAE 20 W/20	SHELL X-100 motoroil SAE 30
Socony Vacuum Oil Co.	Mobiloel Arctic Spezial (HD) SAE 10 W Delvac 910 (HD) SAE 10 W	Mobiloel Arctic (HD) SAE 20 W/20 Delvac 920 (HD) SAE 20 W/20	Mobiloel A (HD) SAE 30 Delvac 930 (HD) SAE 30
Foreign designation	Mobiloil 10 W SAE 10 W	Mobiloil Arctic SAE 20 W/20	Mobiloil A SAE 30
Veedol		Veedol 10–30 Motor Oil (HD)	
	Veedol Motor Oil HD 901 SAE 10 W	Veedol Motor Oil HD 902 SAE 20 W/20	Veedol Motor Oil HD 903 SAE 30
Foreign designation		Veedol 10–30 Motor Oil (HD)	
	Veedol high detergency motor oil SAE 10 W	Veedol high detergency motor oil SAE 20 W-30	
C. C. Wakefield & Co., Ltd.	Castrol CR HD Oil, 10 W	Castrol CR HD Oil, 20 W/20	Castrol CR HD Oil, 30
Valvoline Öl-GmbH.	Ritzol HD 206, SAE 10 W	Ritzol HD 306, SAE 20 W/20	Ritzol HD 506, SAE 30
Foreign designation	Valvoline VL m. HPO, SAE 10 W	Valvoline MA m. HPO, SAE 20 W/20	Valvoline AA m. HPO, SAE 30

Starting and stopping

Check at regular intervals and before every longer drive:

1. Fuel level; the fuel gauge only registers when the ignition is switched on;

2. the water level in the water tank; when the cooling water is cold it should reach up to the marking in the filler pipe;

3. the oil level in the oil container; be careful to effect the oil level check only immediately after the engine has been stopped! If need be, allow the engine to run for about a minute at a high idle running speed before proceeding to check, if the engine his been standing still for some time.

Wipe the dipstick before measuring. The oil level should reach up to the upper marking of the dipstick; do not measure the oil level if the car is standing on an incline.

4. the wheel nuts, to see if they are tight;

5. the tyre pressure; see p. 42 for exact details about the tyre pressure;

6. the effectiveness of the brakes; one should not be able to completely depress the brake pedal;

7. the free play at the steering wheel;

8. the distance and dimmer light.

Starting

Be careful when starting the engine and allowing it to run in the garage; the garage door should always be kept open and you should see to it that the exhaust gases escape. These contain the inodorous and invisible, but **highly poisonous** carbon monoxide gas.

Set the gear-shift lever in idle running position (centre).

Further operation depends on the outer temperatures.

a) Starting the cold engine at normal outer temperatures [of about 86° F (+ 30° C) to about 32° F (0° C)]; see p. 25 "Winter operation" if the temperature is below freezing point.

Pull the pull knob "start" with the left hand – the white control lamp lights up –, turn the ignition key to the right to position "2" with the right hand, thus actuating the starting motor.

At the same time declutch, **but do not depress the accelerator pedal.**

Release the ignition key when the engine is firing regularly, not at the first ignition; it then automatically returns to position 1; however, do not keep it in position 2 for more than 20 seconds without interruption, since otherwise too heavy a strain is imposed on the battery.

As soon as the engine has fired, release the "start" button, which returns to its initial position automatically, whilst the white control light goes out.

As soon as the engine runs smoothly, engage the clutch, rather slowly, however – especially in cold weather – so that the stiff oil in the transmission does not brake the engine.

b) Starting at hot temperatures, in partic ...ar in tropical countries, after longer drives in town on hot days or at high altitudes:

Switch on the auxiliary fuel pump by pulling the pull knob at the instrument panel — the lamp in the pull switch remains lighted as long as the pump is working.
Allow the pump to run for a few seconds, then proceed as for a). When the engine has fired, switch off the pump.

Setting the auxiliary fuel pump in operation also provides a relief when the engine starts running unevenly, say, during a town drive in hot weather or in tropical regions. You should however keep in mind that when the auxiliary pump is also connected, then you cannot be warned that the tank contents are drawing to an end, since the pump also serves to feed the reserve fuel.

Running up the engine

It is harmful to allow the engine running idle until the normal operating temperature [cooling water 167° F–203° F (75–95° C)] is reached, since this takes too long as a result of the slow rate at which the engine heats up in the idle gear. We therefore advise you to drive away at a moderate speed after the engine has fired, if the outer temperature is not below freezing point. In this way, the engine reaches the operating temperature in the most advantageous manner within 4–5 minutes. Only when the temperature is lower, should you allow the engine running idle briefly for 1 minute at the most, before driving away, in order to make sure that the engine is lubricated even when the oil is quite cold. Do not, however, allow the engine to rev up whilst the car is at a standstill.

Driving off

Depress the clutch pedal.

Engage the gear-shift lever in 1st gear. Use only the 1. gear for driving off.
Release the hand brake.

Slowly release the clutch pedal, simultaneously slowly depressing the accelerator pedal with the right foot; that is to say, when driving off, the clutch should be allowed to slip as little as possible and one should only start at a low engine speed.

After driving off, accelerate gradually, not suddenly, shift to 2nd, 3rd, and 4th gear. Only accelerate fully if the clutch is completely engaged.

Stopping

Turn the ignition key to the left while idling. Do not on any account try to stop the engine at a higher speed than the idle running one.

The "first 900 miles" (1500 km)

The engine is not sealed up. The treatment accorded to the engine and the stresses to which it is subjected during the first 900 miles (1500 km) are, however, decisive for the service life and economy of operation of the entire vehicle. The kinder the treatment which you give the engine at first, the greater will your satisfaction with its performance be later. After all, the driving speed is less decisive than the revolutions and the engine load.

During the first 900 miles (1500 km) you should therefore not exceed an engine speed of 4000 r. p. m. and the engine should not be fully loaded for a longer period of time. Above all, however, avoid "tormenting" your engine in the lower speeds and shift back in good time.

The "nonrecurrent" lubrication and maintenance work described on p. 30 is of particular importance for the entire service life and the later quiet run of the engine as well as for the operational safety of the vehicle.

Sheets 1, 2 and 3 of your service book are ...ecially meant for the running-in period. Please do not fail to call at your customer service station in good time.

Gear-shifting

A convenient "central gearshift lever" on a ball pivot on the right beside the driver's seat makes it possible to effect quick gear shifting within the generously proportioned transmission — 4 forward gears, 1 reverse gear.

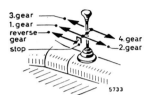

The gear-shifting diagram opposite shows the various gear positions.

The 4 forward gears of the transmission are of the controlled synchromesh type, i. e. a special device in the transmission forces the relevant gear wheels to engage smoothly by a series of couplings. This eliminates the annoying need to declutch twice. The procedure for gear shifting up or down is as follows:

Decelerate, depress the clutch pedal completely, push the gearshift lever from the one gear position to the next one smoothly, then engage the clutch gently and accelerate simultaneously.

Gear shifting can be carried out without exerting oneself. You should merely keep in mind the following points:

1. Before every gear-shifting action: decelerate and declutch completely.

2. Always engage the next gear, never omit a gear.

3. In order to engage the reverse gear, the car must first be brought to a standstill; then declutch and push the gearshift lever in the centre position right over to the left, at the same time overcoming the resistance of a safety stop; after this, slowly push the gearshift lever forward.

The stop along the gearshift lever travel is meant to prevent accidentally slipping into the reverse gear when shifting from the 2. to the 1. gear.

Driving hints

The model 300 SL is a very fast car with great acceleration power. Its outstanding roadholding quality and springing can only too easily result in your not realizing how fast you are actually driving. For this reason, you must remember to decelerate and brake earlier than you would be inclined to do otherwise.

It is well-known that every increase in speed necessarily involves a still higher increase in the braking distance.

In the opposite graph, you can see the relationship between speed and braking distance for various road conditions, making allowance for a second's shock interval. From this, it is apparent that with the best brakes and friction conditions, between the road and the tyres, a speed of 100 m. p. h. requires a braking distance of over 550 fts. including the reaction time.

At high speeds, the air resistance alone has a considerable braking action. Normally, you should therefore decelerate in good time and only then brake with the brake pedal.

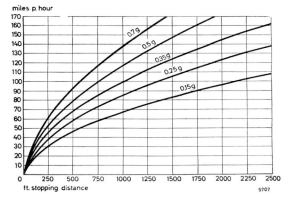

miles p. hour

ft. stopping distance

5707

Braking distances incl. 1 sec. of reaction time

0.7 g (7 m/sec²) dry concrete (autobahn)
0.5 g (5 m/sec²) dry asphalt and macadam
0.35 g (3,5 m/sec²) wet asphalt and macadam this is also the maximum legal braking distance for vehicles driving at 62 m. p. h. (100 km/h)
0.25 g (2,5 m/sec²) maximum braking distance according to the present regulations (not over 62 m. p. h. – 100 km/h)
0.15 g (1,5 m/sec²) Icy roads and maximum permissible braking distance for the hand brake

The brake pedals should, however, never be pushed down hard, but always gently. Jerky and sudden braking should be avoided wherever possible, for sudden braking may cause the car to skid on a smooth road or a following car may run into yours. Moreover, sudden braking will badly affect your tyres. Brake sharply only if danger is imminent.

When driving, use only the foot brake, also on steep gradients. Although braking the car from a high speed with the hand brake alone will neither impair the brake nor damage any other parts, it should be avoided wherever possible as, especially on slippery roads, the rear wheels may get blocked and cause the car to skid. The hand brake should generally be used only for stopping the car and keeping it stationary.

Always watch your speed. The speedometer has been placed well within your angle of vision and you can watch it without taking your eyes off the road. This is essential if you want to change your driving direction after a fast drive, e. g. when turning off the autobahn, as in such moments the actual driving speed is very often underestimated. When overtaking, particularly when overtaking on the autobahn, the driving speed of your car should always be adapted to that of the vehicle you want to overtake. Experience has shown that the vehicle in front, not counting on a fast-driving vehicle coming from behind, may suddenly in its turn want to overtake another car. In an emergency the excellent brakes will correct excessive speed up to about 30 m. p. h. (50 km/h).

With sporty driving, the gears should be shifted in accordance with the revolution counter reading. In order to reach top speed, 5.800 rpm need not be exceeded in the 1st, 2nd and 3rd gears, while in the 4th gear 6.400 rpm are permissible as a maximum.

Owing to favourable synchronization of the gears the sporty driver is given opportunity to fully take advantage of the chassis and the engine. On the other hand, the six-cylinder engine of the 300 SL is, in an extremely wide speed range, so elastic and powerful that

the entire driving range can be covered in the 4th gear alone, with good acceleration. If, after starting, you change over to the 4th gear via the 2nd and 3rd, you will be able to cope in this gear alone with normal city as well as intercity traffic.

It is not necessary to shift gears frequently when driving at normal speed, not even in city traffic. Low speeds down to about 700 rpm will do no harm to the engine, even if the engine accelerator pedal is pushed down as far as "full speed".

Only if you want to accelerate rapidly, in dense city traffic or if you want to overtake a fast truck-train, you should preferably shift down to the 3rd or 2nd gear.

With Model 300 SL fairly steep gradients can be taken in the 4th gear alone (see p. 55). In very mountainous country, however, the fast driver should shift back to the 3rd gear in order to obtain better acceleration values.

Also when driving downhill, particularly on longer steep gradients, it is advisable to shift down to a lower gear. On slopes you should allow the engine to act as a brake by releasing the accelerator pedal. Do not, however, declutch and do not switch off ignition, as otherwise the fuel which had been sucked in by the engine is not burnt and will wash the oil film off the cylinder liners.

If you have to stop your vehicle on an upgrade it will be safer to engage also the 1st gear or the reverse gear and to turn the steering in such a way that, in case the brake is released unintentionally the car will roll towards the hill and not downwards. In winter the car should be secured by blocks.

Model "300 SL" has an oil cooler to prevent overheating of the oil under extreme conditions, such as very fast driving and high ambient temperatures. Max. oil temperatures of 230°–240° F (110–115° C.) are within the range permissible.

It is evident that when driving with lower speed, e. g., in town traffic, or with low ambient temperatures, the oil temperatures reached are much lower.

It is therefore advisable to completely cover the oil cooler at low ambient temperatures.

If the engine is very cold **the oil pressure** will rise gradually some time after the engine has been started, as the pressure increase will become effective but slowly in the narrow line leading to the oil pressure gauge.

If the oil pressure falls while the engine speed remains unchanged or if the usual value is suddenly not reached, stop and proceed as described in "Hints for Emergency Repairs" (p. 52).

Normally the **cooling water temperature** should be 167–203° F (75–95° C). This temperature is reached after the car has been driven at a moderate speed for 4–5 minutes after starting. With driving on long upgrades and at very high ambient temperatures the cooling water temperature of a heavily loaded car may safely rise up to the red mark on the cooling water thermometer. It can be decreased by shifting down to a lower gear. If the car is stopped after having climbed a long way up a steep hill the engine should be allowed to run idle for a while, as otherwise the cooling water may boil over.

If the cooling water rises beyond the red mark, the cooling system is defective; stop and proceed as described in "Hints for Emergency Repairs" (p. 51).

Driving in Winter

During the cold season certain measures have to be taken to protect the engine and the radiator and to safeguard prompt starting.

Protective measures

The engine oil should in any case be a winter oil of the SAE 10 W-Group.

With moderate driving and low ambient temperatures it may happen that the appropriate oil temperature is not reached although the oil cooler has been covered up. In this case you can use engine oil SAE group 5 W in order to obtain satisfactory lubrication also under these circumstances.

A thermostat has been installed which automatically maintains the engine cooling water at the proper temperature by releasing the water circulation from the engine via the radiator only if the water temperature is higher than 167° F (75° C) while the radiator is cut off if the temperature is lower. Thus in winter the water in the cooling block may freeze in, even if the car is running.

Therefore an anti-freezing agent should be added in frosty weather.

Only commercial standard anti-freezing agents should be used for protection and the amount of the additive, which depends on the ambient temperature, should be determined in accordance with the supplier's directions only.

The following table contains the mixing ratios, of water and Glysantin, Genantin or Dixol for various temperatures below the freezing point.

The capacity of the entire cooling system, filled up to the mark at the water tank filler is about 27 Imp. pints/33 US pints (15.5 litres) with DB heating installed.

Freezing point approx.	Dixol Genantin/Glysantin		Water pints	
	Imp.	US	Imp.	US
14° F	7	9	20	24
5° F	10	12	17	21
— 4° F	11	13	16	20
— 13° F	12	15	15	18
— 22° F	13.5	16.5	13.5	16.5
— 40° F	15	18	12	15

Thoroughly flush the cooling system before filling in an anti-freezing agent, particularly if the water has been treated with an additive.

Caution! Do not use an acid anti-corrosion or radiator cleaning agent together with an anti-freeze. A corrosion preventive oil can, however, be used.

With a cold engine fill in coolant only up to the marker plate (abt. 2 ins. below the rim of the filler), as otherwise about 2 pts. of the coolant will be pressed out through the relief pressure valve and get lost, due to warming up and expansion.

Radiator and engine should be flushed well after using an anti-freeze. Please note that the coolant which had been drained off in spring can be filtered through a clean cloth and stored in a clean, well-closed container to be used next winter. Before filling it in again, however, the antifreezing quality of the mixture should be tested by means of a Glysantin/Genantin or Dixol hydrometer.

If an anti-freeze cannot be procured by any means, the radiator should be well covered, also if the car is being driven. The air intakes of the heating and ventilation systems should, however, not be blocked.

If the car in this case cannot be stored in a warm garage, the cooling water should be drained off in a sheltered place while the engine is still hot. To do this open the drain cock at the bottom of the radiator and the engine, left and detach the heating hoses at the bottom of each heating element, in order to thoroughly drain the heater. Also take off the water tank cover. **Caution! Super-pressure cooling system; for opening see p. 13.** Watch the cooling water draining off and if the drain cocks are clogged or frozen, clear them with a piece of wire.

Allow the engine to run for a short time, so that the cooling water will be drained off completely. Leave the drain cocks open until re-filling and attach a warning "water drained off" to the radiator.

Before re-filling do not forget to reconnect the hoses to the heaters and to close the drain cocks.

Measures to ensure safe starting in cold weather.

At temperatures below the freezing point pull the starter button with your left hand while you turn the ignition key clockwise to position 2, with your right hand,

declutch at the same time and
slightly (about 1″) actuate the accelerator pedal.

Then proceed as usual (see p. 20).

If the temperatures are very low, it is advisable to

1. remove the battery and store it in a heated room or bring it to room temperature, as an undercooled battery will yield only a fraction of the starting power of a battery under normal temperature. Or

2. drain coolant out of engine, radiator and water tank after the engine has been stopped, warm it up to approx. 200° F (95° C) before starting and fill it into cooling system. There is no danger, even if a boiling coolant is filled into a cold engine. This procedure, however complicated, will spare your starter motor, engine and battery.

Driving in Winter

Wet, snowy or icy roads are treacherous. Always adapt your speed to the road conditions and drive carefully. On clear winter days smooth ice may be found on places between sunny and shady spots, e. g. at subway crossings, at the outskirts of a town or a wood etc. When frost is just setting in, bridges may already be iced while the roads are still free of ice due to the warmth of the ground. These spots should be passed with special care. The windscreen is defrosted quickly and effectively by turning the two upper ventilation levers outward and the two heating levers to the extreme right (see p. 12).

If the rear cover is frozen, beat the rim of the cover with your fist to loosen the ice between the rim and the rubber moulding. If a door is frozen, first make an attempt in the same way.

The insect screens in the ventilation ducts may get clogged in a storm or by the snow blown up by vehicles driving in front and impair the heating of your car. In this case the insect screens should be thouroughly cleaned or just taken out for this season. The gap which then appears at the air ducts should be well covered with insulating tape or with steel strip. Do not, however, mislay the screens and do not forget to replace them later on.

During the transition periods ground fog may form in the mornings and evenings. We advise you to have a fog lamp fitted for this case.

If no fog lamp has been fitted, the dimmer lights should be switched on. On no account drive with the distance lights on as the little drops of fog will reflect the strong rays of the distance light and dazzle the driver.

The parking light is not sufficient in fog, it is too dim to be noticed in time by an approaching vehicle.

If the car is laid off in the open air in frosty weather, neither pull the hand brake nor engage a gear in order to avoid freezing. In this case the car should be secured by blocks.

To prevent the windscreen from icing up while the car is stationary, put a piece of canvas or a newspaper of the size of the windscreen under the wipers.

Snow chains cannot be used with model 300 SL. For driving in countries with heavy snows we recommend the use of tyres with special snow treads; our customer service stations will be glad to inform you on this subject and to tell you where these tyres are to be had.

Maintenance

We urgently recommend you to have all service and maintenance work carried out by our trained experts at our service stations, and wish to call your special attention upon the importance of having all service work listed in our service book carried out in due time, as this lies in your own interest. Smaller defects, which may cause larger repairs, if not recognized in due time, will be eliminated and your car will thus be kept constantly in excellent condition.

Please note that we shall not be liable for any guarantee claims unless all service work which has become due at the time of such claims have been carried out by one of our approved customer service stations.

Our workshop manual for Model 300 SL gives important details of the workshop routine for all the jobs to be carried out. It can be ordered from our Central Customer Service Department.

Model 300 SL has grease-nipple lubrication. The different lubrication points are indicated on the following tables and the lubrication scheme.

The nipples at the upper wishbone bearing pin (right and left) and at the universal steering joint should be lubricated **from above**, lubrication of other nipples and checking the oil level and the transmission oil change and changing the oil in the rear axle housing as well as draining the oil off the oil container and the engine should be carried out **from below** on a pit, lifting platform etc. The lubrication points can be reached through bores in the bottom protection plate or after removing small covers at the protection plate (for transmission and rear axle) and the nipples can be serviced as usual or by applying an extension piece to the standard grease gun. Only the two nipples at the angular drive of the tachometer shaft and the two nipples at the angular drive of the revolution counter shaft are accessible only after removing the transmission tunnel and the front panels of the bottom protection plate. These nipples, however, will have to be lubricated only every 60 000 miles (96 000 km).

The oil in the engine and the oil tank as well as the oil in the transmission and the rear axle housing should be changed immediately after a drive while the oil is still hot, as it will thus flush away all impurities.

Cleaning of the Vehicle and Care of the Coachwork painted with Nitro-Polishing Lacquer*

Nitro-polishing-enamel is an air-drying lacquer which must be ground and polished to obtain high gloss and should be repolished regularly. Its characteristics are high-polishing gloss and smooth grain-less areas. If the painting of a car is rubbed over with a white cloth soaked in a diluted nitro-solution, nitro-lacquer will quickly stain the cloth while resin-polish will show only slight swelling and corrosion.

Nitro-lacquer should be attended to as follows:

1. The **cold** coachwork should be washed thoroughly with cold water and a clean sponge, if possible with a slight spray. Direct sunlight should be avoided. Chassis, wheels, bumpers and chromium-plated parts should thoroughly be cleaned at the same time. The sponge and brush used for cleaning the chassis and the wheels should not be used for cleaning the coachwork painting. Windscreen and the other window panes should also always be cleaned with a clean chamois leather which is used for this purpose only, in order to avoid smears. After this the entire coachwork should be rubbed dry with a clean chamois leather, in order to prevent the water from drying on the lacquer and thus stain it. Special care should be taken with very hard water.

   Washing the car frequently will improve the durability of the lacquer, which is otherwise impaired by the chemical action of dirt and dust particles staying on too long. The car should be washed as often as possible, particularly after longer drives. Tar stains should be removed only with "Mercedes-Benz Tar Remover", as many commercial tar removers contain solutions which are harmful to our paintwork.

2. If the preservative treatment of the lacquer has become ineffective (see picture overleaf), the coachwork, which had first been cleaned as described under 1), should be re-polished to high gloss with "Mercedes-Benz Neuglanz" or any other car polish recommended by us. To do this put some polish on polishing cotton wool and apply it to sections of about ½ sq.yard at a time by stroking firmly and rhythmically always in the same direction. If high gloss has been obtained, the remaining polish is carefully removed with clean cotton wool. Polishing and grinding compounds should not be used unless the lacquer has been seriously damaged. Jobs like these should only be carried out at our Customer Service Stations, as these compounds may easily damage the lacquer if applied by an unskilled hand.

3. If the lacquered surface of the car is to be given an especially effective protective treatment, the highly polished coachwork should be slightly sprayed with the protective agent "Mercedes-Benz-Kristall" – always about ¼ to ½ sq.yards at a time – and this agent distributed equally over the surface with a piece of flannel or soft cotton wool and finally polished to high gloss with circular movements, applying a moderate pressure.

   By this treatment a protective film is formed on the coachwork.

This treatment of the coachwork should also be applied after the painting had been repaired or tar stains removed.

Note: Cars painted with nitro-lacquer should never be shampooed, not even if the polished surface has been treated with a protective agent.

* Special instructions for resin-baked painting.

Chromium-plated parts: All chromium-plated parts should be rubbed dry after having been cleaned with water and sponge and after this tar stains, if any, should be removed with "Mercedes-Benz Tar Remover" (see above). Sharp-edged tools – knives etc. should on no account be used for this purpose in order not do damage the chromium-plating. Finally a thin layer of the chromium polish "Mercedes-Benz Brillant" should be applied with a soft cotton cloth (flannel); allow to dry and polish the parts with a clean flannel. Eventual pores are closed by this treatment and corrosion is thus prevented. This treatment of the chromium-plated parts should be carried through every time the car has been washed, particularly in winter. The costs of this treatment are low and the effect will be surprising.

If the car is heavily strained, particularly in winter, when the snowy streets have been strewn with gravel and cattle salt, the chromium-plated parts should be treated with a protective compound which is highly effective due to its high wax content. We advise you to apply this treatment before every drive in snowy and slushy weather after the chromium-plated parts have been cleaned with clear water from snow and salt-water.

The chromium protective compound is also applied with polishing cotton wool. After having been allowed to dry for a short while, polish with more cotton wool. If the weather is so bad as to necessitate a special protection of the chromium-plated parts, apply a thick layer of the protective compound and do not polish at all.

The efficacy of the protective treatment of the lacquered as well as the chromium-plated parts is shown by drops of water or rain which are repelled from the surface, i. e. they form beads and not patches. As soon as patches of water will form on the surface, the protective treatment has become almost ineffective and should be repeated.

 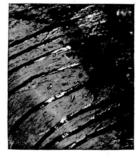

Protective treatment effective, repelling water and retaining gloss.

Protective treatment ineffective. Patches of water forming, lacquer becomes dull.

Covers and upholstery are cleaned only with a brush which should not be too stiff. Do not try to remove oil or grease stains with any solution available, as unsightly patches may appear caused by the lining.

There is no universally effective solution for removing stains, the solution to be used will have to be determined for each individual case. In most cases it will be quite sufficient to rub the upholstery off, after brushing, with diluted liquid ammonia (1 part of commercial liquid ammonia to about 3–4 parts of water), with gauze, soft muslin etc., moist, however, not wet and after this to allow it to dry. Sugar stains are removed with warm water. Grease stains should be rubbed off with some soap solution, not, however, liquid soap, as it often contains alkali which attacks the paintwork. Oil paints and resin can be removed with a little turpentine. Rust and ink stains are repeatedly treated with a diluted solution of citric acid. In every case finish off by rubbing over with diluted liquid ammonia.

In general we would advise you to consult one of our Customer Service Stations only about the removing of stains.

Also as to the treatment of leather upholstery and of stains which have penetrated into the leather please apply to one of our Customer Service Stations or to a leather expert.

Cleaning of Car Windows and Windscreens.

The panes are cleaned best with a sponge and some lukewarm water to which a little fuel alcohol or some mild soap solution have been added. The panes are rubbed clean with a soft cloth. If commercial window cleaning solutions are used, those containing grinding agents should be avoided. Insects, butterflies etc. should previously be soaked in some mild soap solution.

The rubber sleeves on the rear axle housing should be cleaned only with lukewarm water or fuel alcohol, never with fuel.

Also the bottom part of the floor unit should be cleaned and occasionally sprayed with oil.

The windscreen wiper blades should be cleaned from time to time by wiping them with a clean cloth, if necessary with soapy water or fuel alcohol, to remove dirt and dust from the rubber. The wiper blades should be replaced by new ones once or twice a year. To take off the wiper blade, push the small lever which protrudes at the back of the blade below the fastening point in the direction of the arrow. Clean the fastening point. The new wiper blade can be inserted after the small lever has again been pushed in arrow direction (see above).

Initial "Nonrecurrent" Lubrication and Maintenance Work

After the first 30–60 miles (50–100 km):

Check all wheel nuts for tight seat, if necessary adjust.

After the first 300 miles (500 km):

1. Clean oil filter element and check housing for tight seat.
2. Drain oil out of oil container and engine housing (while the oil is still hot), fill in fresh oil according to oil chart.
3. Oil change in transmission (while oil is still **hot**). Before draining off check oil level (up to the rim of the filler opening). In case of loss of oil check for tightness.
4. Oil change in rear axle housing (while oil is still **hot**). Before draining off check oil level (up to the small hexagonal plug at the housing wall rear right) and in case of loss of oil check for tightness.
5. Check oil level in oiler at ignition distributor, replenish, if necessary.
6. Check valve clearance, adjust, if necessary.
7. Check tension of fan belt, re-tighten, if necessary.
8. Clean element of fuel ante-filter.
9. Check footbrake and handbrake for proper function. If necessary, adjust handbrake.
10. Check wheel nuts, tighten, if necessary.
11. Check tyre pressure, correct, if necessary.

After the first 1250 miles (2000 km):

1. Clean oil filter and check housing for tight seat.
2. Drain oil out of oil container and engine housing (while oil is still **hot**), fill in fresh oil according to oil chart.
3. Check tension of fan belt, if necessary re-tighten.
4. Check all nuts of intake and exhaust lines for tight seat.
5. Check gap between breaker contacts of ignition distributor, adjust, if necessary, but do not refinish contacts.
   On no account grease felt in cam bore with oil before having completed 15 000 miles (24 000 km) to avoid contamination of the breaker contacts.
6. Re-tighten fastening screws of shock absorbers.
7. Check brake fluid, engine oil, fuel and cooling water hoses for tightness and chafed spots.
8. Check wheel nuts, if necessary, adjust.
9. Check tyre pressure, correct, if necessary.
10. Check toe-in.
11. Check function of footbrake and handbrake on a test drive, bleed, if necessary and adjust handbrake.
12. Grease hinges of engine hood, doors and rear cover.

After the first 2500 miles (4000 km):

1. All lubrication and maintenance work due after every 2500 miles (4000 km) (see p. 31).
2. Check free travel of clutch pedal.
3. Check toe-in.

Regular Lubrication and Maintenance Work

After every miles	Page	Part of Car	Nature of Work
1	42	Tyres	Test pressure of cold tyres.
	20	Oil container	Wipe dipstick; check oil level, replenish, if necessary.
2,500	34 — 36	Oil filter [2]	Take out element and clean it.
		Oil container and engine	Oil change [2].
		Flap nipple of the intake line	Apply a few drops of oil to the following points: a) spring pressure pin at throttle valve lever, b) part throttle valve, c) bearings for the control of cold starting gate valve. After detaching the hose connection and taking off the connecting tube, apply one drop of oil to the following points inside the flap nipple: a) cold starting gate valve via the 2 bores, b) bearings of throttle valve shaft.
	33	Front axle [3]	Grease the following 20 grease nipples with a grease gun — clean lubricators first. a) 2 nipples each at the upper left and the upper right wishbone bearing pin, b) 2 nipples each at the lower left and the lower right wishbone bearing pin, c) 3 nipples each at the left and right steering knuckle. d) 1 nipple each at the steering-gear arm, at the intermediate steering lever, at the bearing of intermediate lever and at the steering shock absorber, e) 1 nipple each at the outer part of the tie rods.
	33	Pedals [3]	Grease the two nipples with a grease gun, clean lubricators first.
	—	Joints and bearings for pedals and levers, cables and linkage for handbrake and injection pump	Check and lubricate.
	—	Brake fluid, engine oil-, fuel-, cooling water hoses and hose connection to vacuum tank	Check for tightness, chafed spots and impressions.
	34	Air filter	Remove, clean with gasoline and moisten with engine oil. Clean more frequently on dusty roads.
	34	Fuel ante filter	Take out element and clean it.
	34	Fan belt	Check tension, adjust, if necessary.
	37	Exhaust pipe	Check flanged nuts for tight seat.
	43	Battery [4]	Check level and density of acid.
	—	Electrical consumer points	Check for proper function.
	40	Wheels	Re-balance [5]; interchange.

[1] From time to time and before every longer drive.
[2] *In city traffic or on very dusty roads every 1250 miles; observe viscosity prescriptions.*
[3] *On very muddy, slushy or otherwise very bad roads every 1250 miles.*
[4] *At least every four weeks.*
[5] *Can be carried out at a Service Station only.*

After every miles	Page	Part of Car	Nature of Work
2,500	38	Brakes	Check footbrake and handbrake, adjust handbrake, if necessary.
5,000	—	Ventilation ducts, front	Clean insect screens.
	33	Injection pump	After removing oil dipstick fill in engine oil up to rim; apply 3–5 drops of oil to flap oiler of governor.
	—	Ignition distributor and oil pump-drive	Check clearance [1].
	36	Ignition distributor	Check breaker contacts for contamination. Check gap, adjust, if necessary.
	37	Spark plugs	Clean, check electrode gap.
	37	Valves	Check clearance, adjust, if necessary; test compression [1].
	33	Transmission	Check oil level (up to the rim of filler opening); in case of loss of oil check for tightness.
	33	Rear axle housing	Check oil level (up to the small hexagonal plug, rear right at housing wall); in case of loss of oil check for tightness.
	33	Brake fluid container	Check level of fluid; if necessary replenish with brake fluid up to the dipstick.
	38	Brakes	Take off brake drums, check drums and brake linings. Smooth surface of linings with emery cloth. Check position of switch for electrical vacuum valve (solenoid valve) at brake pedal.
	43	Wheels	Check toe-in.
	—	Locks of doors, rear cover, engine hood	Keep door locking bolts clean and free from oil; clean catch of hood lock and rear cover lock with gasoline, grease carefully, do not apply oil to the keyholes [2].
	—	Hinges of engine hood, doors, rear cover	Lubricate.
		Door sealings	Rub in some tallow.
		Window guides	Clean them and keep them free from grease.
10,000	43	Battery	Clean terminals, check for tight seat and grease.
	47	Water pump	Check oil level.
	37	Intake and exhaust line	Check all nuts for tight seat.
	38	Clutch	Check free play of pedal, adjust, if necessary.
	—	Shock absorbers	Check for oil-tightness, tighten fastening bolts.
	—	Nuts, bolts and cotter pins of steering, engine suspension, drive shaft and rear axle	Check on a pit or lifting platform and tighten, if necessary.
	38	Booster brake	Take off air filter, clean in a solution, allow to dry and reinstall.

[1] Can be carried out only at a Customer Service Station.
[2] Some flaky graphite (Messrs. Krystagon-Graphit-Kompanie Driver KG, Düsseldorf 10) can, however, be applied to these locks.

After every miles	Page	Part of Car	Nature of Work
10,000	33	Front wheel bearings	Top up with grease.
	33	Transmission	Oil change (while oil is still hot). Check oil level before draining off (up to the rim of filler opening), in case of loss of oil check for tightness.
	33	Rear axle housing	Oil change (while the oil is still hot). Check oil level before draining off (up to the small hexagonal plug, rear right at the housing wall), in case of loss of oil check for tightness.
	33	Steering-gear housing	Check oil level.
	33	Drive shaft	Grease with a grease gun: Front: Grease nipple at joint and grease nipple at the splined end. Rear: Grease nipple at the joint (Extension s. page 27).
	33	Auxiliary fuel pump	Lubricate.
	—	Windscreen wiper [1]	Lubricate drive shaft of linkage.
	46	Headlights	Check aiming.
15,000	36	Ignition distributor	Replenish oiler with engine oil. Take off distributor disc and rotating arm; apply 3–4 drops of engine oil to the felt in the cam bore — Caution, do not apply too much as otherwise the terminals may get contaminated. Slightly grease distributor cams; make sure there is still a wedge of grease in the sliding edge of the cam, if necessary put in some more Bosch-grease Ft 1 v 4.
	35	Fuel filter	Exchange paper insert.
	47	Cooling system	Flush and replenish with treated water.
30,000	—	Ignition distributor [2]	Check [2] (special directions).
	—	Generator [2]	Remove; check condition of collector and, if necessary, turn it; clean carbon brush holder, replace carbons by new ones.
	—	Clutch [2]	Check for proper function [2] (special directions).
	—	Rear axle [2]	Check wheel bearings (special directions) [2].
	—	Front axles [2]	Check wheel bearings (special directions) [2].
	—	Steering shaft	Check steering for free play adjust, if necessary.
	—	Steering universal joint	Grease nipples with grease gun (pointed extension s. page 27).
	—	Tie rods [2]	Check joints and sealing [2].
	—	Brakes [2]	Check master brake cylinder and wheel brake cylinder for tightness. Check subpressure and tightness of booster brake.
	—	Hand brake	Check brake cables.
	—	Wheels	Check for exterior damage.
60,000	—	Angular drive of tachometer shaft	Press grease into the 2 grease nipples (extension s. page 27).
	—	Angular drive of revolution counter shaft	Press grease into the 2 grease nipples (extension s. page 27).

[1] We advise you to have the wiper blades replaced every 6 to 12 months, according to their degree of wear (s. page 29).
[2] Can be carried out only at a Customer Service Station.

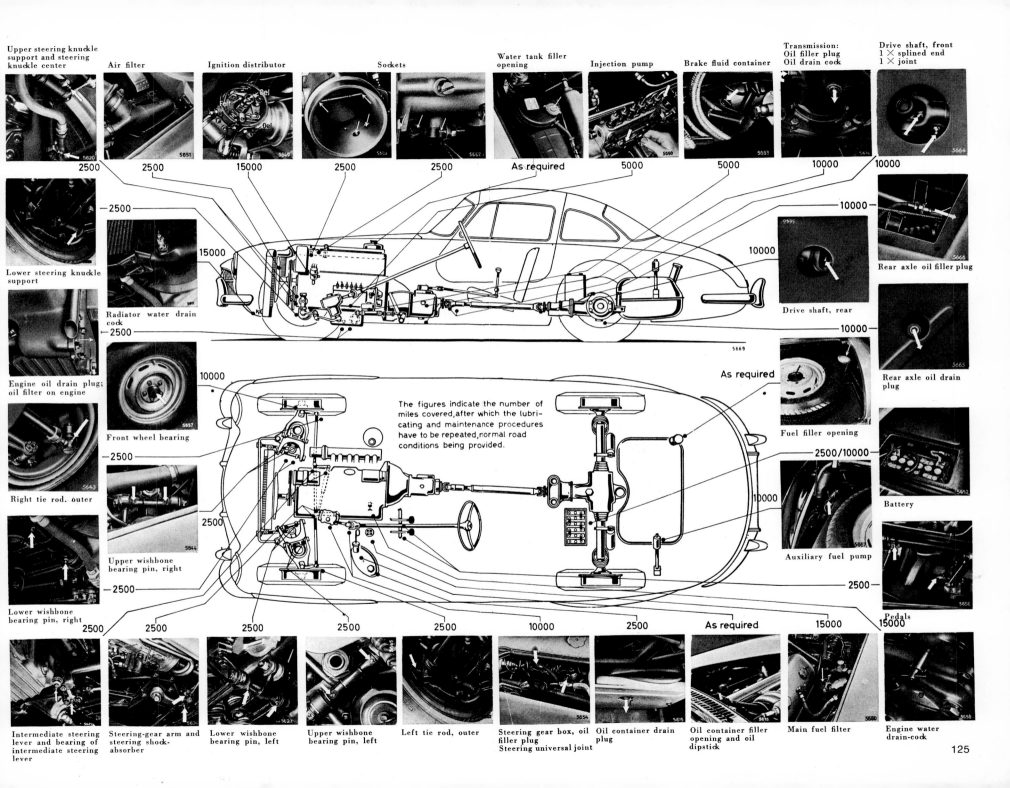

Upper steering knuckle support and steering knuckle center
2500

Air filter
2500

Ignition distributor
15000

Sockets
2500

2500

Water tank filler opening
As required

Injection pump
5000

Brake fluid container
5000

Transmission:
Oil filler plug
Oil drain cock
10000

Drive shaft, front
1 × splined end
1 × joint
10000

Lower steering knuckle support
2500

Radiator water drain cock
2500

15000

Front wheel bearing
10000

2500

Right tie rod. outer

Engine oil drain plug; oil filter on engine

10000

10000

Drive shaft, rear
10000

Rear axle oil filler plug

Rear axle oil drain plug

Fuel filler opening
As required

2500/10000

10000

Battery

Auxiliary fuel pump

Pedals
15000

The figures indicate the number of miles covered, after which the lubricating and maintenance procedures have to be repeated, normal road conditions being provided.

Upper wishbone bearing pin, right
2500

Lower wishbone bearing pin, right
2500

2500

2500

2500

2500

2500

10000

2500

As required

15000

Intermediate steering lever and bearing of intermediate steering lever

Steering-gear arm and steering shock-absorber

Lower wishbone bearing pin, left

Upper wishbone bearing pin, left

Left tie rod, outer

Steering gear box, oil filler plug
Steering universal joint

Oil container drain plug

Oil container filler opening and oil dipstick

Main fuel filter

Engine water drain-cock

125

Car tools: The tools supplied with the car, i. e. the jack with lifting arbor and wheel nut wrench as well as the spare wheel are housed in the rear part of the car and easily accessible.

Points of special attention.

Engine:

Check fan belt: If it shows worn spots, replace it by a new one; fit it on as described below. Caution! Do not try to force it on with a screw driver or a similar tool.

The belt should not be too loose nor too tight. Therefore the tension of the belt should be checked regularly: Distance A, by which the belt is deflected if moderately pressed with your thumb at the generator side, should be at least 0.2 in. (5 mm) and not more than 0.4 in. (10 mm).

Adjusting: Loosen the three (1), (2), (3) fastening nuts at the fan support. The belt can then be correctly adjusted by turning the hexagonal nut (4) of the tensioner with a wrench. Afterwards the three nuts (1) (2), (3) should be tightened again.

To clean the oil filter (coil type filter): Loosen nuts of housing cover fastening screws and pull it out together with the filter element. Take the element apart – loosen retaining nut at bottom ring which can then be taken off the cover as well as the filter coil. Clean the filter coil with a soft brush (no wire brush!) and some washing gasoline inside and outside and blow through with compressed air. Reassemble filter element and housing cover and replace into housing, make sure the gasket at the housing is in perfect condition. Tighten fastening nuts equally.

To clean air filter: Loosen the two tommy screws and the hose strips. Take off air filter. It cannot be taken apart. Dip the whole filter into washing gasoline, move it to and fro, allow to dry for a short while, moisten with engine oil and reinstall.

To clean fuel ante-filter: This filter is situated at the left side of the engine behind the steering box (ill. page 35).

To clean it loosen tommy screw, fold bracket downwards at the side (ill. p. 35).

Take off upper part, compress spring at the bottom of the upper part and pull off.

Pull out strainer, clean thoroughly with a soft brush, not a wire brush, and with clean washing gasoline; rinse filter bowl in clean gasoline. Clean gasket at the bottom part and check for perfect condition.

Reassemble in reverse order; make sure the bracket is replaced vertically and the tommy screw is tight.

The main fuel filter is situated at the left side of the engine behind the oil filler socket. Its element cannot be cleaned, it should be replaced by a new one at least every 15,000 miles: after releasing the clamp at the filter housing cover the housing can be pulled off downwards. The cover remains at the engine. Take out dirty element, clean the housing, insert new element and fasten the housing at the cover with the clamp. With very dirty fuel the element should be exchanged more frequently.

Cylinder-head bolts. Due to the inner arrangement of the cylinder-head gasket of the 300 SL the cylinder-head bolts must be tightened according to a new principle. When heated the gasket should be subjected quickly to a high tightening torque.

Repairs should be carried out as follows:

To take off the cylinder head loosen the bolts in reverse order to the illustration below and only when the engine is cold.

Before mounting the cylinder head apply some "Auto-Kollag" to the contact surfaces of the cylinder-head bolts and the washers. Only quality 12 K bolts should be used. The cylinder-head bolts with thread M 12 should be tightened according to the illustration below

first torque: to 28.9 ft. lbs.

second torque: to 50.6 ft. lbs.

third torque: to 72.3 ft. lbs.

Tightening up: As soon as the engine is thoroughly warm, i. e. about 5 minutes after the cooling water has reached 176° F check all M 12 bolts with 79.5 ft. lbs.

Checking torque: After the trial run, at the latest, however, after 10 miles at approx. 176° F cooling water temperature check all M 12 bolts with 79.5 ft. lbs.

M 8 bolts should be tightened with a hand wrench.

It is not necessary to re-tighten after the first 300 miles.

126

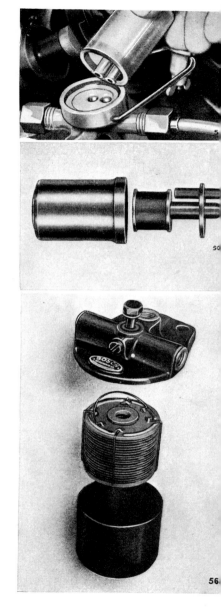

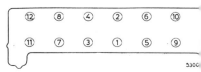

Ignition distributor

The ignition distributor rotor is lubricated with engine oil at the oiler which is fitted with a turning cover. The oil level in the oiler should be checked after the "first" 300 miles and every 15,000 miles the oiler should be replenished with the engine oil. Release clamp at distributor disc, take off distributor disc. Make sure the breaker contacts are free from grease, clean them, if necessary. Any deposits at the contacts should be removed with a contact file, never with emery paper. After that clean contacts of filings. Check the gap, which should be 0.011–0.015 in. (0.3–0.4 mm): Turn the engine until the heel of the projection on the contact breaker arm is resting on the center of the cam; this is done best by jacking up the rear wheel and turning the wheel after engaging the 4th gear. At this point the breaker contacts have the largest gap (A). The gap is correct, if a feeler plate of 0.011–0.015 in. (0.3–0.4 mm) thickness, in an emergency a doubled up post-card can be pulled through between the breaker contacts. To adjust slacken fastening screw (1) below the breaker contact and turn adjusting screw (2) at the other end of the angular piece until the correct distance is obtained. The gap is made wider by turning to the left and narrower by turning to the right. Tighten fastening screw (1), check gap. The contacts must be free from dirt and fibers. Turn the engine (see above) until the contacts are closed. As a final check lift contact lever with a small piece of wood while the ignition is switched on. If a spark appears, condenser and contact are in good order. If there is no spark, the condenser or the ignition coil are defective and should be repaired at a Customer Service Station only.

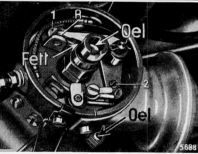

Inside the cam with the revolving part of the distributor there is a piece of felt soaked in oil; apply 3–4 drops of oil to it after every 15 000 miles. Do not apply too much!

Furthermore, it should be checked every 15 000 miles whether there is still grease enough at the contact breaker slide, if not, the wedge of grease should be made up with Bosch grease Ft 1 v 4 by means of a 0.2 in. (5 mm) wide spatula. The distributor cams should be greased slightly at the same time.

The movable parts of the **flap-type socket** of the intake line should always be well oiled. Therefore a few drops of oil should be applied at least every 2500 miles to the flexible pressure pin at the throttle lever at the outside of the socket, to the partial load valve and the bearings of the cold starting slide control.

The cold starting gate valve and the supports of the throttle valve within the flap-type socket which are accessible after the connecting hose has been taken off should also move smoothly. These points, however, should be oiled only with one drop of oil, in order to avoid contamination of the intake air.

The flap-type socket has several functions, in accordance with the different operational stages: idle running regulation according to the cooling water temperature (below 113–122° F, below 158° F, above 158° F), then the partial load regulation and the full load regulation.

The opposite illustrations show the arrangement of jets, connections and airs ducts.
It is not advisable for you to adjust the flap-type socket yourself; this should be done at a service station only.

Exhaust and intake lines: Check all nuts, especially the flanged nuts at the exhaust manifold, for tightness. Defective gaskets can be recognized by

a) blowing off at the exhaust line

b) unsatisfactory idling at the intake line.

To check spark plugs: Screw off only with a special wrench, clean dirty plugs with a brush and a cloth soaked in gasoline, blow through. Gap between electrodes $0.023^{+0.004}$ in. $(0.6^{+0.1}$ mm), check with a plug gauge. If necessary, only the ground electrode should be bent, never the central electrode. Exchange defective plugs. It may be necessary to exchange the spark plugs every 10,000 miles, according to the brand of fuel used.

To check valve clearance: The gap between the valve stem and the adjusting screw should be, with a **cold** engine, 0.002 in. at the intake valve and 0.008 in. at the exhaust valve. The adjusting screws will be accessible after the three kurled screws at the cylinder head cover have been loosened and the cover has been taken off. The valve clearance can be measured only if the respective cam does not touch the rocker arm and the valve is completely closed. This cam can be set to this position by engaging the 4th gear, jacking up the rear wheel and spinning it. The valve clearance is measured by gauges of appropriate thickness (see above). If the gauge can just be passed between the valve stem and the adjusting screw, the valve clearance is correct.

When replacing the cylinder head cover make sure the gasket is in good condition. It is advisable to have the valve clearance set at a Customer Service Station only.

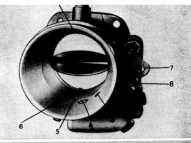

1 Idling air duct
2 Idling air throttle
3 Inlet to the cold starting vacuum air duct
4 Inlet to cold starting air duct
5 Inlet to partial load jet
6 Inlet to vacuum connector
7 Control piston lever
8 Cold starting control piston
9 Lever at the throttle shaft
10 Flexible stop with lock nut.
11 Partial load valve
12 Screw plug for partial load valve
13 Vacuum connector for ignition distributor
14 Vacuum connector
15 Screw plug for cold starting air jet
16 Screw plug for idling nozzle
17 Screw plug for vacuum cold starting nozzle

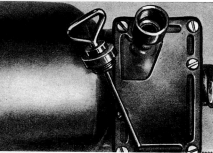

Clutch

To check free travel of the clutch pedal: The free travel of the clutch pedal should be 1 in., measured from the upper edge of the foot plate before pressure is applied. If it is less, adjust the clutch. To do this, slaken the lock nut (1) from below, give the adjusting nut (2) a few turns until the clutch rod is long enough to permit a free travel of 1 in. Tighten lock nut. If the clutch cannot be adjusted any more, take your car to a Customer Service Station.

Brakes

The hydraulic footbrake affects all four wheels simultaneously and is fitted with a **vacuum booster brake,** which will relieve the driver by supplying part of the braking power. The vacuum from the engine intake line affects the booster piston, whose power is in addition to the foot power of the driver transferred to the master brake cylinder and from there to the brakes at the wheels. Moreover, a vacuum container has been attached which will allow about 4 braking actions also after the engine has been stopped. The vacuum in this container is maintained by means of a special magneto valve; when braking this valve is opened by a control at the brake pedal. The adjustment of this control should be checked every 5,000 miles: by revving up the idle running engine for a moment, and decelerating, a vacuum will be formed in the container. After about 2 minutes press brake pedal slowly, the magneto-valve should then open as soon as the pedal has been pressed down about 0.2 in. and should close as soon as the pedal is released. Both operations are accompanied by a clearly audible clicking. If no or only one noise can be heard, the valve has remained open and there is no more vacuum in the container which will be felt by the increased pressure to be applied to the brake pedal. The control will then have to be re-adjusted, if possible at a Customer Service Station. If the valve does not close when the brake is released the magneto coil will get too hot.

The booster brake cylinder is connected to the outside air by a filter at the booster brake. This filter should be removed and cleaned in washing gasoline after every 10,000 miles on very dusty roads even more frequently. Allow to dry a short while and re-install.

The reservoir of the master brake cylinder should contain so much fluid that the dipstick will touch the surface. Use only **the original brake fluid ATE blue or Lockheed brake fluid.**

If the resistance at the brake pedal slackens (long travel of the brake pedal), actuate the pedal several times; if there is still no resistance to be felt, bleed the brakes (see p. 39) and check lines for leaks.

To bleed the brakes:

Special equipment: 1 bleeder tube, 1 glass jar.

1. During bleeding the brake fluid container should be repeatedly replenished (see 6).

2. At one front wheel: take off wheel brake cylinder cap and attach bleeder tube to the nipple.

3. Slip a spanner over the bleeder tube and place it on the bleeder screw.

4. Place the other end of the tube into the glass jar and fill the latter with enough brake fluid to cover the end of the tube.

5. Give the bleeder screw a few turns but do not screw it right out.

6. Push brake pedal down and release slowly until there are no more air bubbles in the glass jar. Caution! Do not allow the level of the fluid to sink, as otherwise fresh air will get into the lines.

7. Push brake pedal and keep it down until the bleeder screw has been tightened. Only then the brake pedal should be released.

8. Detach bleeder tube from nipple and replace cap.

9. Proceed in the same manner at the other wheels.

10. Replenish main reservoir and close it.

To adjust the brakes:

Footbrake: automatic adjustment, no outside control.

If the brake drums have been taken off, the brake shoes should be pushed inwards over the automatic adjustment device before replacing the drums. After the drums and the wheels have been re-mounted **the brake pedal should be pushed down firmly several times before the car is being driven,** in order to bring the brake shoes into the correct position.

Handbrake: Turn the adjusting nut at the hand-brake lever clockwise only far enough that the rear wheels will still spin freely while the handbrake is released.

If the handbrake adjustment is correct the brake shoes should grasp as soon as the hand-brake lever is set to the 3rd or 4th indent.

Final check: With released brakes the car should stop without jerking. After having driven several miles without braking, the wheels should only be slightly heated.

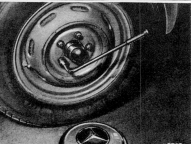

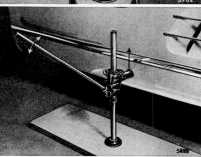

Wheels

Front wheel lubrication:

Take off the ornamental cover with the flat end of the wheel nut wrench and pull off the hub cap which has thus been exposed (special tool). Fill hub cap with grease and replace. The grease will thus be pressed into the ball bearings. Replace ornamental cover.

The rear wheel bearings are lubricated direct from the rear axle housing.

To change the wheels. Spare wheel, wheel nut wrench and the jack with lifting arbor are housed in the rear compartment. The flattened end of the wheel nut wrench is used for taking off the ornamental cover. Before changing the wheels pull the handbrake. If possible, the car should be placed on level ground and not on a slope. On upgrades it should be secured by blocks. Take off ornamental cover, slacken wheel nuts but do not screw them off. Place the lifting jack in the supports right and left of the car and jack the car up until the wheel spins freely. Take off wheel nuts and pull off the wheel. Put on the new wheel with the mounting fork which you will find among the tools:

Push the mounting fork through the two upper securing holes of the wheel and slip it over the bolts at the brake drum; keep your foot at the wheel which you lift into place with the mounting fork. Keep in mind that certain tyres should be put on in a particular driving direction (which is indicated by an arrow on the cover). Replace all wheel nuts but do not tighten yet. Lower the lifting jack and tighten the wheel nuts always omitting one. Correct tyre pressure (s. page 42) and have damaged tyres quickly repaired.

To balance the wheels

Unbalance is the unequal distribution of material and weight in a rotating body, e. g. wheel and tyre. Excessive lack of balance at the wheels may at a speed of over 50 miles p. h., cause steering difficulties, vibration of the body and jumping of the wheels even on smooth roads. Tyre wear, too, is increased and will become unequal.

After a new tyre has been mounted or a tyre which has become flat through a defective tube or valve, the wheel should be rebalanced.

Tyre wear may also gradually cause unbalance of the wheels. Therefore the wheels should be rebalanced every 2500 miles.

The static balancing method which is usually applied is in general insufficient for top speeds – the wheels should be balanced dynamically. The special balancing weights should be fastened in the slots provided for this purpose at both sides of the wheel flanges; it is not advisable to wedge the standard balancing weights between wheel flange and tyre, as they will not keep in place at high speeds. Special directions for the fastening of the balancing weights will be found on the enclosed leaflet.

Attention! If balancing the wheels at the car do not balance at the rear axle but only at the front axle in order to avoid overstressing of the differential gears, i. e. place the rear wheels to the front axle for balancing purposes.

We urgently recommend to have the wheels balanced at a Customer Service Station only.

To interchange the wheels

In order to obtain even wear on the tyres and the longest possible life we would recommend you to have the tyres interchanged every 2,500 miles according to the opposite scheme.

Tyres

The high speeds of Model 300 SL will severely strain the tyres and not all makes on the market will prove adequate to this strain. We therefore urgently recommend to **consult our Customer Service Stations about the tyre brands tested and approved by us.**

If the vehicle is to be driven in a competition it will have to be fitted with racing tyres. In this case it would be best to contact the makers direct and ask their advice about the type of tyres to be used.

To change a tyre

To pull a tyre off a rim, never use a sharp-edged tool and do not apply force, as the vehicle is fitted with light-metal rims. If the tube is to be exchanged, the size of the new tube must match the cover.

Place the slightly inflated tube into the cover in such a way that the valve lies at the red dot on the cover which indicates the lightest spot of the cover. Before inflating to full check the position of the beading.

Inflate to the required pressure (s. page 42).

After a tyre has been exchanged the wheel should be rebalanced (s. page 40).

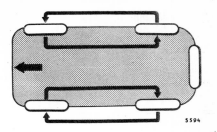

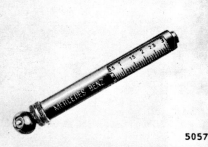

129

Tyre pressure

Make sure the correct tyre pressure is maintained!

This is decisive for the driving safety, the long life of the tyre and the comfort.

Too low a pressure will increase tyre wear and result in bad cornering, too high a pressure will impair the springing and cause severe strain of the body on bad roads.

Tyre pressure with cold tyres:

Up to a max. speed of 110 mph

Front wheels	28.5 lbs./sq.in.	(2.0 atü)
Rear wheels	31.5 lbs./sq.in.	(2.2 atü)

At a speed of over 110 mph

Front wheels	31.5 lbs./sq.in.	(2.2 atü)
Rear wheels	34 lbs./sq.in.	(2.4 atü)

For racing:

Front wheels	42.5 lbs./sq.in.	(3.0 atü)
Rear wheels	50 lbs./sq.in.	(3.5 atü)

The tyre pressure should be checked before every longer drive, at least, however, once a week.

As the pocket pressure gauges which are usually available are not always in good condition, the tyre pressure should be measured only with the precision pressure gauge supplied by us. This instrument should be checked from time to time at our customer service station.

If the tyre pressure drops by more than 3 lbs./sq.in. the valve or the tube is untight and should be repaired as quickly as possible. Experience has shown that nails in the tyre do not cause the air to escape immediately but will effect only a slow dropping of the pressure. On a longer drive the damage is increased by the fast motion of the tyre until the tyre is suddenly flat.

Deformation of the tyre on the road is higher with low tyre pressure than with the normal pressure. Also the less experienced driver will, after some practice, notice a difference if he carefully examines the tyres. Therefore, before every drive, just give them a quick glance.

Tyre wear

As tyre wear mainly depends on the manner of driving, every driver is personally responsible for the service life of the tyres of his car:

Sharp cornering, sudden braking and starting will considerably increase tyre wear, whereas the tyres are not noticeably affected with fast driving straight ahead, e. g. on the autobahn.

Tyre wear is naturally higher in summer than in winter, as warm rubber is less resistant than cold one.

Rough roads wear off the tyres quicker than smooth roads.

A tyre cannot be at a time skid-proof to a high degree and highly resistant to wear. Always keep in mind that highly skid-proof tyres are subject to greater wear.

Premature and unequal tyre wear may have the following causes:

1. Tyre pressure too low. This is shown by a greater wear at the sides of the tread than in the middle.

2. Unsuitable tyres: Our Customer Service Station will be pleased to advise you on the most suitable brand of tyres under the given circumstances.

3. Faulty toe-in at the front axle. This is the case if the tyre is worn off prematurely yet evenly along the circumference. In extreme cases there will be saw-tooth-shaped patches across the tyre.
The toe-in is correct if the distance between the two front wheels, measured at the edge of the rim in the center of the wheel, is by 0.07–0.15 in. smaller at the front than in the rear.
To compensate for any possible bend in the rim, the mean of the two measurements should be taken, the second measurement being made after the wheel has been turned by 180°.

4. Lack of balance. Balancing see page 40.

5. Defective shock absorbers.

6. Brakes which grip unevenly.

7. Faulty toe-in of the front wheels or a bent rim or splined shaft caused by running into something.

The damages mentioned under 3–7 can be checked and remedied only at a Customer Service Station.

Care of the tyres

Check tyres as often as possible and remove any pieces of grit, gravel etc. imbedded in the cover. The best opportunity for this is every 2500 miles when the wheels are interchanged. Cuts and any other damage to the rubber should be repaired by an expert. The resistance to skidding of worn tyres can be increased by re-soling (slight retreading across the direction of travel).

Complete retreading of worn-off tyres is not permissible due to the high top speed.

For repainting use only the special tyre paints on the market. Check the rims! Dented, bent or rusty rims damage the beading. The rims should be unrusted once a year.

Electrical equipment: Wiring diagram see page 45.

Battery: 12 V, 56 Ah. The battery is in the luggage compartment behind the seats and is accessible after taking off the protective cover.

Keep the exterior of the battery clean and dry. The fluid level should lie 0.4–0.6 in. above the upper edge of the plates. Replenish only with distilled water. Special electrolytes should not be used, because they may shorten the life of the battery. In a well kept battery the charge is indicated by the acid density (at a temperature of the acid of 68° F), therefore check the charge of the battery by means of an acidimeter.

Charged: acid density 1.285 = 32° Bé
Half charged: acid density 1.20 ≈ 24° Bé   } if too low, recharge via an
Not charged: acid density 1.12 ≈ 16° Bé   } outside source of current

Clean terminals with hot soda lye (Caution! No lye into the battery). Rinse with cold water, grease terminals with acid protecting grease.

Fuses: The fuses are in a box on the front left side of the dashboard (seen in driving direction).

The lead to the ignition is not secured by a fuse. If a fuse burns through repeatedly, have the lines checked for earthing at a service station and defective fuses replaced.

Note: The parking lights, the reading lamp, the socket and the wireless set – if any – can be switched on independent of the ignition key; all other consumer points are switched off as soon as the ignition key has been drawn out.

List of the fuses from right to left (facing the fuse box):

No.	Fuse DIN 72 581	Lead	Consumer point
1	8	30	Socket; magneto valve for vaccuum booster brake; electrical clock
2	8	30	Reading lamp, parking lights, wireless set [1]
3	25	54	Choke control lamp, windscreen wipers, horns and horn relay
4	25	54	Gasoline gauge, auxiliary fuel pump, cigar lighter, blower right and left for de-frosting the parked car
5	8	54	Brake lights, blinkers and control lamp distance light blinkers [1]
6	8	58	Right parking light, right tail light, licence plate lighting, reverse drive lamp [1]
7	8	58	Left tail light, left parking light, instrument panel lighting
8	8	58	Fog lamp [1]
9	8	56 a	Right distance light, distance light signal lamp
10	8	56 a	Left distance light
11	8	56 b	Right dimmer light
12	8	56 b	Left dimmer light

[1] Will be supplied only on request and against special charge.

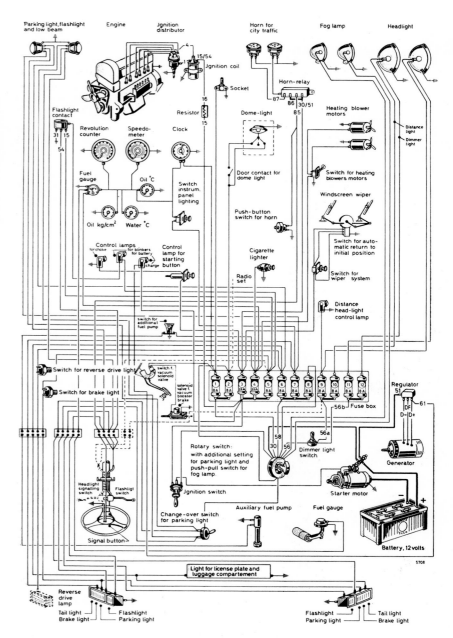

Wiring diagram of the electrical fittings (Sealed Beam)

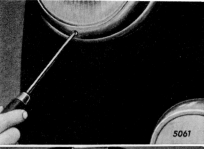

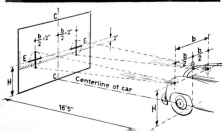

Headlights

Do not clean the reflector of the headlamps. Finger prints impair the reflector surface. The headlight should be opened only to exchange the bulb, see below.

To exchange head-light bulbs: unscrew lens-head countersunk screw at the lower part of the headlight, take off ornamental ring. Unscrew lower retaining screw of the headlight which can then be removed. Remove the bulb holder from the back of the reflector, push the bulb back, turn in anti-clockwise and pull it out. Insert new two-filament bulb, turn clockwise and pull it back as far as the stop. Caution: do not touch the bulb with moist or oily fingers, the moisture will evaporate later on, deposit on the reflector and thus considerably decrease its efficiency. Clean dirty lamps with methylated spirits and not with gasoline. After inserting the new bulb wipe it with tissue paper or the like. Replace the bulb holder in the headlamp and the latter in the mudguard. Tighten lower retaining screw. Check aiming of headlights and adjust, if necessary (see below). Replace ornamental ring and tighten lens-head countersunk screw.

To check headlight alignment:

Place a normally loaded car on level ground about 16 ft. from a vertical wall.

I. To be measured at the headlamp lenses:

1. Distance of the center of the lens from the ground = (H) ins.
2. Horizontal distance between the center of the lenses = (b) ins.
3. Horizontal distance of each headlight from the center line of the car: should be $\left(\frac{b}{2}\right)$

II. Mark on the wall:

1. A center line vertical to the axis of the car (C–C).
2. Two crosses for the alignment in the following position:
   a) Distance from the ground = H ins.
   b) Distance of each cross from the central line $\frac{b}{2}$ + 2 ins.

III. To switch on distance light:

The spots of light cast by the headlamps must coincide with the crosses. If necessary, each headlamp can be adjusted independently by means of two adjusting screws at the rim. Turning the upper adjusting screw (1) will adjust the headlamp vertically, turning the screw at the side (2) will adjust the headlamp horizontally. The other headlamp and all other lamps should be covered up while a headlamp is adjusted. Do not forget to replace the ornamental ring and to tighten the lens-head countersunk screw.

Cooling system

To clean the cooling system:

If the cooling water temperature rises above normal, the cooling system is dirty. It should then be degreased, descaled and cleaned. Caution! Superpressure cooling system; for opening see page 13.

a) **Degreasing:** Pour two hands full of soda or P 3 into the cooling system through the filler opening. Drive with this solution for one day. Drain off solution at the two drain cocks – at the radiator bottom left and at the engine bottom left. Flush cooling system thoroughly with running fresh water while the engine is operating.

b) **Descaling:** The cooling system should preferably be descaled at one of our Customer Service Stations. The most suitable method is a treatment with hydrochromium solution, as the process can be checked by means of the test strips supplied by the manufacturer. Strictly observe the directions:

Pour about 0,44 pint of hydrochromium solution into the cooling system which had been filled with untreated water. After a longer drive, at the latest, however, after 1 day, dip a test strip into the cooling water through the filler opening. The colour chart which is supplied along with the directions and the test strips by the manufacturer will inform you about the pH-value of the shade. If it is over 6, drain off cooling water, thoroughly flush the cooling system and repeat the procedure. If after a longer drive the pH-value lies below 6, the cleaning is perfect. Drain off cooling water once more, thoroughly flush cooling system and treat the cooling water according to the directions (see page 13).

c) **Cleaning:** Blow through radiator with compressed air from the engine side or spray with water to clean the radiator ribs thoroughly from all foreign bodies. Check rubber hose connection between radiator and tubing for tightness and exchange, if defective.

To remove and clean **thermostat.**

Check **water pump** oil level every 10,000 miles at the oil level check screw of the water pump (at the side of the bearing case about 2 ins. below the center of the shaft).

The oil level should be checked also if the water pump has been dismantled.

Jobs at the water pump, especially installing a replacement water pump, should be carried out at a service station only, as there are special directions for lubrication.

To garage and lay up the car:

Make sure the place you have chosen for your garage is well aired and dry. Caution! Do not allow the engine to run in a closed garage, the exhaust gases are poisonous.

If the car is to be laid up over a longer period, it should be thoroughly cleaned inside and outside and lubricated. The painted parts should be checked for scratches and repainted, the chromium-plated parts should be treated with a protective paste. Also the chassis should be checked for damaged painting and repainted with chassis-enamel. All non-painted parts, including springs and spring suspension should be greased with corrosion protective vaseline or corrosion protective grease.

Add 1% of soluble corrosion protective oil to the cooling water. It should be drained off only, if there is danger of frost and no anti-freeze has been added. Directions for draining see page 25. Drain fuel out of container.

Screw off spark plugs and spray about 0.61 cu.in. of corrosion protective oil for engines, SAE 10, through the spark plug ports. Replace plugs and turn engine with starter motor for **1 second only**. Take off cylinder head cover and spray the valves with corrosion protective oil for engines, SAE 10, replace cylinder head cover.

If the vehicle is to be laid up for several months, please contact a Customer Service Station for the necessary additional protective measures for the injection system, the transmission and the rear axle housing.

The battery should, if possible, be removed and stored in a place protected against frost. It is urgently recommended to check its charge every 4–6 weeks and, if necessary, to carefully recharge.

The tyre pressure should be maintained at the prescribed height. If the car is laid up over a longer period of time, the car should be jacked up to take the weight off the tyres. To do this, take off the bottom protective plate and place the jacks or whatever is used in the rear under the cross member ends and in front under the cross members of the front axle. On no account place the jacks under the frame tubing or under the rear axle housing. Keep the tyres on a pressure of 7 lbs./sq.in. to 14 lbs./sq.in.

Hints for Emergency Repairs

If you service your car yourself in accordance with our directions or, better still, have it regularly attended to at our Customer Service Station, there is little danger that the engine does not start or that you will have trouble with your car on the open highway, apart from possible tyre defects.

If your car should nevertheless break down on the road the following hints will help you to realise the possible cause from the symptoms and to remedy it.

To open the engine hood see page 7.

The tools, the jack with lifting arbor, the wheel nut wrench and the spare wheel are housed easily accessible in the rear compartment.

The starter motor does not turn

To find out the cause of the trouble, switch on the headlight and then switch on the starter motor. If now

1. the lamps suddenly go out, there is a bad contact at one of the two battery terminals or at one of the starter terminals. Thoroughly clean the terminals until the metal shines;

2. if the lamps go out slowly, the battery is insufficiently charged. Have the battery recharged by an outside source of current;

3. if the lights remain unchanged there is a defect in the starter motor itself which can be remedied only at a Customer Service Shop.

The engine does not start although the starter motor turns

The cause may be:

I. Faulty servicing:

A. **Fuel tank is empty.** The fuel gauge is operating only as soon as the ignition is switched on; it does not indicate the last gallon in the tank.

If the fuel system has been driven empty, the main filter should be replenished with fuel via the filler screw.

B. **The starter button has not been pulled out while the engine was cold.**

C. **The auxiliary fuel pump is not engaged while the engine was warm.**

II. **Defects in the car itself:**

A. **Troubles with the ignition**

The following examination is carried out best with a leather glove on or with a clean cloth and, in order to avoid a short circuit, a dry piece of wood and no metal tool. The cable at the battery should not be disconnected either, except if the defect has been found and is to be remedied.

Test as follows: Remove the lead from the spark plug; touch only the insulated part. Have the starter motor operated by someone else while **the ignition is switched on** and **the gears are in the neutral.** Hold the end of the cable at some distance off the cylinder head: a spark 0.3–0.4 in. long should leap from the end of the cable to the cylinder head. If no spark appears or if the gap is narrower than 0.3 in., the ignition is defective.

Check now:

1. whether a) the cable leading to the ignition coil (terminal 15),
   b) the high-tension cable (thick) and the low-tension cable (thin) between ignition coil and ignition distributor,
   c) the cable leading to the spark plugs
   are not broken and have good contact at both ends. At the same time check the electrode gap of the ignition coils and make sure they are clean (see page 37).

2. whether the current reaches the ignition coil: detach the cable leading to the ignition coil at terminal 15. Press the free end of the cable to the brass sleeve of the plug for the hand lamp and hold its center contact against the cylinder head. If the hand lamp lights up, the current supply is in good order. If the lamp does not light up, one of the cables is broken or the ignition switch is defective. Makeshift repair: Attach an extra emergency cable from terminal 15 (thick cable) of the dynamo regulator to terminal 15 of the ignition coil.

   If, however, the engine is not running, the emergency cable should be taken away on any account, as with this makeshift solution current is constantly being taken away from the battery also while the engine is stopped. Take your car to a Customer Service Station as soon as possible and have the trouble remedied by an expert.

3. whether the ignition coil is in order; to check it, disconnect the thin cable leading from the ignition coil to the condenser, terminal 1 at the ignition distributor, press the free end of the cable against the brass sleeve of the plug of the hand lamp and the middle contact of the latter against the cylinder head.
   If the lamp does not light up and if the current supply has been in order when tested as under 2, the trouble lies with the ignition coil (breaker) and can be remedied only at a Customer Service Station.
   If the lamp lights up, re-connect the cable to the ignition distributor and check:

4. whether the ignition distributor is in order: see page 36. If the ignition distributor is, at the final test, found to be in perfect condition and if the cause of the trouble has not yet been detected, check again:

5. whether a spark will leap from a plug cable to the cylinder head, if the engine is turned by means of the starter motor.

If not, the high-tension coiling of the ignition coil is defective and should be exchanged at a Customer Service Station.

B. Fuel supply defective

The causes may be:

1. Fuel ante-filter dirty: clean it, see page 34.

2. Main fuel filter dirty: exchange element against new one, see page 35.

3. Lines untight.

Cold engine does not start smoothly or does not turn over:

The cause may be: Cold starting is stuck: release it and if necessary, renew the springs (the thermostat holder may be bent).

Hot engine does not start smoothly although the auxiliary fuel pump is engaged:

1. Auxiliary fuel pump defective: replace pump driving motor or the pump. Check electric parts of the pump.

2. Nonreturn valve in the fuel line is stuck: clean nonreturn valve.

Engine does not idle smoothly and at partial load range:

The cause may be:

1. Air jets in the flap-type socket are clogged, clean air jets. Setting of jets see page 37.

2. Fuel line leading to the fuel feed pump untight: replace gaskets or flexible line.

3. Overflow valve stuck: clean the overflow valve.

4. Fuel feed pump defective: exchange it.

5. The pressure pin in the flexible stop of the partial load valve is stuck: renew flexible stop. Do not tighten the nuts too much, otherwise the pressure pin may grip.

6. Vacuum connection or vacuum line untight: check subpressure.

7. Governor diaphragm untight: exchange injection pump.

The defects listed under 3–7 can be repaired only at a Customer Service Station.

Idling engine makes sawing noises

The causes may be:

Idling jet too big or too small. Jet seat see page 37. The size of the idling jet should be chosen so as to safeguard minimum "sawing"; should be done at a Customer Service Station only.

"Sawing" can be watched at the oil pressure gauge.

Irregular idling of the engine

The release spring does not completely shut the throttle valve. If necessary, shorten release spring. Can be done only in a Customer Service Station.

With new vehicles the idling speed sometimes rises after some time, as the resistance to friction in the engine lessens. In this case the idling speed will have to be regulated with the idling jet see page 37, which should be done at a Customer Service Station only.

The engine runs backward

It may happen with the injection engine that after stopping the engine will turn a few backward revolutions. This does not necessarily indicate a defect. Engage a gear in this case and stop the engine by clutching.

Engine fuel consumption too high (black smoke at the exhaust pipe)

The cause may be:

1. The chocke is stuck: check choke and release spring.

2. An injection nozzle untight: check injection nozzles and if necessary replace.

3. Cold-starting thermostat defective, gate valve does not disconnect: renew thermostat.

4. Vacuum line or governor diaphragm untight: can be checked and repaired only at a Customer Service Station.

Irregular operation of engine in all ranges

The cause may be:

1. An injection line broken: renew line.

2. Defective pressure valve at the injection pump: exchange injection pump.

3. Control rod stuck: exchange injection pump. After removing the screw cap the control rod can be checked for easy operation.

4. Fuel overflow valve stuck: clean it.

5. Cam box ventilation of the injection pump clogged: clean ventilation. If the oil in the injection pump housing contains much fuel, check the oil supply to the leaking oil stop. To do this remove nonreturn valve, dismount and clean it.

The defects listed under 2–5 can be repaired only at a Customer Service Station.

The engine fails at a high speed (output decreases)

Nonreturn valve in the fuel line dirty: clean nonreturn valve; can be done only at a Customer Service Station.

Cooling water is boiling

The cause may be:

1. **Too little water in the cooling system. Caution! Superpressure cooling system.** Open only if the cooling water temperature is below 194° F. Turn first to stop I and allow superpressure to blow off, turn round and take off screw cap. To close turn until stop II. Replenish slowly and only while the engine is running.

   Check hose connections between water tank, radiator and engine and between engine and heater for tight seat and tighten.

2. **Radiator may be covered up too much.**

3. **V-belt for fan and the water pump not tight enough** (see page 34) or broken.

4. **Cooling line clogged.**

5. **Water pump defective.**

6. **Retarded ignition:** in this case the output will be too low.

7. **Cylinder-head gasket defective.**

8. **Cooling water thermostat defective:** exchange.

   The defects listed under 5–8 should be repaired at a Customer Service Station only.

The red charging control lamp lights up during a drive.

If the charging control lamp lights up while the car is being driven, i. e. at medium or higher speeds, the electrical system is defective. Stop and look for the cause, which may be:

1. **Defective dynamo,** which should be repaired as soon as possible at the nearest Customer Service Station, as the battery will not be re-charged if the dynamo fails to work.

2. **V-belt slack or defective:** re-tighten, see page 34.

3. The **cable** leading from the charging control lamp to the dynamo or to the battery is **earthing.**

Oil pressure drops suddenly. The cause may be:

1. **Too little oil.**

   Lack of oil can be noticed by a dropping oil pressure in a curve, while the oil pressure remains unchanged when driving straight ahead: the oil level in the oil container should reach at least the first mark at the oil dipstick.

2. **Oil relief pressure valve at the engine dirty or untight:**
   Remove oil relief pressure valve, dismantle and clean.

3. **Line between engine housing and oil filter untight.** Tighten connecting bolts.
   If points 1–3 are in good order:

4. **Check oil pressure gauge:**

   Disconnect connecting line at filter. If oil escapes at the connection while the engine is running, the fault lies with the oil pressure gauge itself or the line leading to the oil pressure gauge which should then be exchanged. If not, there is a defect in the engine which should be repaired at a Customer Service Station only.

The clutch slips.

If, when accelerating, the number of revolutions rises without increasing the speed of the car, the clutch is slipping. You will then just be able to drive on slowly to the nearest Customer Service Station, accelerating very carefully, so as to prevent the clutch from slipping. This is possible by engaging a low gear. The cause may be:

1. **The clutch pedal has not the correct free travel.**
   Adjusting see page 38.

2. **Clutch is oiled up.**

3. **Clutch facing or the clutch itself defective.** Should be repaired at a Customer Service Station.

Brakes

Checking the brakes **before driving off,** the brake pedal should have a point of resistance. If not, the following may happen:

1. **The brake pedal can be pushed right down slowly or quickly.**
   The cause may be:

   a) A wheel brake cylinder or brake line are untight. Before driving off, tighten up connections or take your car to a Customer Service Station.

   b) Master brake cylinder defective. There will be no outward sign of leakage. The master brake cylinder can be repaired at a Customer Service Station only.

2. **The brake pedal can be pushed down against a clearly perceptible elastic resistance.**
   Air in the brake lines: bleed, see page 38 and, if necessary, replenish reserve tank with brake fluid.

During a drive.

1. **If the brake pedal can be pushed right down during a long downhill drive:** release and press down quickly twice; the resistance should again be felt. If the brakes do not grip all the same, stop the vehicle with the handbrake and, if necessary, by shifting back to a lower gear.
   Check whether the defect is not of the nature described under 1a or 1b. Have the brake system checked at a Customer Service Station as soon as possible.

2. **Braking action insufficient.** The cause may be:

   a) No vacuum in the booster brake due to leakage in the lines, reserve tank, nonreturn valves, the booster brake itself or at the intake line or throttle valve at the side of the engine: check rubber sleeves of lines, exchange them, if necessary – the distance between the line ends at the hose coupling should not be less than 0.15 in. and not more than 0.3 in. and the line ends should be level –; repair or exchange storage tank; have the nonreturn valve and the booster brake checked at a Customer Service Station.

   b) The electrical valve between the storage tank and the booster brake
      1. does not react: check fuses and electrical wiring between fuse box, the switch at the brake pedal and the magneto valve.
      2. gets hot: check adjustment of switch at brake pedal, if necessary have it adjusted at a Customer Service Station (see page 38).

   c) Brake linings defective: have them checked at a Customer Service Station.

3. **Brake becomes effective too late.** The causes may be:
   The subpressure in the booster cylinder rises slowly: check lines of vacuum system; if crushed, have them replaced.

4. **The brake is released slowly.** This is mostly due to hard operation of the valve and the booster piston or to jamming of the pedal linkage. Have this checked at a Customer Service Station.

5. **Unsatisfactory gradation:** The cause may be:

   a) hard working linkage including pedal plate: grease linkage and make sure it operates smoothly

   b) hard-moving booster piston: have the booster brake checked at the Customer Service Station.

6. **The pedal cants or vibrates when the brake is actuated or released.** The cause may be: booster piston sticks: have it checked at a Customer Service Station.

7. **Chattering of the brake.** The cause may be:

   a) Brake drums out of true (motion can be felt at the pedal). Have the brake drums re-adjusted

   b) Brake linings burnt (brake tends to grab). Exchange linings, have the drums adjusted.

Defects at the electrical system

All fuses will be found in a box in front at the right side of the dashboard (see page 44).

The causes of failure of an electrical device may be:

1. Bad contact of the fuse: turn the fuse, polish contact surfaces, readjust contact spring, if necessary.

2. Defective fuse; it is either burnt out or the fuse wire in the partridge is not making contact. This cannot be ascertained from the outside. Replace only by soldered fuses.

3. Bad contact at a connection: tighten terminals.

4. A line is earthing: check cables for chafed spots.

5. The device itself is defective: defects listed under 3–5 should be repaired at a Customer Service Station.

Technical Data

Design .... MB Type M 198
Principle of operation .... Four-stroke gasoline injection
Engine output .... 240 gross HP acc. to SAE standards
Number of revolutions at 60 mph .... 2510 rpm; 2640 rpm; 2810 rpm
   at reduction ratio i = ... 3.25 : 1   3.42 : 1   3.64 : 1
Maximum revolutions .... 6400, in the different gears 6000 rpm
Number of cylinders 6
Bore/stroke .... 11/32 – 15/32 in. (85/88 mm)
Total eff. capacity .... 183 cu. ins (2996 c. c.)
Compression ratio .... 8.55 : 1
Oil filling in oil container .... 3 Imp. gals/4 US gals. max. (15 ltrs)
   2 Imp. gals/3 US gals. min. (11 ltrs)
Cooling .... water circulation by pump,
   Thermostat with short-circuit line,
   Ventilator

Capacity of cooling system
with DB-heating .... 3.4 Imp. gals./4.0 US gals. (15.5 ltrs)
Valve clearance with cold engine
   intake .... 0.002 in. (0.05 mm)
   exhaust .... 0.008 in. (0.20 mm)
Firing order, cylinder 1 at the radiator 1–5–3–6–2–4
Spark plugs .... Bosch W 280 T 2
   or Beru 280/14/3 Lu
Standard timing adjustment .... 6° after UDC
Ignition control .... automatic by centrifugal force or vacuum and
   by hand for compensation of octane rating
Ignition distributor .... Bosch VJU R 6 BR 25
Ignition coil .... Bosch TK 12 A 9
Starter motor .... Bosch EGD 1,0/12 AR 5
Dynamo .... Bosch LJ/GJJ 150/12–1600 R 4
Injection pump .... Bosch PES 6 KL 70/320 R 2
Injection nozzles .... Bosch DC 10 A 30 R 1/4
Injection pressure .... 568–682 lbs. sq. in.
End of injection .... 60° after UDC
Fuel feed pump .... Bosch FP/KLA 22 K 1
Auxiliary fuel pump .... Daimler-Benz
Oil cooling .... oil-air-heat exchanger

Chassis

Transmission ...... Daimler-Benz 4-gear transmission baulked synchromesh in all gears
Steering .... Daimler-Benz recirculating balls or ZF steering, special design Model 542
Camber of front wheels .... about 0° 30′–0° 45′ loaded
Toe-in .... about 0.078–0.15 in. loaded
Caster .... about 5°
Camber of rear wheels .... —3° ± 20′

Rear axle ratio		1st gear	2nd gear	3rd gear	4th gear
3.64 : 1	Driving speed mph	appr. 39 (64 km)	67 (108)	96 (155)	145 (235)
(Standard)	Climbing ability	1 in 1.3	1 in 2.8	1 in 4.7	1 in 8.2
3.42 : 1	Driving speed mph	appr. 42 (68 km)	71 (115)	101 (164)	155 (250)
(on request)	Climbing ability	1 in 1.4	1 in 3.1	1 in 5.2	1 in 9.0
3.25 : 1	Driving speed mph	appr. 44 (71 km)	75 (121)	107 (173)	161 (260)
(on request)	Climbing ability	1 in 1.5	1 in 3.3	1 in 5.7	1 in 9.6

Wheels .... Steel sheet disc-wheels
Type of rims .... Drop-base rim
Size of rims .... 5 K × 15
Size of tyres 6.50–15
Tyre pressure, front } see page 42
Tyre pressure, rear }
Overall length .... 177.95 ins. (4520 mm)
Overall width .... 70.47 ins. (1790 mm)
Overall height, unloaded .... 51.18 ins. (1300 mm) approx.
Wheelbase .... 94.48 ins. (2400 mm)
Track, front .... 54.52 ins. (1385 mm)
Track, rear .... 56.49 ins. (1435 mm)
Diameter of turning circle .... 37.5 ft. approx. (11.5 m)
Ground clearance (with 2 passengers) .... 5.12 ins. approx. (130 mm)
Maximum clocked speed, according to rear axle ratio, up to 161 mph (260 km/h)
Engine oil consumption .... 147 m. p. US pt./177 Imp. pt. (0.2 l/100 km)
Fuel consumption, acc. to the manner of driving
    14–23 m. p. Imp. gal./12–20 m. p. US gal. (12–19 ltrs./100 km)
Standard fuel consumption .... 30 m. p. Imp. gal./25 m. p. US gal. (9.5 ltrs./100 km)
Capacity of fuel tank .... approx. 28 Imp. gals./34 US gals. (ca. 130 ltrs.)
Chassis with superstructure dry, without spare wheel and tools ..... 2556 lbs. (1160 kg)
Curb weight of car (empty weight to DIN 70020) .... 2849 lbs. (1295 kg)
Permissible total weight .... approx. 3333 lbs. (1515 kg)
Payload .... 484 lbs. (220 kg)
Permissible axle load, front .... 1463 lbs. (665 kg)
Permissible axle load, rear .... 1870 lbs. (850 kg)

Subject to Modifications

MERCEDES-BENZ TYPE 300SL ROADSTER

OWNER'S MANUAL

Edition B

DAIMLER - BENZ AKTIENGESELLSCHAFT

STUTTGART - UNTERTÜRKHEIM

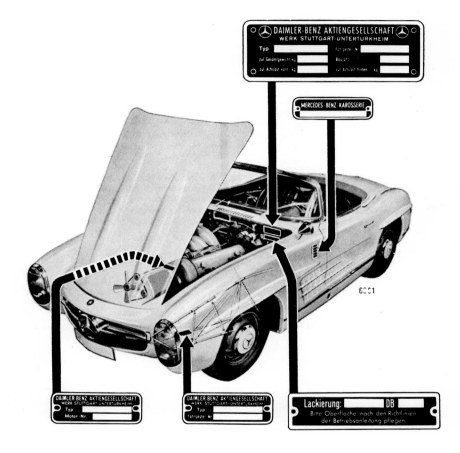

Make a note of the chassis and engine numbers of your car including the complete model designation which you will find over them.

Should you require any spare parts — and this also applies to the ignition key and key to the door lock (which also fits the cover of the tank) or luggage compartment key (which also fits the glove box) — we will only be able to deal with your order satisfactorily and quickly if you indicate the chassis number and the engine number together with the complete model designation on your order.

A few general hints

to be read before you drive your new car for the first time.

Safety first!

Keep this in mind whenever you drive. Make sure that all the parts of your car are in a good condition, in particular, the brakes, the clutch, the steering, the tires and the entire lighting system.

The Mercedes-Benz Type 300 SL ROADSTER is a vehicle with very high acceleration and top speeds. On account of its outstanding roadholding ability and springing, it is only too easy for you not to realize how fast you are really travelling. All the more reason to firmly resist every temptation to be careless.

Adapt your driving speed to the traffic and to the condition of the roads over which you travel and the ease with which they can be surveyed. Wet, snowy or icy roads are treacherous. The braking distance increases progressively with the speed. The relevant facts and figures are snow in a diagram in the section "Driving hints" on p. 19. **You should, therefore, start to decelerate and brake earlier than you are otherwise inclined to do.**

Watch your consumption figures

Fast sporty driving inevitably results in higher consumption values than normal travelling speeds. Nevertheless, if you drive smoothly, you can attain favourable consumption figures with your Type 300 SL ROADSTER. You can see from the diagram below how the fuel consumption depends on the driving speed. The figures refer to the rear axle ratio of 3.64 : 1.

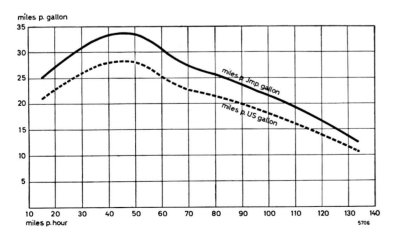

Maintenance is important.

The best lubricants are just good enough for your car. See to it that only those brands are used which correspond to the season and to our viscosity prescriptions.

Dirt in the oil damages the bearings and the working surface of the cylinders. Make sure that the oil filter is regularly cleaned. Change the engine lube oil at the prescribed intervals, if at all possible, immediately after a longer drive, as long as the oil is still hot and thin and can flush the dirt out.

Keep the air filter thoroughly clean and in a good condition, for dust which is sucked in with the air grinds the bearings and contact surfaces and impairs the proper fit of the valves. If you drive for longer periods over very dusty roads, then it is advisable to clean the air filter more frequently than is prescribed in the operating instructions for normal conditions.

The Type 300 SL ROADSTER has no central lubrication; there are, however, a number of grease nipples at the front and rear axle, at the pedal linkage and at the propeller shaft, into which grease must be pressed at the prescribed mileage intervals. Never forget these maintenance jobs.

Have the fuel filter cleaned or the filter element exchanged, if necessary, and have the distributor and the spark plugs checked as prescribed in the maintenance schedule.

Do not forget to have your battery serviced. A new battery is expensive.

Have the wheels interchanged and balanced as prescribed by our instructions.

See to it that the tires are always inflated to the prescribed pressure. This will reduce wear and tear on the tires while the steering gear and springing will remain good. If the tire pressure is too low, there is a danger of the tires heating up too much at very high speeds, and the rubber layer may even come off.

If you follow these hints,

the type 300 SL ROADSTER will never disappoint you and you will come to know it as a very fast, comfortable and sporty touring car.

Operating instructions

Doors
Opening from the outside.
Unlock; the door key also fits the lock of the fuel tank cover.
Depress the projection at the end of the handle with your thumb, whereupon the handle will protrude out of the recess so that you can grasp it. Pull it outwards as far as it will go whereupon the locking mechanism will be released. Open the door.
The passenger door can only be opened from the outside if the interior locking mechanism has been released (see below).
The door can be opened **from the inside** by actuating the inside door handle. There is a tipping lever next to the handle at the passenger's door. If it is turned back, the door is locked and cannot be opened from the

outside.

Driver's seat

1. Foot dimmer switch: push down to switch from "dim" to "bright" and vice-versa. The blue warning lamp at the lower part of the combi-instrument (see p. 10) lights up when the bright light is switched on.

2. Clutch pedal.

3. Brake pedal.

4. Accelerator pedal.

5. Hand brake lever.

6. Gear shift lever; 4 forward speeds, fully-synchronized, 1 reverse gear (see p. 18).

7. Tommy handle to actuate the supplementary ventilation (see p. 11).

8. Contact ring for horn and blinkers: push down to actuate the horn. Turn to the right or left to switch on the corresponding blinkers. The red warning lamp in the combi-instrument remains lighted as long as the blinkers are switched on. The contact ring only functions when the ignition is switched on.

9. Control knob for the windshield washing system and wipers. Pushing down to a stop switches on the windshield wipers. Pushing down beyond this stop actuates the windshield washing system. If you push back to the stop, the windshield wipers which now operate alone will dry the windshield. See page 30 for agents to fill into the windshield washing system.

10. Tommy handle for engine hood lock. See p. 10 for opening and closing of the engine hood.

11. Control lever for the overtaking signal light. This is combined with a horn. If it is pushed back beyond a stop, the horn is actuated in addition to the overtaking signal light.

12. Ventilation and heating levers for the left side of the car (see p. 11).

13. Ventilation and heating levers for the right side of the car (see p. 11).

14. Electric clock: this is set by depressing and turning the knob at the clock.

15. Lockable glove compartment; when the lid is opened, it is illuminated by an interior light.

16. Electric cigarette lighter: press the button for a few seconds until the heating coil glows red.

17. Ash tray. To empty it, pull out the ash tray; the lower part can be removed by pressing on the sides.

18. Rear view mirror. Fold back the control lever to bring it into anti-glare position.

19. Speedometer with total and trip mileage recorder (see page 9).

20. Combi-instrument (see p. 10).

21. Tachometer.

22. Cushion-mounted sun visor (1 each on the right and left side). The sun visor is only supplied upon special request.

23. Light of interior department; is also used as courtesy light. A screen over the light serves to switch on and over:
Screen closed: light is switched off.
Screen half-opened: courtesy light. When the driver's door is opened, the light is switched on by a door contact switch and remains lighted as long as the driver's door is opened.
Screen completely opened: map light; light burns constantly.
When you get out of the car, you should always set the screen to the "courtesy light" position.

The seats can be adjusted backwards and forwards.
Depress the lever at the seat, shift the seat backwards or forwards, and let the lever go.

The back rests can be pushed forward; moreover, they can be adjusted in an oblique direction.

Take out the cushion, push the back rest forward, pull out the two retaining bolts below at the back of the seat frame and insert into the next bore required (3 positions). Both bolts should be adjusted to the same degree.

If the seats are upholstered in leather, the upholstery is fitted with longitudinal air grooves and small holes (ventilated seats).

Instrument panel

1. Ventilation lever for the left side of the leg space. Lever to the left: ventilation turned off (see p. 11).

2. Temperature control lever for the left side of the car. Lever to the left: heating turned off (see p. 11).

3. Ventilation lever for the left side of the windshield. Lever to the left: ventilation turned off (see p. 11).

4. Pull knob "Start". Pulling out switches on the starting device of the injection pump. The white control lamp in the combi-instrument remains lighted as long as the start button is pulled out.

5. Main light turn button; 4 possible positions:

Neutral position (operating knob vertical):	"Daylight driving"; the following units can be set in operation when the ignition lock (9) is turned to position "1": starter control light, windshield wipers, signalling horns, fuel gauge, auxiliary fuel pump, cigarette lighter, brake lights, stationary defrosting unit, blinkers and the bright light blinking system.
From neutral turned to the right to 1st stop (1):	The following units are switched on: identification plate light, tail light, parking light, instrument panel light, and, after the reverse gear has been engaged, the back-up light. In addition, the consumers for "daylight driving", as listed above, can also be set in operation.
Turned to the right to the 2nd stop (2):	The bright or dimmed light, depending on the position of the dimmer switch, are switched on in addition to the units listed under (1).
Turned from neutral to the left to the stop:	Only the clearance lights – depending on the position of the clearance light change-over switch (6) – are switched on; all the other outside lights are switched off.

The fog lamps are also switched on by the light turn button, which should he turned to position 1 or 2, as the case may be, and then pulled out.

6. Clearance light change-over switch. Depending on whether it is turned to the right or left, the right or left clearance lights are switched on (no central position). The clearance lights are switched on by turning the light turn button (5) to the left.

7. Two-stage push-pull switch for the blowers for stationary defrosting: pulling out switches the blowers on.

> Half pulled out: slow operation
> Pulled completely out: fast operation.

A dark-green control lamp in the combi-instrument (p. 10) remains lighted as long as the blowers are in operation.
The blowers are only installed upon special request.

8. Pull switch for the auxiliary fuel pump: pulling out sets the pump in operation.
The pump automatically begins to function quite independently of this pull switch if the ignition is switched on (ignition key in position 1); however, as soon as there is oil pressure in the engine, it is automatically switched off by an oil pressure switch.
A colored control lamp in the pull button of this switch remains lighted as long as the pump functions, regardless of whether the pump has been set in operation manually or automatically.

It is necessary to switch on the pump if
a) the engine is to he started in a warm condition (see p. 17).
b) you notice that the engine is running unevenly, either because the fuel in the tank is drawing to an end or because steam bubbles are forming in hot weather. The pump then conveys the remaining contents of the fuel tank into the engine or flushes the injection pump.
The pump can safely remain in operation for a longer period of time, but only if the engine is running.

9. Ignition lock and starter button. Turning the key to the right to position 1 switches the electrical system on, turning further to position 2 – whereby the key should be simultaneously pushed slightly forward – switches the starter motor on.
After the engine has fired, immediately release the key which will return to position 1.
Any instruments which are mounted upon special request can be switched on by turning to the left when the ignition is switched off.

10. Two-stage pull switch for the electric windshield wipers.
> Half pulled out: wiper blades move slowly.
> Completely pulled out: wiper blades move quickly.

11. Ventilation lever for the right side of the leg space. Lever to the left: ventilation shut off (see p. 11).

12. Temperature control lever for the right side of the car. Lever to the left: heating turned off (see p. 11).

13. Ventilation lever for the right side of the windshield. Lever to the left: ventilation shut off (see p. 11).

14. Speedometer with total and daily mileage recorder.
The daily trip recorder can be reset to 0 by turning the rotary button on the far right.
The red sector marks the maximum speeds which have to be strictly adhered to when using "touring special" tires (see page 41).

15. Combi-instrument (see p. 10).

16. Tachometer. Do not exceed the red mark.

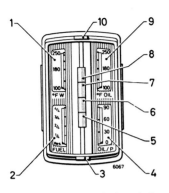

Combi-instrument

1. Cooling water thermometer. The cooling water temperature should not rise beyond the red limit mark.

2. Fuel gage: only starts to function when the ignition is switched on but remains set at the last value recorded after the ignition has been switched off. When the hand points to "Reserve", the auxiliary fuel pump must be switched on. Don't forget to refuel in good time .

3. Blue control light for bright beam; remains lighted as long as the bright beam is switched on.

4. Oil pressure gage: only functions when the engine is running.

5. Dark-green control light for the heater blowers; remains lighted as long as the blowers are in operation.

6. Red Generator light; if the electric system is in order, this lamp lights up when the ignition key has been inserted and goes out as soon as the idling speed has been exceeded (normal driving).

7. White control lamp for the knob „Start"; remains lighted as long as this knob is pulled out.

8. Red control lamp for the turn signals; flashes as long as the turn signals are switched on.

9. Oil temperature indicator.

10. Switch for instrument panel light.
This switch turns the instrument panel light full on. Actually, this light starts burning as soon as the rotary light button is turned to position 1 or 2; as long as this switch is not turned on it will only give a dim light, however. (Bright-dim switch).

Moreover, there are illuminated rings under the various control knobs which enable you to recognise them in the dark even if the instrument panel light is switched off.

Opening the engine hood: Pull the handle for the hood lock (10, p. 6) below the instrument panel; this releases a hook lock, and, after a safety catch on the left side of the car has been disengaged, the engine hood can be opened against the driving direction. When it is fully opened, spring pressure makes the hood automatically snap into a bracket on the left side of the car.

Closing the engine hood: Press the bracket forward in driving direction and close the hood.

Socket for electric instruments (12 volts):
A socket (12 volts) for connecting a reading lamp or some other electric appliance will be found at the dashboard of the engine compartment, on the right side in the driving direction, beside the fuse box.

Luggage compartment lock. This is opened by a half turn of the key. The key can **only be removed again after the lock has been turned back to its initial position.** When the luggage compartment lid is slammed shut, the lock snaps automatically in the same way as the front door of a house. For this reason, make sure that you never leave the key inside the luggage compartment. The key of the luggage compartment lock also fits the lock of the glove box.

Ventilation and Heating

A ventilation system in which fresh air flows through ducts which lead from the cowl along the right and left sides of the engine compartment into the inside of the car ensures that the interior is kept pleasantly ventilated even if the top is closed. Upon special request, a heat exchanger and a two-stage blower can be fitted into each duct, which makes it possible for the ventilation system to function as a heating system too.

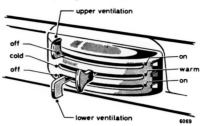

The control of the fresh air supply and of the heating is effected separately for each side of the car through levers which are fitted to the instrument panel. The 3 on the left are for the driver's side, the 3 in the center for the passenger's side.

The driver can, therefore, easily operate all the control levers from his seat.

Control of the fresh air supply (blue mark)
The upper levers control the supply to the windshield, the lower ones the supply to the leg space; to turn the air supply on, the levers should be shifted from left to right.

Lever on the left: air supply cut off.

Lever on the right: air supply full on.

Any intermediate position can be selected as required.

A supplementary ventilation system, in which fresh air enters directly from the outside through an opening in front of the windshield which is covered by an ornamental grille and flows into the passenger compartment under the instrument panel is available for driving in city traffic and during hot weather. This supplementary ventilation is set in operation by the tommy handle (7, p. 6) under the instrument panel. This can be set into two positions: half and fully opened. However, the supplementary ventilation does not pass through the heat exchangers.

The temperature control is effected through the central levers (red mark). When they are moved from the left to the right they allow the engine cooling water to pass through the heat exchanger so that when the

lever is pushed over to the left as far as it will go: the heating is turned off and when it is

pushed over to the right as far as it will go: the heating is turned full on.

Every intermediate position is effective provided that the supply of air has not been cut off by the air control lever.

As a rule, both ventilation and heating should only be turned on in winter if the cooling water has reached a temperature of about 122° F (50° C). In order to heat the passenger compartment, open the ventilation and heating levers completely for a short while; after an interval of about 5–10 seconds, move them back to the desired heating position without waiting for the full heating effect to make itself felt.

In order to defrost the windshield, open the heating levers as well as the upper ventilation levers completely, and, if it is extremely cold, switch on the blowers too until the panes have thawed. Then reset the temperature to the level which you find most comfortable.

Thanks to the separate controls, both ventilation and heating can be adapted to the driver's and passenger's wishes. The following point should, however, be kept in mind: **If you drive behind a vehicle which is producing clouds of dust or emitting thick exhaust fumes, then cut off the supply of fresh air temporarily to prevent exhaust gases from the vehicle in front from penetrating into the passenger compartment.**

Instructions for the roadster top

The top can be opened and closed by one person. Caution! The top compartment cover and the luggage compartment lid should never be opened at the same time.

Opening the top

Caution! The top should not be folded back if the material of the top is wet or damp.

1. There is a removable protective pad (1) fastened with snap fasteners each on the right and left side along the linkage of the top. Before the top is folded back, these pads must be removed. They can then be stowed in the top compartment.

2. Swing the two locking handles (2) at the top towards the inside; this loosens the top.

3. Fold the top (3) back a little way (as shown in figure 2).

4. Take the back of the top out of the rail (4) at the rear edge of the top compartment cover and pull the top fabric towards the front.

5. Open the central lock (5) (move against the driver's seat) of the top compartment cover (6) and open it completely.

6. Fold the top (3) back into the top compartment; make sure that the rear top window is lying completely flat on the foundation of the top compartment.

7. Swing the locking handle (7) in the top compartment inwards; this securely fixes the top.

8. Close the top compartment cover (6).

Closing the top

1. Open the central lock (5) of the top compartment cover (6) (move against the driver's seat).

2. Swing the locking handle (7) in the top compartment towards the outside and erect top.

3. Close the cover of the top compartment (6).

4. Attach the back of the top to the rail (4) at the rear edge of the top compartment cover.

5. Pull the top completely forward and fasten at the windshield frame with the two locking handles (2).

6. Affix protective pads at the snap fasteners (8) of the top linkage.

When the top is closed, the top compartment can accommodate small luggage items. If you wish to take these items out without having to open the top compartment cover, you can just push the backs of the seats forwards.

Care of the top (see p. 31).

Injection engine (brief description)

The "300 SL" is equipped with an injection engine for gasoline. In its construction, it can generally be compared with a carburetor engine with this difference, that the fuel injection system (injection pump, governing units, fuel feed pump, nozzles, accessories) replaces the carburetor.

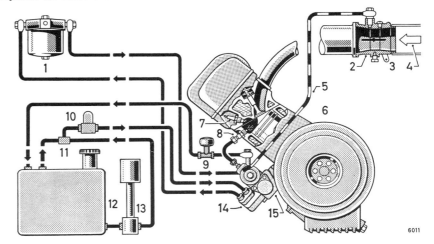

1. Main fuel filter	7. Spark plug	11. Non-return valve
2. Throttle housing	8. Injection nozzle	12. Fuel tank
3. Lever to the throttle linkage	9. Steam container in the return line	13. Auxiliary fuel pump
4. Air inlet		14. Fuel feed pump
5. Vacuum line	10. Fuel pre-filter	15. Injection pump
6. Engine		

The difference as compared with a carburetor engine lies in the mixture formation.

In a carburetor engine, the fuel-air mixture is produced in the carburetor, that is to say, outside the cylinder. In the injection engine of the "300 SL", however, this process only takes place in the cylinders: during the intake stroke, unmixed air is sucked into the cylinders while finely vaporized fuel is simultaneously injected by the injection pump through the nozzles into the combustion chamber of the cylinders. When the compression stroke, which follows the intake stroke, begins, the mixing process in the cylinder must be completed. **The feeding end of the injection pump is, therefore, set to 60° AUDC of the intake stroke of the engine.** During the compression stroke, the fuel-air mixture which has been formed in the cylinder is compressed and then brought to combustion in the normal way with the aid of a normal ignition system (coils, distributor, spark plugs).

In a conventional engine, the fuel and air quantities must be so carefully related to each other under all operational conditions that the optimum operational mixing ratio of fuel to air is always maintained.

This is the function of the governing units of the injection system of the "300 SL" engine: The "throttle housing" (see p. 36) in the intake line and the "diaphragm block" with feelers for air pressure and air temperature.

"Throttle housing" and "diaphragm block" are inter-connected through the vacuum line. These governing units automatically ensure — regardless of variations in the ambient and cooling water temperature or differences of altitude — that the fuel-air mixture is correctly dosed over the entire engine speed ranges from the idling speed upwards.

Difficulties which might arise when starting with a hot engine are prevented thanks to a special auxiliary fuel pump which flushes the injection pump, thus clearing it of vapor bubbles. This auxiliary fuel pump also serves to supply the reserve quantity of fuel when the contents of the tank are drawing to an end.

Fuels, coolants and lubricants

Fuels

Maximum filling quantity of the fuel tank: about 22/26.4 imp./US gals. (100 lit.), of which about 2/2^{1}/$_{3}$ imp./US gals. (9 lit.) are the reserve supply which should suffice for an additional 25–30 miles (40–50 km).

To operate without pinking the engine of the "300 SL Roadster" requires premium fuel. **In order to ensure maximum output without any pinking the engine has been set by the factory using a fuel of 93–95 octane rating according to the Research Method (ROZ).**

The use of fuels, in which the specified resistance to pinking is secured by the addition of alcohol, is not allowed since it results in too meagre a mixture with the present setting of the injection pump. Fuels with an unduly high lead content are also not suitable. Substitute fuels, e. g. gasolines with too high a boiling point may not be used either pure or in a mixture. In particular, you are warned against manufacturing gasoline-benzene or gasoline-benzene-alcohol mixtures yourself.

Coolants

The cooling water container with the filler nipple is located separately from the radiator on the right side under the engine hood.

Filling quantity of the entire cooling system, including water tank and DB-heating: about 4.4/5.3 imp./US gals. (20 lit.); without DB-heating: about 4/4.8 imp./US gals. (18.25 lit.).

Caution! Superpressure cooling system. Only unscrew the cap of the water container when the cooling water temperature is below 194° F (90° C). To do so, turn to notch I and allow the excess pressure to blow off. Then go on turning and remove the cap. To close, turn to the stop (notch II). Only caps marked 100 may be used.

The cooling water only boils at a temperature of 239° F (115° C) – which is marked by a red line on the cooling water thermometer. When driving in mountainous country or in areas with high ambient temperatures, the cooling water temperature may rise to 239° F (115° C).

Use clean water with as low a lime content as possible or well-filtered river water.

The cooling water should be "treated", i. e. a rust inhibitor should be added to it before you drive the car for the first time. If you drive with untreated water, scale, rust and other corrosion by-products will form. Since the latter are poor conductors of heat, they reduce the cooling effect and impair the efficiency of the cooling system. The following agents which can safely be used together with an anti-freeze may be used to treat the cooling water:

Brand	Manufacturers	Total quantity	Concentration
Anticorit MKR	Fuchs, Mineralölwerk, Mannheim	3–6 cu.ins. (50–100 c.c.)	0.6–1.2 cu.in./US gall. 0.7–1.4 cu.in./Imp. gall. (2.5–5 ccm/lit.)
Korrosionsschutz-mittel für Kühler	Voitländer, Kronach	,,	,,
Korrosionsschutzöl	Rheinpreußen GmbH., Homberg/Niederrhein	,,	,,
Kutwell 40	Esso AG., Hamburg	,,	,,
Phosphatol	Houghton Chemie, Hildesheim	,,	,,
Shell Donax C	Deutsche Shell AG., Hamburg	,,	,,
Valvoline Korrosi-onsschutzöl S 2	Valvoline-Öl-Gesellschaft, Hamburg	,,	,,
Veedol Anorust 50	Veedol GmbH., Hamburg	,,	,,

If the engine is hot, only add cold water if the engine is running; on the other hand, you may safely add hot water if the engine is cold.

Caution! If a DB-heating unit is installed, proceed to top up the cooling water as follows:

1. Fully open both heating levers.

2. Fill in the cooling water slowly up to the rim of the filler nipple.

3. Allow the engine to run for about 1 minute at an increased idling speed, leaving the filler nipple open.

4. Return to a lower idling speed and slowly fill up the cooling system completely, as follows:
   a) if the cooling water is cold, up to the mark at the filler nipple,
   b) if the cooling water is warm, up to the rim of the filler nipple.

If the temperature of the cooling water gradually heats up beyond the normal level, then this points to the cooling system being dirty. It should then be degreased and descaled (see p. 47), if possible, in a service workshop. During frosty weather, the instructions for winter operation (see p. 21) should be adhered to.

Lubricants

Lubricants have just as important a contribution to make to the satisfactory running of your car as any structural part. Both must stand up to various strains and stresses and ensure smooth functioning.

When selecting lube oils, look for

quality and viscosity.

The quality must be of a high standard, for performance, service life and operational safety of all makes and models are closely related to the lube oil used. These requirements are met by so-called mixed lube oils, i. e. oils with special chemical additives.

In view of our experiences, we specify the use of the lube oil types tested by us, e. g. for the engine only heavy-duty (HD) engine lube oils.

If, in exceptional circumstances, no HD-oil is available for refilling, you can drive with other engine lube oils for a short while. However, when you fill in HD-oil again, you must adhere to special change-over instructions. In that case, you would do well to get some advice from one of our service stations.

The engine has dry sump lubrication. The engine lube oil is not filled into the engine direct but into a separate oil container which is located on the left beside the engine under the engine hood. The oil dipstick with the upper and the lower oil level mark is in the cap of the oil container. From the oil container, the oil is fed by a pressure pump through the oil filter to the lubricating points. The oil collects at the bottom of the oil pan of the engine; from there it is constantly drawn off by a further pump and conducted back into the oil container through an oil cooler located on the right beside the radiator. When the engine is running, the engine lube oil constantly travels along the following circuit: oil container – pressure pump – oil filter – engine lubricating points – oil pan – suction pump – oil cooler – oil container.

When the engine is not running, this circuit is interrupted. It is, therefore, necessary to **proceed as follows when checking the oil level:**

Allow the engine to run at a higher idling speed for about ^{1}/$_{2}$ minute, then stop the engine and measure the oil level which must come up to the lower mark of the oil dipstick at least.

During cold weather it is advisable to cover the oil cooler.

The viscosity must correspond to the seasonal ambient temperature. We therefore advise you to always adhere to the viscosity groups of the Society of Automotive Engineers (SAE).

	Lubricating point	Lubricant *	Filling quantity in imp./US pints (ltr.)	Viscosity		
				Min. ambient temperature [1] °C (°F)	SAE classification	
Engine	Oil filling (container, engine, filter, lines)	HD engine oil	total max. of 19⅓ / 23¼ (11); min. 14/17 (8) for sporty driving: max. 26⅓/ 31⅔ (15); min. 19⅓/ 23¼ (11)	above + 86° F (+ 30° C)	30	
				above + 50° F) (+ 10° C)	20 W/20 or 10 W–20	
				below + 50° F) (+ 10° C)	10 W or 10 W–20	
				below — 13° F) (— 25° C)	5 W or 5 W–20	
	Distributor: oiler cams	HD engine oil Bosch grease Ft 1 v 4		[1] The temperature will, of course, have to prevail at least several days or more.		
	Transmission	Automatic transmission fluid	2,45/2,95 (1,4)	all the year round	—	
	Drive axle	As per the list at the end of this booklet	3,95/4³/4 (2,25)	all the year round	SAE 90	
	Steering gear housing (DB-steering system)	Hypoid transmission oil	0,5/0,6 (0,3)	all the year round	SAE 90	
	Water pump	Hypoid transmission oil	—	all the year round	SAE 90	
	Front wheel hubs	Bearing grease	2,8 ozs. (80 g) [1] each 4¼ ozs. (120 g) [2] each	all the year round	—	
	Lubricators	Chassis grease	—	all the year round	—	
	Turn signal switch	Kollag grease M 1/2	0,035 oz. (1 g)	all the year round	—	
	Battery terminals	Bosch grease Ft 40 v 1	—	all the year round	—	
	Auxiliary fuel pump	lithium-saponified grease, e. g. Retinax A	—	all the year round	—	

* At the end of this booklet, you will find a list of commercial products which may be safely used as they have been tested by us from among the great number of products on the market.
In case this list is no longer available, please contact one of our Service Stations which will furnish expert advice on all problems concerning lubricants.

[1] Normal hub with wheel pin   [2] Hub with Rudge serration

Starting and Stopping

Check the following points at regular intervals and before every longer drive:
1. the fuel level;
2. water level in the water tank; if the cooling water is cold, it should reach the mark in the filler nipple;
3. the oil level in the oil container; it is important to check the oil level immediately after the engine has been stopped. If the engine has not been in operation for a longer period of time, allow it to run at a higher idling speed for about 1 minute. Before measuring, wipe the oil dipstick. The oil level should reach up to the upper mark of the dipstick; do not measure when the car is parked on sloping ground.
4. the tire pressure; see p. 41 for exact details about the tire pressure;
5. the effectiveness of the brakes; a certain degree of resistance must make itself felt at the brake pedal, which it should not be possible to push down completely; if this is not the case, see hints for emergency repairs, page 53;
6. the bright and dim beam of the headlights, the parking, blinker, tail and brake lights.

Starting

Be careful when starting and allowing the engine to run in the garage; always keep the garage door open and make sure that the exhaust gases can draw off. The latter contain the inodorous and invisible, but **highly poisonous** carbon monoxide gas.
Move gearshift lever into idling (centre) position.
Turn the ignition key to the right to position "1".
What is to be done next depends on the ambient temperature.

a) Starting the **cold** engine at normal ambient temperatures (from about 86° F [30° C] down to about 32° F [0° C]; for temperatures below 32° F (0° C), see winter operation, p. 22.
Pull the knob "Start" out with the left hand – the white control lamp in the combi-instrument lights up – and turn the ignition key to the right to position 2 with the right hand, which sets the starter motor in operation.
At the same time, disengage the clutch, but **do not depress the accelerator pedal.**
Release the ignition key when the engine is firing regularly, but not earlier; it will then automatically return to position 1; on the other hand, you should not keep it in position 2 for longer than 20 seconds at a time, since the battery will be subjected to too great a strain otherwise.
As soon as the engine has started running, let go the knob "Start" which will automatically return to initial position; the white control light will go out.
As soon as the engine is running regularly, engage the clutch; in cold weather, be careful to do so slowly to prevent the cold oil in the transmission from braking the engine.

b) Starting **in hot weather**, in particular, in tropical areas, after prolonged city drives on hot days or at a high altitude:
As soon as the ignition key is turned to position "1", the auxiliary fuel pump (which serves to flush the injection pump) automatically starts to function. A red control lamp in the pull switch at the instrument panel (8, page 8) will remain lighted as long as the pump is in operation.
In hot weather allow the pump to run for a few seconds and then turn to the right to position "2", which sets the starter motor in operation. Push down the accelerator pedal slightly, but do not pull the knob "Start".
When the engine has fired, release the ignition key which will automatically return to position "1".
As soon as there is oil pressure in the engine, the auxiliary pump automatically stops functioning. Setting the auxiliary fuel pump in operation with the pull switch (8, page 8) also helps if, for instance, the engine begins to run unevenly during a city drive in hot weather or in tropical regions. The pump may be in operation for a longer period of time provided that the engine is running; it is, however, in these circumstances possible to drive until the fuel tank is empty without your getting any warning.

Warming up the engine

It is not advisable to let the engine idle until the normal operating temperature (cooling water 158°–203° F (70°–95° C) has been reached, since this would require a very long time in view of the slight degree of heat produced by the engine when idling. When the ambient temperature is above 32° F (0° C) we advise you to drive off at a moderate speed after the engine has fired. The engine will thus reach the operating temperature in 4–5 minutes in the most advantageous way. At lower temperatures, you should allow the engine to idle for 1 minute at the most before driving off, in order to ensure that the engine is lubricated even if the oil is completely cold. Do not allow the engine to idle at an excessive speed, however.

Driving off

Press the clutch pedal down.

Move the gearshift lever into 1st gear. **Important: drive off in 1st gear only.**

Disengage the hand brake.

Slowly release the clutch pedal and simultaneously slowly depress the accelerator pedal with the right foot; that is to say, make sure that the clutch slips as little as possible when starting and only drive off at a low engine speed.

After you have driven off, accelerate gradually, not abruptly; shift to the 2nd, 3rd and 4th gear. Don't press the gas pedal down completely until the clutch is fully engaged.

Stopping the car

Turn the ignition key to the left **when the engine is idling.** Under no circumstances should you try stop the engine if it is running at a speed higher than that of the idling range.

The first 900 miles (1500 km)

The engine is not sealed. The way the engine is handled and the strains to which it is subjected during the first 900 miles (1500 km) decisively affect the service life and economy of operation of the entire vehicle. The more carefully you treat the engine at first, the more satisfied will you be with its performance later. The driving speed is not so important in this connection as the engine speed and the load to which it is subjected. During the first 900 miles (1500 km), you should not exceed an engine speed of 4000 r. p. m. and the engine should not be subjected to full load for a longer period of time. Above all, avoid "worrying" your engine at lower engine speeds during this "breaking in" period and shift back to a lower gear in good time.

The "first" lubricating and maintenance jobs listed on p. 25 vitally influence the service life of the car, the quietness with which the engine will run later and the operational safety of the vehicle.

Sheets 1, 2 and 3 of your service book are specially provided for the "braking in" period. Please remember to call on your service station in good time.

Gear shifting

A handy central gearshift lever on a ball joint is located on the right beside the driver's seat and makes for quick shifting of the transmission – 4 forward gears, 1 reverse gear.

The diagram shows the various gear positions.

The 4 forward gears of the transmission are fully synchronized, i. e. a special device in the transmission automatically ensures through couplings that the corresponding gears inter-mesh smoothly. This makes it unnecessary to engage the clutch twice and to step on the gas in between. To shift upwards or downwards, proceed as follows:

Decelerate, press down the clutch pedal completely, **briskly shift the gearshift lever from its present gear position to the next one, engage the clutch smoothly accelerate simultaneously.**

All gearshifting operations can be effected easily and effortlessly. You need only remember to:

1. Decelerate and disengage the clutch completely before every gearshifting operation.

2. Always engage the next lower or higher gear, never omit a gear.

3. To engage the reverse gear, the car must first be brough to a standstill. Then disengage the clutch and shift the gearshift lever in central position completely over to the left, whereby the resistance of a safety notch has to be overcome; afterwards slowly move the gearshift lever forward.

The safety notch along the gearshift travel prevents you from unintentionally engaging the reverse gear when shifting from the 2nd to the 1st gear.

Driving hints

The Type 300 SL is a very fast car with powerful acceleration. Its outstanding road-holding ability and springing only too easily prevent you from realizing how fast you are actually driving. It is, therefore, all the more important for you to **slow down and brake earlier than you tend to do normally.**

Every increase of speed automatically involves an even greater increase in the braking distance.

The diagram opposite illustrates the relation between speed and braking distance under different road conditions and when a reaction time of 1 second has been taken into account. You can see from it that with the best brakes and optimum friction values betwen road and tires a speed of 100 m. p. h. (160 km/h) involves a braking distance of over 590 feet (180 m), after allowance has been made for a reaction time of 1 second.

When travelling at high speeds, the air resistance alone brakes the car to a considerable extent. You should therefore normally decelerate

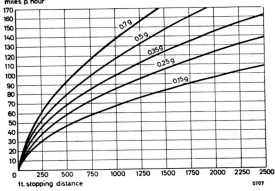

Braking distances incl. 1 sec. of reaktion time

0.7 g   dry concrete (express highways)
0.5 g   dry asphalt and macadam
0.35 g   wet asphalt and macadam
         also max. distance officially allowed for vehicles
         travelling at a speed of over 62 m. p. h. (100 km/h)
0.25 g   max. distancee officially allowed according to the
         present regulations (not over 62 m. p. h. –100 km/h)
0.15 g   icy surfaces, also max. distance allowed for the
         hand brake

in good time and only then apply the foot brake. Always depress the brake pedal smoothly, and not abruptly, however. Jerky and sudden braking should be avoided if at all possible, as the car might start skidding on a slippery road or a vehicle coming up behind might collide with it; moreover, it damages the tires to a considerable extent. You should only brake quickly and energetically in a real emergency.

When driving, only use the foot brake, even on steep inclines. If necessary, the hand brake can also be used as a driving brake, but normally it should only serve to arrest the car. If you brake the car with the hand brake only when travelling at high speed, this does not actually damage the brake or other parts of the car. But if you do so, the rear wheels may lock, especially on a slippery road, and this again may be responsible for the car starting to skid.

When driving in a quick, sporty fashion in dry weather – which subjects the brakes to very severe strains – it is possible to remove the two small round rubber covers from each anchor plate before setting off on your drive; this provides additional and very effective interior brake ventilation. When driving in a conventional way and in rainy weather, this ventilation is not necessary. The rubber covers then prevent dirt and humidity from penetrating into the brake.

Constantly check your speed when driving. The speedometer is located so advantageously that you can read it without taking your eyes off the road ahead. This is particularly important when you are going to turn off a straight road after driving at high speed, e. g. when turning into a lane off an express highway, for at such moments one nearly always under-estimates one's actual speed.

Exercise special care when overtaking, particularly if you do so on an express highway. You should always be prepared for sudden surprises, for the driver whom you wish to overtake may overlook the possibility of your being closely behind him and suddenly swerve off to overtake the car in front of him. Thanks to our cars excellent brakes, you may be able to cut down on your speed by up to 30 m. p. h. (50 km/h) if need be.

When driving in a sporty fashion, we advise you to be guided by the tachometer whenever you wish to shift from one gear to another. For quick acceleration in the 1st, 2nd and 3rd gear, a speed of 5.800 r. p. m. need not be exceeded, whereas in exceptional cases a speed of 6.400 r. p. m. is permissible in the 4th gear.

The first-rate tuning of the gears allows the sporty driver to take full advantage of the qualities of chassis and engine. On the other hand, the 6-cylinder engine is so flexible and powerful over an extraordinarily wide speed range that it is possible to rove along the entire driving range in the 4th gear alone and to achieve very good acceleration while doing so. If you shift up to the 4th gear via the 2nd and 3rd ones after starting, you can therefore cope with normal city traffic and inter-urban trips without continual gear shifting.

When driving normally, frequent gear shifting is not required, not even in city traffic. Low engine speeds down to about 700 r. p. m. do not harm the engine in any way, even if the accelerator pedal is pressed completely down.

It is only wise to shift back to the 3rd or 2nd gear if you wish to accelerate very quickly indeed in dense city traffic or when overtaking a truck which is travelling at high speed. The Type 300 SL masters very high grades in 4th gear alone (see page 55). Fast drivers are, however, advised to shift back to 3rd gear in very mountainous country since it is then possible to attain better acceleration values.

When hill-climbing, in particular when driving down long and steep slopes, it is a good idea to shift back to a lower gear. When you drive downhill, allow the engine to act as a brake inasmuch as you decelerate but do not disengage the clutch; on no account should you switch off the ignition, for in that case the fuel which is sucked in by the engine, but not consumed, might wash the oil film off the cylinder walls.

If you have to park your car on a slope, engage the first or the reverse gear to be on the safe side, and set the steering wheel at such an angle that the car can only roll

against the ascending side and not into the precipice if the brake is unintentionally released. In winter, the car should be secured by placing blocks in front of the wheels.

An oil cooler is installed in Type 300 SL. Under extreme conditions, i. e. fast driving and high ambient temperatures, maximum oil temperatures of 230°–239° F (110°–115° C) can still be tolerated. Obviously, when one does not drive in such a sporty fashion, e. g. in city traffic, and when the weather is cool, much lower oil temperatures are reached. It is, therefore, advisable to cover the oil cooler completely when the weather is cold.

When the engine has cooled down completely, the oil pressure gauge will only indicate a rise in the oil pressure after some time has passed, and then only slowly, as the increased pressure only slowly makes itself felt in the narrow connection line to the oil pressure gauge.

If the **oil pressure** suddenly falls while the engine speed remains constant, or if it one day fails to reach its usual level, then you should stop and proceed according to the section "Hints for Emergency Repairs" (page 52).

The **cooling water temperature** normally amounts to 158°–203° F (70°–95° C). After starting, this temperature is reached in about 4–5 minutes if you drive at a moderate speed. In extremely hot weather and if the car is heavily loaded, the cooling water temperature may safely reach the red mark at the cooling water thermometer when driving over prolonged grades. In that case, it can, if need be, be reduced by shifting to a lower gear. If the car is brought to a standstill after prolonged uphill driving, the engine should still be allowed to idle for a short while, since if it is immediately put out of operation, the cooling water may boil.

If the cooling water temperature rises above the red mark, there is some defect in the cooling system; you should then stop driving and proceed according to the section "Hints for Emergency Repairs" (page 52).

Winter driving

In the winter, certain measures have to be taken to protect the engine and radiator and to ensure that the car will start at any time. It is also advisable to drive more carefully than usual.

Safety precautions

A winter oil in accordance with the instructions on page 16 should be used as an engine lube oil. In addition, the battery must be well charged.

The built-in thermostat automatically maintains the cooling water in the engine at the correct temperature, for it only releases the water circuit from the engine via the radiator when the water has reached a temperature of about 167° F (75° C); below this temperature the radiator is kept out of operation. This means that the water which is in the radiator block can freeze in the winter even whilst the car is being driven.

In frosty weather, you should, therefore, use an antifreeze.

A commercial branded antifreeze only should be used. The instructions of the makers will tell you which amounts to add to the cooling water at different ambient temperatures.

The table overleaf shows how the mixing ratio of water and Glysantin or Genantin as the case may be varies depending on the temperature.

When DB-heating is installed, the capacity of the entire cooling system, filled up to the mark on the filler nipple of the radiator, amounts to about 4.4/5.3 imp./US gals. (20 ltrs.).

Antifreeze protection down to about		Genantin/Glysantin imp. / U.S. ltrs.			Water imp. / U.S. ltrs.		
°F	°C	pints			pints		
14	—10	7	8.45	4	28	33.8	16
5	—15	9.65	11.62	5.5	25.4	30.63	14.5
— 4	—20	11.85	14.25	6.75	23.25	28	13.25
—13	—25	14	17	8	21	25.3	12
—22	—30	15.3	18.5	8.75	19.75	23.75	11.25
—40	—40	18	21.65	10.25	17.1	20.6	9.75

Before filling in an antifreeze, the cooling system should be thoroughly flushed, in particular, if the cooling water had been treated with a special agent.

Caution! A rust inhibitor which contains acids or a radiator cleaning agent may not be used together with an antifreeze; this does not apply to anti-corrosion oil, however.

When the engine is cold, fill in coolant up to the mark only (about 2 ins. (5 cm) below the edge of the filler nipple); otherwise when it expands through heat about 1¾–2 imp. US pints (1 ltr.) of coolant will be pressed out through the relief pressure valve and consequently lost.

Both radiator and engine must be flushed well after an antifreeze has been used. In the spring, filter the coolant which has been drained off through a clean cloth and store it in a clean well-closed container until the next winter. Before filling it in again, the mixture should be tested with a Glysantin/Genantin areometer to find out whether the antifreeze is still effective and the cooling water must be treated with anti-corrosion oil.

Should it prove impossible to obtain an antifreeze, then the radiator must be covered up, even if you are driving; the air inlet to the heating and ventilation system should not be obstructed, however.

In that case, if the car cannot be parked in a warm garage, the coolant must be drained whilst the engine is still warm, and, if possible, this should be done in a sheltered spot. To do so, open the drain cocks on the left side of the radiator, below, and on the left side of the engine, below, and disconnect the heating hose at each heater in order to ensure that the heater is completely drained. At the same time, remove the radiator cap. **Caution! Superpressure cooling system; to open, see p. 14.** Watch the coolant run out, and if the drain cocks are clogged or frozen up, clear the opening with a piece of wire. Afterwards, allow the engine to run again for a short while to ensure that no coolant is left in the entire cooling system. Leave the drain cocks open until you fill in coolant again, and affix a notice "water drained off" at the radiator.

Do not forget to connect the hoses to the heaters and to close the drain cocks before you fill in the coolant again.

How to make the engine start in cold weather
When the temperature is below 32° F (0° C), pull the knob "Start" with the left hand whilst you turn the ignition key to the right to position 2 with the right hand, disengage the clutch and "play" with the accelerator pedal slightly (0,08–0,12"/2–3 mm). Then proceed as described on p. 17.

When the weather is very cold indeed, it is advisable

1. to dismount the battery and to store it in a heated room or to warm it to the corresponding temperature, for a battery which has cooled down produces only a fraction of the starting power of a battery which has been kept at normal temperature. Or
2. drain the coolant from the engine, radiator and water tank. Before starting, heat it to a temperature of about 203° F (95° C) and fill into the cooling system. Even boiling coolant can be safely filled into the engine if the latter has cooled down. This procedure may be somewhat complicated but it spares the starter motor, the engine and battery to a considerable extent.

Driving in winter
Wet, snowy or icy roads are treacherous. You should, therefore, adapt your speed to the condition of the road and always drive with care. On clear winter days, you will find patches of slippery ice between sunny and shady spots, e. g. at underpasses, on the outskirts of villages or at the edge of a wood. When the weather is slightly frosty, ice may well form on roadways over bridges while the roads are still free of ice as a result of the ground warmth. Exercise special care near such danger spots.

The windshield can be safely and quickly defrosted if the two upper ventilation levers and the two heating levers are pushed completely to the right (see page 11).

You can prevent the windshield from freezing up when the car is stationary if you insert a piece of canvas or a newspaper of the size of the windshield under the windshield wipers.

If the lid of the luggage compartment is stuck because it is frozen, then knock all round the edge of the lid with your fist; this loosens the ice between the edge of the lid and the rubber moulding and releases the lid. Use the same method if one of the car doors is stuck through frost.

In a severe snowstorm, or if cars which are driving in front of you whirl up a great deal of snow, the insect screens in the ventilation ducts may get clogged up so that the heating of the vehicle no longer functions satisfactorily. The only remedy is to thoroughly clean the insect screens or to take them out completely in winter. In that case, the cavity in the ventilation ducts must be sealed well with adhesive or insulating tape or with a piece of metal of the correct size. Don't mislay the screens, however, and don't forget to put them back in the spring.

According to § 33 of the German Highway Code the following regulations must be followed in Germany in foggy weather or when it is snowing:

Section 4: Low-beam headlights must be switched on in the daytime if there is dense fog or snow is falling.

Section 5: Fog headlights may only be switched in conjunction with the low-beam headlights in foggy weather or when snow is falling.

Abroad, it is possible to use different methods of lighting the way. However, we urgently advise you to adhere to the traffic regulations of the country in which you are driving.

If the car is parked in the open air in frosty weather, do not engage the hand brake or one of the gears as they might freeze and get stuck. Secure the car by placing blocks in front of the wheels.

In areas where it often snows, it is advisable to have all 4 wheels fitted with **tires with a special tread for snowy ground.** Snow chains of the usual design cannot be used for the 300 SL; special snow chains which have been designed for the 300 SL and which should only be fitted to the rear wheels are available, however. Our service stations will be pleased to give you detailed information concerning these special snow chains and the tires with special treads.

An important note for all those who are going abroad

A widespread Mercedes-Benz service organization will gladly help you when you go abroad. Our "List of authorized Mercedes-Benz agencies in export countries" will tell you all you need to know in this connection. Upon request, our Service Department in Stuttgart-Untertürkheim will supply you with this list.

Nevertheless, in very remote areas, you may occasionally be compelled to consult workshops which do not belong to our organization. To meet this possibility, we have assembled a "Travelling assortment of the most indispensable spare parts (such as seals, etc.)" and worked out suggestions about which tools can usefully be added to the set which forms part of the car's standart equipment. It is a good idea to get these extra items before you go abroad.

Moreover, we advise you to take spare tires and tire valves along with you and in certain circumstances also an agent to treat the cooling water and distilled water for the battery. A first aid kit should also form part of your travelling equipment.

It is important to make sure that no impurities get into the engine when **fuel, lubricants or coolant** is being filled in.

See to it that only fuel with the specified **minimum octane rating** (see p. 14) is filled in.

The engine lube oil must also meet the requirements listed on page 15. At all events, one of the HD-oils mentioned in the enclosed list, – most of which are available all over the world, – must be used; make sure that the viscosity is correct.

Maintenance

We urgently advise you to entrust all maintenance and service work to the trained staff of our service stations. In particular, it is in your own interest to have all the jobs listed in your service book effected at the specified intervals. This not only ensures that the general condition of your car is satisfactory but also makes it possible to eliminate any small defects before they cause serious damage. In this connection, we should like to remind you that **the warranty shall not apply if all the service jobs which should have been carried out until the moment when the claim is presented have not been executed in time in one of our authorized service stations.**

Our workshop manual for Type 300 SL, which can be ordered from our Service Department, contains detailed instructions for all service and maintenance work.

Type 300 SL has **grease nipple lubrication.**

Grease should be applied to the nipples at the upper wishbone bearing pins (right and left) and at the steering universal joint **from above** and to the other nipples **from below;** checking the oil level and changing the oil in the transmission and rear axle housing and draining the oil from the oil container and engine are also operations which should be effected **from below** in a pit, on a lifting platform or some other similar equipment. Grease can then be applied to the nipples as usual, although it may be necessary in some cases to fit an extension piece to the normal grease gun. Only the 2 nipples at the angular drive of the odometer shaft cannot be serviced until the transmission casing has been removed; the grease need only be renewed every 60.000 miles (96.000 km), however.

If a high-pressure grease gun is used, its greasing pressure should not exceed 5690 p. s. i. (400 kg/cm²); if need be, the pressure should be correspondingly limited by a safety device at the gun.

It is advisable to point this out to the mechanic who carries out this work.

The oil in the engine and oil container as well as in the transmission and rear axle housing should always be changed at the end of a drive whilst the oil is still hot and can flush all the impurities out.

If the fuel tank is completely empty, the strainer at the bottom of the tank should be unscrewed and cleaned before any freh fuel is filled in.

See pages 29 to 31 for regular care and protective treatment of the paintwork and of the chromium parts.

„**First**" **lubrication and maintenance jobs, which need only be carried out once**

After the first 30–60 miles (50–100 km):
Check all wheel nuts to see if they are tight, if nec., tighten.
After the first 300 miles (500 km):
1. Clean the oil filter element.
2. Drain the oil in the oil container and engine housing (while the oil is still **hot**) and refill with fresh oil as specified in the oil table.
3. Change the oil in the transmission (while the oil is still **hot**). Before draining the oil, check the oil level (up to the rim of the opening) and if any oil has been lost, check for leaks.
4. Check the oil level in the oiler at the distributor; if nec. fill up.
5. Check the cylinder head bolts for tightness with a torque wrench; if nec. tighten.
6. Check the valve clearance; if nec. correct.
7. Check the tension of the fan belt; if nec. tighten.
8. Clean the element of the fuel pre-filter.
9. Check the main fuel filter.
10. Check the foot and hand brakes to see if they function satisfactory. If nec. adjust the hand brake.
11. Check the wheel nuts; if nec. tighten.
12. Check the tire pressure; if nec. correct.

After the first 1250 miles (2000 km):
1. Clean the oil filter element.
2. Drain the oil in the oil container and in the engine housing (while the oil is still **hot**) and refill with fresh oil as specified in the oil table.
3. Check the tension of the fan belt; if nec. tighten.
4. Check the gap of the breaker contacts of the distributor; if nec. correct. Do not re-file the contacts.
   On no account should oil be applied to the cams before a distance of 15,000 miles (24,000 km) has been covered, as impurities may then collect on the breaker contacts.
5. Check all the nuts of the intake and exhaust pipes to see if they are tight.
6. Tighten the fastening screws of the shock absorbers.
7. Check the lines, connecting hoses and joints for engine lube oil, coolant, fuel, brake fluid, and vacuum, to see if they leak or have any worn spots or dents.
8. Check the wheel nuts; if nec. tighten.
9. Check the tire pressure; if nec. correct.
10. Check the toe-in and camber. – This can only be done in a service workshop.
11. Oil the hinges of the engine hood, of the doors, of the lid of the luggage compartment and of the top compartment cover.
12. Check and grease the arresting straps of the doors.
13. Powder the rubber sealing strips of the doors with talc.
14. Check the door locks; if nec. tighten the setting rings at the strikers.
15. Check the foot and hand brakes to see if they function satisfactorily; if nec. bleed – do not forget the Ate-T-50/12 booster brake when you do so – and readjust the hand brake.

After the first 2500 miles (4000 km):
1. All the lubrication and maintenance jobs which have to be regularly done every 2500 miles (4000 km) (see ps. 26 and 27).
2. Check the toe-in and camber. – This can only be done in a service workshop.

Regular lubrication and maintenance jobs

After every miles (km)	Page	Part	What has to be done.
)[1]	41	Tires	Check the tire pressure while the tires are **cold**.
	17	Oil container	Wipe the dipstick; check the oil level, if nec. fill up.
2,500 (4,000)	32	Oil filter [2]	Take out and clean the element.
	—	Oil container and engine	Change the oil. [2] Check whether the seal rings on the drain screws can be used again, if need be, renew.
	36	Throttle housing of the intake line	Apply a few drops of oil at the following spots: a) to the spring-loaded pressure pin of the throttle housing lever b) to the partial load valve c) to the bearing points for the cold start gate valve control In addition, after the hose strap has been loosened and the connecting hose removed, apply 1 drop of oil only to the following points inside the throttle housing: a) over the two bores to the cold start gate valve b) to the bearing points of the throttle housing shaft.
	32	Air filter	Dismantle, clean with gasoline and moisten with engine lube oil. Clean more frequently when driving over dusty roads.
	32	Fuel pre-filter	Take out and clean the element.
	36	Exhaust pipe	Check the flange nuts for tight seat.
	32	Fan belt	Check the tension, if nec. adjust.
	27	Front axle [3]	Apply grease to the following 20 lubrication nipples with a grease gun – clean the lubrication heads previously: a) 2 nipples each at the upper left and right wishbone bearing pin b) 2 nipples each at the lower left and right wishbone bearing pin c) 3 nipples each at the left and right steering knuckle d) 1 nipple each at the steering arm, at the intermediary steering arm, at the bearing of the intermediary steering arm, at the steering shock absorber e) 1 nipple each at the outside of the tie rods.
	27	Pedal linkage [3]	
	27	Rear axle [3]	Apply grease to the lubrication nipples with a grease gun; clean the lubrication heads first.
	27	Drive shaft [3]	Front: grease the lubrication nipple in the joint at the key way with a grease gun. Rear: grease the lubrication nipple in the joint with a grease gun.
	—	Joints for pedal linkage and levers, cable lines, and linkages to the hand brake and injection pump	Check and grease.
	—	Lines, connection hoses and connections for engine lube oil, cooling water fuel, brake fluid, and vacuum	Check for leaks, worn spots and dents.
	36	Clutch	Check the "lash" of the pedal, if nec. adjust.
	43	Battery [4]	Check the level and density of the electrolyte.
		Electric consumers	Check whether they function properly.

[1] Occasionally and before every longer drive.
[2] **Every 1,250 miles (2,000 km) when using the car for city drives exclusively or when operating in dusty areas;** remember the viscosity instructions.
[3] **Every 1,250 miles (2,000 km) when driving over very muddy or slushy roads as well as when driving on extremely poor roads.**
[4] At least every 4 weeks.

After every miles (km)	Page	Part	What has to be done.
2,500 (4,000)	39	Wheels	Rebalance [1]; rotate in acc. with diagram on page 40.
	27	Brake fluid container	Check the level of the fluid, if nec. fill up with brake fluid up to $^2/_5''$ (1 cm) below the rim; if a great deal of fluid has been lost, check the brake system for leaks.
	37	Brakes	Check the foot and hand brakes to see if they function properly if nec. adjust the hand brake.
5,000 (8,000)	—	Ventilation ducts, front	Clean the insect screens.
	27	Injection pump	Check the oil level with the dipstick – the oil should reach up to the upper dipstick mark –; if there is too little oil, fill up at the flap oiler only.
	—	Distributor and oil pump drive	Check the gear backlash [1].
	34	Distributor	Check the breaker contacts to see if they are dirty and if the gap is correct; if nec. adjust.
	35	Spark plugs	Clean; check the electrode gap.
	33	Valves	Check the clearance, if nec. correct; check the compression [1].
	27	Transmission	Check the oil level (up to the rim of the filler opening); if any oil has been lost, check for leaks.
	27	Rear axle housing [2]	Check the oil level (up to the rim of the filler opening); if any oil has been lost, check for leaks.
	—	Brakes	Remove the brake drums. Hone the surface of the linings with emery cloth. Remove the dust which has accumulated. Check the brake drums, linings and dust covers of the wheel cylinders.
	—	Wheels [1]	Check the toe-in and camber.
	—	Seats	Tighten the screws for the guide rails of the seats.
	—	Draft excluders of doors	Apply some talcum powder to the rubber parts of the draft excluders.
	27	Door hinges	Apply grease to the lubrication holes; tighten the fastening screws.
	—	Door locks, lock of luggage compartment cover, lock of engine hood, cover of top compartment	Check the fastening screws at the door locks and the strikers, if nec. tighten; if nec. tighten the setting rings at the strikers. Check the plate of the lock of the luggage compartment cover; if nec. adjust. Slightly grease the safety latches of engine hood lock, of the lock of the top compartment cover, and of the lid of the luggage compartment; do not apply any oil to the keyholes, however [3]. Tighten the mounting of the lock at the engine hood.
	—	Hinges of engine hood, of lid of luggage compartment and of cover of top compartment	Grease.
10,000 (16,000)	43	Battery	Clean the terminals, check for tight seat and grease with acid-proof grease.
	35	Spark plugs	Replace by new ones.
	47	Water pump	Check the oil level.
	36	Intake and exhaust pipe	Check all the nuts for tight seat.

Continued on page 28

[1] Can only be effected in a service workshop.
[2] After the "first" 5,000 miles (8,000 km) oil change.
[3] On the other hand, you can apply some flaked graphite to these locks (manufactured by Edelgraphit-Gesellschaft mbH., Godesberg/Rh.)

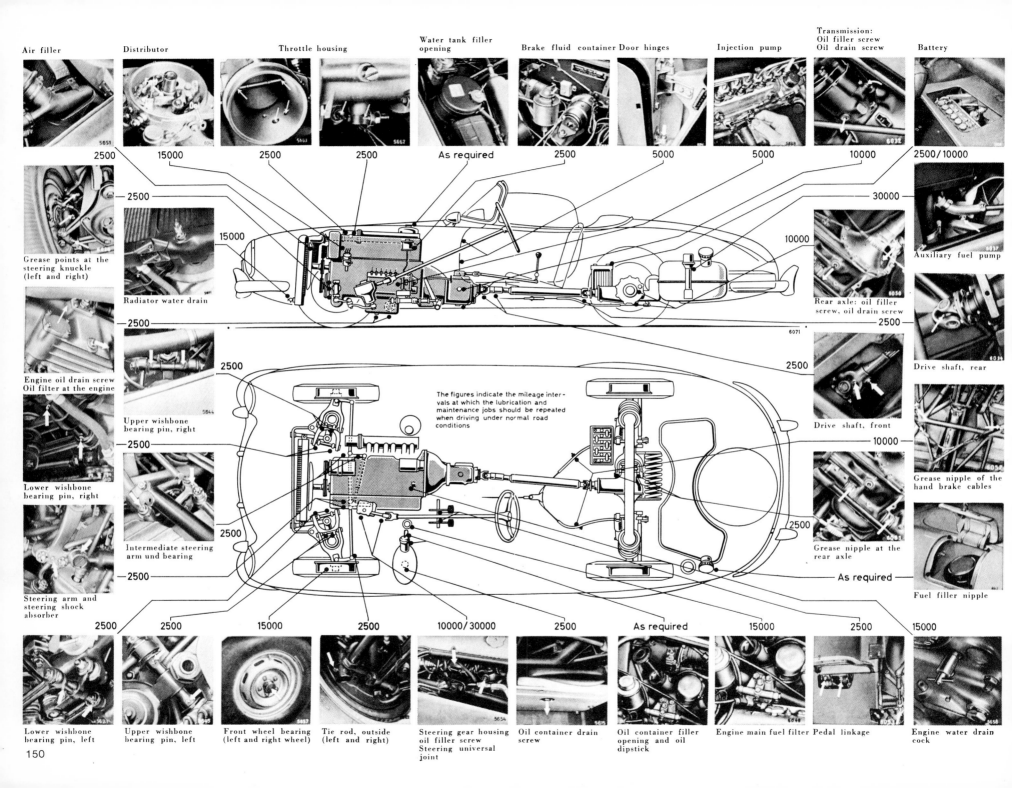

Air filler

Distributor

Throttle housing

Water tank filler opening

Brake fluid container Door hinges

Injection pump

Transmission:
Oil filler screw
Oil drain screw

Battery

2500

15000

2500

2500

As required

2500

5000

5000

10000

2500/10000

2500

15000

2500

Grease points at the steering knuckle (left and right)

Radiator water drain

30000

Auxiliary fuel pump

10000

2500

Rear axle: oil filler screw, oil drain screw

2500

Engine oil drain screw
Oil filter at the engine

Upper wishbone bearing pin, right

2500

Drive shaft, rear

2500

The figures indicate the mileage intervals at which the lubrication and maintenance jobs should be repeated when driving under normal road conditions

Drive shaft, front

10000

Lower wishbone bearing pin, right

2500

Intermediate steering arm und bearing

Grease nipple of the hand brake cables

2500

Steering arm and steering shock absorber

2500

Grease nipple at the rear axle

As required

Fuel filler nipple

2500

2500

15000

2500

10000/30000

2500

As required

15000

2500

15000

Lower wishbone bearing pin, left

Upper wishbone bearing pin, left

Front wheel bearing (left and right wheel)

Tie rod, outside (left and right)

Steering gear housing oil filler screw
Steering universal joint

Oil container drain screw

Oil container filler opening and oil dipstick

Engine main fuel filter

Pedal linkage

Engine water drain cock

150

After every miles (km)	Page	Part	What has to be done.
10,000 (16,000)	—	Shock absorbers	Check for oil leaks, tighten the fastening screws.
	—	Nuts, screws and cotter pins of steering, engine mounting, drive shaft and rear axle housing	Check in a pit or on a lifting platform and if nec. tighten.
	27	Transmission	Change the oil (while it is still **hot**). Before draining the oil, check its level (up to the rim of the filler opening), and if any oil has been lost, check for leaks.
	27	Rear axle housing	Change the oil (while it is still **hot**). Before draining the oil, check its level (up to the rim of the filler opening), and if any oil has been lost, check for leaks.
	27	Steering gear housing[1]	Check the oil level.
	37	Booster brake system (Ate-T-50/12)[1]	Remove the air filter; replace the element by a new one.
	—	Windshield wipers[2]	Grease the ball-and-socket joints of the linkage.
	46	Headlights	Check the adjustment.
	27	Hand brake cables	Apply some grease to the lubrication nipples.
15,000 (24,000)	34	Distributor	Fill up the oiler with engine lube oil right up to the top. Remove the breaker plate, the rotor – after the fastening screw at the side has been loosened – and the dust cover. Slightly grease the cam with Bosch grease Ft 1 V 4. Caution! Do not apply any grease to the contacts. Replace the dust cover, the rotor – screw on the fastening screw at the side – and the distributor cover.
	27	Front wheel bearings	Refill grease.
	33	Main fuel filter (at the engine)	Replace the paper element by a new one.
	47	Cooling system	Flush and fill up with treated water.
30,000 (48,000)	—	Distributor[1]	Check[1] (special checking instructions).
	—	Generator[1]	Dismantle: check whether the commutator is in a good condition and if nec. turn on a lathe; clean the carbon brush holders and replace the carbon brushes by new ones.
	—	Clutch[1]	Check to see whether it functions[1] (special instructions).
	—	Rear axle[1]	Check to see whether it functions (special instructions).
	—	Front axles[1]	Check the wheel bearings (special checking istructions).
	—	Steering spindle[1]	Check the steering for lost motion, if nec. readjust.
	—	Steering universal	Grease the lubrication nipples with a grease gun (pointed prolongation).
	—	Tie rods[1]	Check the joints and seals[1].
	—	Brakes[1]	Check the master brake cylinder and the wheel brake cylinders for leaks. Check the booster brake system for vacuum and leaks.
	—	Hand brake	Check the brake cables.
	—	Wheels	Check for defects on the exterior.
	—	Auxiliary fuel pump	Refill grease (use lithium-saponified grease).
	—	Blinker switch[1]	Grease notched plate and roll.
60,000 (96,000)		Angular drive of the speedometer shaft	Apply grease to the 2 lubrication nipples (prolongation).
		Angular drive of the tachometer shaft	Apply grease to the 2 lubrication nipples (prolongation).

[1] Can only be effected in a service workshop.
[2] Moreover, we advise you to have the wiper blades renewed at intervals of 6 months to a year, depending on the degree of wear to which they have been subjected.

Cleaning and care of the body

Synthetic resin finish: [1]

Do your best keep the paintwork free from scratches or scores, that is to say do not use a whisk, brush hard cloth, coarse absorbent cotton or unsuitable preservatives. Our service stations will gladly give you detailed information about suitable preservatives and about all other questions connected with the finish. Any repairs to the paintwork which may be required will also be carried out there in accordance with our instructions. **Regular and frequent washing** is indispensable if you wish to keep the finish of your car in a good condition, for dirt may permanently damage the paintwork.

You should never wash or polish the car in the sunshine or while the engine hood is warm.

At first wash the car thoroughly with a weak spray which will loosen any caked dirt and wash it away. See below for instructions on how to remove tar or dead insects.

Then wash the paintwork with a soft, clean sponge, working from the top downwards. The sponge should be frequently and thoroughly rinsed in cold water to avoid scratches on the finish. Be sure to use a special sponge or a soft brush to clean the chassis and the wheels.

Afterwards, dry the car with a clean chamois skin so that the water cannot leave any spots.

If you wish to give your car a "shampoo", our service stations will tell you which brands have been tested and approved by us. Only mild products may be used and even then, care should be taken to mix them to the correct strength. You should always wash the car down with a lot of clear water afterwards to prevent the solution from drying onto the car. We advise you to apply "Mercedes-Benz synthetic resin polish" to the paintwork after it has been shampooed.

For the synthetic resin finish, we recommend "Mercedes-Benz synthetic resin polish".

This special agent can be applied with very little work, acts as a preservative and gives highly-effective results. On no account should you use abrasive products, such as nitro-lacquer polishes, standard polishes, etc.; these agents may facilitate your work but they will leave scratches on the synthetic resin finish.

The synthetic resin polish is used to remove the traces of dirt and oil, which have remained after the finish has been washed down, without scratching the paintwork; in addition, it has a preservative effect. **The finish will retain its gloss and unimpaired quality for a much longer period if it is regularly treated with synthetic resin polish at intervals of 8 to 10 weeks. Finishes of a light metallic shade require more frequent treatment.**

After the car has been washed and thoroughly dried with a chamois skin and any tar spots have been removed, the polish should be sparingly applied to clean, soft absorbent cotton. It should then be evenly applied in strokes to the paintwork until the required gloss has been achieved. The amount of pressure which you will have to apply will depend on how dirty the finish is. Finally, remove any traces of polish with clean absorbent cotton until the surface is completely free of film.

If synthetic resin polish has not been regularly looked after or has become very dull for other reasons, you will generally not be able to restore a satisfactory gloss by using synthetic resin polish any more. In that case, you can inquire about other more suitable agents at our service stations.

Spots on the paintwork, such as splashes of tar, traces of oil, dead insects, etc., can usually not be removed by washing; as a general rule, they must be removed as soon as possible, however, since they may cause permanent damage to the finish otherwise.

Tar spots should only be treated with "Mercedes-Benz tar remover", since some of the other commercial products for removing tar damage the paintwork. **Dead insects** are very difficult to remove; if at all possible you should therefore try to detach them with

[1] The type of finish used on your car is mentioned on a plate under the engine hood. Different instructions apply for the care of nitro-lacquer (only supplied upon special request).

lukewarm water on the very same day. Should this prove ineffective, then a mild, 1–2% (but not more) soap solution which is free from alkalis should be used. Afterwards, you should thoroughly rinse the finish with a great deal of water.

Windows and windshield

The windshield wiper blades can be folded back, which makes it much easier to do any work at the windshield.

It is best to clean the panes with "Mercedes-Benz Window-Cleaner". This is thinly applied to the pane and after a white film has dried onto the surface, this is removed with a soft cloth. In the same way, you can wash the panes with a sponge and a solution consisting of 1 part of "Mercedes-Benz window washing compound" and 6 parts of lukewarm water; polih off with a soft cloth afterwards. Insects which are sticking to the panes should previously be detached with this solution.

A mixture of "Mercedes-Benz window washing compound" and water should also be used for the **windshield washer**; the mixing solution should be 1 : 6 in winter and 1 : 12 for the rest of the year. Be careful to keep these mixing ratios, as stronger concentrations damage the finish.

The solution which is to be used in winter (1 : 6) will not freeze until a temperature of 15.8° F (— 9° C) has been reached. If the car is parked for a longer period of time in the open air when the temperature is below 15.8° F (— 9° C), the container of the windshield washing system should be emptied.

When the windshield is being washed, the **blades of the windshield wipers** should also be cleared of accumulated dirt and sand. To do so, use a clean cloth, and wipe the rubber with soapy water or alcohol.

Moreover, it is advisable to replace the wiper blades once or twice a year by new ones.

To remove, press the small lever at the back of the wiper blade downwards and remove wiper blade. Insert the new wiper blade in the wiper arm, until it audibly clicks and the small lever snaps.

As a test, pull at the wiper blade; it should not be possible to loosen it.

Chrome-plated and light metal parts. These parts should be cleaned with water and a sponge and then rubbed dry. Remove any tar spots with "Mercedes-Benz Tar Remover" (see above); under no circumstances should you use sharp-edged tools, such as knives.

Then apply the **chrome preservative "Mercedes-Brilliant"** sparingly with a soft flannel cloth; allow it to dry for a short while and then polish the parts with a clean corner of the cloth until they are bright. This should always be done very thoroughly after the car has been washed, particularly in the winter; this method involves relatively little work and produces excellent results.

When the car has to cope with very unfavorable conditions, above all, **in the winter months,** when snow has fallen and fine gravel and salt have been strewn on the roads, we recommend using **chrome preservative paste** which is even more effective on account of its higher wax contents. Use absorbent cotton to apply and rub in the chrome preservative paste; wash off snow and salt water with warm water first. Allow the chrome parts to dry for a short while and polish with clean absorbent wool until they are bright.

Upholstery

On principle, we advise you to immediately consult one of our service stations regarding the removal of spots.

Leather upholstery should be cleaned with a soft brush or a cloth which has been dampened in a mild soap solution. Be careful not to let the water form any pools on the leather upholstery, for the water may trickle off through the seams. Coarse sand-soap and hard brushes are not suitable. The soap solution should be rinsed with clear water and the upholstery dried with a cloth. Afterwards, treat the leather with **"Mercedes-Benz Karneol"** in accordance with the instructions; make sure that no visible excess remains in the graining of the leather.

Steering wheel, lights and rubber parts

If possible, avoid touching a white steering wheel with gloves which color off or wrapping it which a colored plastic cover. Steering wheels of all colors, plastic lights, rubber parts and weather strips should only be cleaned with ordinary soapy water On no account should organic solvents (e.g. gasoline, stains remover, diluted solutions, etc.) be used.

The best way to brighten up the finish of **the instrument panel and of the wooden ornamental moldings** is to apply "Mercedes Benz synthetic resin polish" and to polish off with a soft cloth. This does not remove scratches, of course; these can only be smoothed out in a service workshop.

Cleaning and care of the top

1. Brush the top frequently with a soft brush, always working from the front to the rear; this is especially important before you wash the top.

2. Clean with a neutral detergent. The material of the top should be washed with a lot of lukewarm water and a soft brush or sponge; always work in the same direction, from the front to the rear.

3. Rinse thoroughly with clear water.

4. The top must be stretched for cleaning. Even if you only want to wash certain parts of it, it is advisable to finish by wetting the entire top; allow the stretched top to dry in the open air (but not in the sunshine).

5. If the top is very dirty, do not use gasoline or any other detergents which dissolve rubber. Any persistent spots should be removed at one of our service stations.

6. The top should occasionally be waterproofed.

7. We advise you to park in shady spots if at all possible, since prolonged exposure to the rays of the sun harms every kind of textile, color and rubber.

8. Under no circumstances should wet tops be left folded back for a longer period of time.

9. Bird excrement on the top should immediately be removed. The organic acid causes the rubber to expand and this impairs the impermeability of the top.

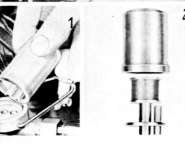

Tools: The tools which are supplied with the car, i.e. the jack with lifting support and the wrench for the wheel nuts as well as the spare wheel, are housed in the luggage compartement where they are easily accessible.

What requires regular attention?

Engine:

Checking the fan belt: as soon as the latter shows signs of being worn, have it replaced by a new one. See below for instructions on how to fit it on. Caution! Do not force the belt on with a screwdriver or some similar object. The belt should be neither too tight nor too loose. For this reason, the tension of the belt should be regularly checked: The amount by which it should be possible to depress the belt when applying moderate pressure on the generator side with the thumb must be at least 1/5″ (5 mm) and must not exceed 2/5″ (10 mm).

Readjusting the fan belt: Loosen the three (1), (2), (3) retaining nuts at the fan bracket. The tension can then be exactly adjusted with a screw wrench at the hex. nut (4) of the clamping device of the belt. Tighten the three nuts (1), (2), (3) again.

Cleaning the oil filter: (laminated filter). Loosen the nuts of the retaining screws of the housing cover and take them out together with the filter element. Disassemble the element — to do so, loosen the retaining nut in the bottom ring, after which the latter and the filter coil can be separately pulled out of the housing cover, — wash the inside and outside of the filter coil with washing gasoline, using a brush (not a wire brush) and blow through with compressed air. Reassemble filter element and housing cover and insert in the housing. At the same time make sure that the seal ring at the housing is in a good condition. Tighten the nuts of the fastening screws evenly.

Cleaning the air filter: Loosen the two knurled screws and the hose straps and take out the air filter. This filter cannot be disassembled. Dip the whole filter thoroughly rinse it in washing gasoline, allow it to dry for a short while, moisten with engine lube oil and mount again.

Cleaning the fuel pre-filter: This filter is located on the left side of the engine behind the steering housing.

To clean, loosen the knurled screw and push the clamp downwards to the side.

Remove the upper part, press the spring at the bottom of the upper part together somewhat and pull it out. Pull out the strainer and wash it well with a brush (but not a wire brush) and clean washing gasoline; thoroughly rinse the filter bowl in clean gasoline. Clean the seal ring at the lower part and make sure that it is in a good condition. Reassemble in the reverse order; make sure that the clamp is set in vertical position and the knurled screw tightened well.

The **main fuel filter** is located on the left side of the engine behind the oil filler nipple. Its element cannot be cleaned and it is essential that it be replaced by a new one at least every 15.000 miles (24 000 km): after the tension bolt on the cover of the filter housing has been loosened, the housing can be pulled out downwards. The cover is not pulled away from the engine. Take out the dirty element, clean the housing, insert the new element and fasten the housing to the cover by tightening with the tension bolt. If the fuel tends to become very dirty, it is advisable to replace the element at more frequent intervals.

Cylinder head bolts. The 300 SL has a special kind of cylinder head gasket which makes it necessary to adopt a new method of tightening the cylinder head bolts. When they are in a warm condition, the gasket must be vigorously tightened as quickly as at all possible. Should any **repairs** prove necessary, proceed as follows:

To remove the cylinder head, the bolts should be **loosened in the reverse order** to that shown in the diagram; **this should only be done when the engine is cold** .

When **mounting** the cylinder head, apply "Auto-Kollag" to the contact surfaces of the cylinder head bolts and to the washers before installation. Use quality 12 K bolts only. Tighten the cylinder head bolts with thread M 12 in the order shown in the adjoining diagram, with the following torques:

first tightening torque: up to 29 ft. lbs. (4 mkg)

second tightening torque: up to 50 ft. lbs (7 mkg)

third tightening torque: up to 72 ft. lbs. (10 mkg).

Final tigthening operation: As soon as the engine has warmed up properly, i. e. about 5 minutes after a cooling water temperature of 176° F (80° C) has been reached, retighten all M-12 bolts with a torque of 80 ft. (11 mkg).

Check-up: After the trial drive, but at the latest after covering about 12 miles (20 km), check all M-12 bolts with a torque of 80 ft. lbs. (11 mkg) when the cooling temperature amounts to about 176° F (80° C).

Tighten bolts with threat M 8 with a wrench.

After the "first" 300 miles (500 km) have been covered, the tightness of the cylinder head bolts should be checked with a torque wrench and if nec. tightened in accordance with the above-mentioned values.

Checking the valve clearance: The gap between the valve stem and the setscrew should amount to 0.003 in. (0.08 mm) at the intake valve and 0.008 in. (0.20 mm) at the exhaust valve when the engine is cold. Access is gained to the setscrews after the three knurled screws on the cylinder head cover have been loosened and removed. The clearance of a valve can only be checked when the cam no longer presses on the rocker arm, so that the valve is completely closed. If need be, the cam can be brought to the correct position by engaging the 4th gear, jacking up a rear wheel and then turning it.

Gauges which have the appropriate thickness (see above) are used to measure the valve clearance. If it is just possible to draw these gauges along between the valve stem and the setscrew, then the valve clearance is correct. When replacing the cylinder head cover, make sure that the gasket is in a good condition.

We advise you to have the valve clearance only corrected in a service workshop.

Distributor

The engine of the 300 SL Roadster is equipped with a distributor with dual breakers and with two ignition coils. The two pairs of breaker contacts are set at an angle of 180° to each other so that the distributor shaft only requires three cams. Each pair of breaker contacts therefore supplies the required ignition voltage to three cylinders through its ignition coil.

In order to guarantee the correct firing order, the plug cables must be connected to the distributor in the following way:

Cylinder 1 at the marked connection, then in clockwise direction cylinder 6, 3, 4, 2, 5. Connecting the ignition coils:

1. Ignition coil to terminals 1a or 4a as the case may be,
2. Ignition coil to terminals 1b or 4b as the case may be

of the distributor. See the electric wiring diagram on page 44.

The distributor drive shaft is lubricated by engine lube oil which is applied to an oiler which is fitted with a revolving cover. The oil level in the oiler should be checked after the "first" 300 miles (500 km) and then after every 15.000 miles (24.000 km); if nec. fill up the oiler completely with the appropriate engine lube oil. The cam axis need not be lubricated when this design of distributor is fitted and it is also not necessary to have a grease reserve at the breaker lever. Instead, the cams should be slightly greased with high-viscosity grease (Bosch grease Ft 1 v 4) every 15.000 miles (24.000 km). To do so, loosen the side holding screw of the rotor and remove the rotor and dust cover. This gives you access to the cams which should be slightly greased. Caution, keep grease off the contacts. If nec. the contacts can then be cleaned. If there are any deposits on the contacts the max. height of which exceeds 0.02 in. (0.5 mm), these should be removed with a corundum file; emery paper should not be used. Remove the file dust from the contacts and check whether the contact gap amounts to 0.011–0.013 in. (0.3–0.35 mm). The closing angle should be at 87 ± 3° distributor shaft revolutions. The closing angle should only be checked in a service workshop with a special instrument.

When correcting the contact gaps, make sure that the breaker contacts are set at an exact angle of 180° to each other and that the ignition point at the two breaker contacts is accordingly also set at an angle of 180°.

Correcting the contact gaps (A): The locking screw (2) under each breaker contact should in each case be loosened, after which the setscrew (1) at the other end of the breaker arm should be turned until the gap is correct. Turning in an anti-clockwise direction increase the gap, turning in a clockwise direction reduces it. Then tighten the locking screw (2). Moreover, if necessary, the two pairs of breaker contacts can be adjusted after the locking screws (4) and (5) have been loosened at the setscrew (3). **Make sure that there is no oil, grease, dirt or fibres on the contacts.**

Crank the engine – this is best done by turning a rear wheel which has been jacked up whilst the 4th gear is engaged – until the contacts are closed.

As a final check, lift each contact lever with a small wooden stick, while the ignition is switched on. If you can see a spark, the condenser and connection are in order. Otherwise, there is a defect in the condenser or in the coil; it is advisable to have this remedied in a service workshop.

Checking of the correct position of the breaker after the contact gaps have been corrected should normally only be effected on a distributor test stand. In exceptional cases, this check can be effected at the engine using a droplight and a scale on the crankshaft or with the stroboscope when the engine is running, by comparing the ignition points of cylinder 1 and cylinder 6 (same dead center marks).

Ignition timing – factory setting

The 300 SL is very sensitive as regards ignition timing. The ignition timing which will produce the best engine performance depends on the compression ratio and other factors; for this reason, it varies for each engine. The compression ratio and the ignition timing which has been specially determined for the engine involved and related to an engine speed of 5500 r. p. m. are, therefore, stamped on all engines of the 300 SL ROADSTER on the cylinder head above the chain tightener. In addition, the compression ratio is also stamped on the cylinder crankcase below the type designation plate. Moreover, a graduated scale from 50° BUDC to 20° AUDC is to be found on the flywheel of the vibration damper and a metal hand is affixed to the crankcase. In addition, there is a mark on this flywheel at 60° AUDC for the feeding end of the injection pump.

With these details, it is possible to exactly check or adjust the ignition timing with the aid of a scintillation stroboscope of high intensity such as that e. g. of Messrs. Sun, Chicago, model X–35, even if a new distributor has been installed. The engine is brought to a speed of 5500 r. p. m. The distributor must be set to completely advanced ignition. When the stroboscope ligths up, the angle value of the flywheel indicated at the cylinder head (e. g. 24° crankshaft BUDC) must appear at the metal hand of the crankcase.

Within certain limits the ignition timing can be reset at the knurled screw (7) after the locking nut (6) has been loosened:

Turning the knurled screw (7) in a clockwise direction retards the ignition, turning it in an anti-clockwise direction advances it.

Do not forget to retighten the locking screw (6) afterwards.

Spark plugs

Only those spark plugs which have been tested by us may be used. At the moment the following makes have been released:

For normal operation: BERU 260/14/3 Lu 3 or BOSCH W 260 T 20 or CHAMPION NA 10;

For races with low average speed without long straights: BOSCH W 280 T 20 or CHAMPION NA 10;

For fast races: BOSCH W 280 T 20.

The CHAMPION plug NA 12 can also be used for races, but only if a solid copper or aluminium ring 0.06 in. (1.5 mm) high is used in addition to the normal spark plug seal ring.

The free thread length from the pressed seal ring to the first full crest of the thread may not exceed 0.55 in. (14 mm) under any circumstances. This applies to all spark plugs. The specified value of the spark plugs electrode gap of 0.2 in. (0.5$^{+0.1}$ mm) must always be adhered to exactly with a 300 SL; otherwise the engine may fail to fire at high speeds and when it is subjected to high load. If the electrodes are to be re-bent, this should be effected at the outer ground electrode only and never at the middle electrode.

When looking at the spark plug face, you should remember that injection engines generally produce a somewhat lighter face than carburetor engines.

The spark plugs should be replaced by new ones every 10,000 miles (16,000 km).

Anti-interference device for radios

The cars are only equipped with anti-interference devices by us if the plant supplies them with a built-in radio set. If such a set is subsequently installed, the anti-interference devices (anti-interference resistor, condensers, etc.) must be built in too.

The size of the overall anti-interference resistor depends on the wave band in which the radio is to function. Full interference suppression for all wave bands inevitable impairs the ignition capacity for the engine as a result of the high resistance values; in view of the sporty character of the 300 SL engine, this can affect the smoothness with which it runs in the range of higher revolution speeds and engine loads.

The total of anti-interference resistors should not exceed 15.000 ohm per cylinder under any circumstances.

All anti-interference resistors should be taken out if you are going to participate in sporting events.
Our service stations will gladly give you further information about the installation of radio sets and anti-interference devices. We urgently advise you to have any subsequent installation of a radio set and of the necessary anti-interference devices only effected by one of our service stations.

1 Adjustable stop for the throttle
2 Throttle lever
3 Spring-loaded pressure pin
4 Partial-load valve
5 Idling air throttle
6 Cold start thermostat
7 Lever to actuate gate valve J
8 Gate valve J for cold start
9 Screw plug for cold start
10 Screw plug for partial-load nozzle
11 Screw plug for the idling nozzle
12 Vacuum connection to the diaphragm housing at the injection pump
13 Screw plug for cold start air nozzle

The **throttle housing** ensures in conjunction with the diaphragm housing that the fuel-air mixture is correctly dosed.
If its throttle is opened because of the accelerator pedal being depressed, the vacuum on the vacuum side is decreased. This effects the pressure ratio in the diaphragm housing through the vacuum line in such a way that the control rod of the injection pump is moved in the "full load" direction so that more fuel is injected. The engine accelerates up to the speed which corresponds to the position of the throttle. This process is reversed when the throttle is closed as a result of the accelerator pedal being released; the amount of air which is sucked in is reduced, the vacuum increases and the control rod is shifted in the "stop" direction.
When the engine is idling or during partial-load operation in the lower and medium engine speed ranges, the pressure ratio in the diaphragm housing is influenced by the connecting and disconnecting of air nozzles which are located in the throttle housing so that the best mixing ratio of fuel and air is always guaranteed. When idling, the partial-load valve is kept closed by the spring-loaded pressure pin in the throttle lever. During partial-load operation, it is opened by its spring.
The movable parts of the throttle housing should always move smoothly. A few drops of oil should therefore be applied to the spring-loaded pressure pin at the outside of the throttle housing at the throttle lever (3), the partial-load valve (4) and the bearing points for the cold start gate valve operation. The cold start gate valve and the bearing points of the throttle shaft, which are inside the throttle housing and which are accessible after the connecting hose has been removed, should also always move smoothly. Apply **only 1 drop of oil** to each of these points, however, to prevent the intake air from being fouled by oil.
Any alterations at the nozzles or adjustments at the lever and linkage positions of the throttle housing should only be effected in a service workshop.
Intake and exhaust line: Check all the nuts, in particular the flange nuts on the manifold of the exhaust line, for tight seat. Defective gaskets can be recognised
a) at the exhaust line: by blowing off
b) in the intake line: through unsatisfactory idling.

Clutch
Checking the free travel of the clutch pedal: This should amount to 1 in. (25 mm) when measured at the upper edge of the pedal plate before pressure makes itself felt. If it is less than the specified amount, readjust. To do so, loosen the counternut (1) from below, unscrew the nut (2) by a few turns until the clutch rod has been lengthened so far that the free travel amounts to 1 in. (25 mm). Tighten the counternut. If the clutch cannot be readjusted any more, call at a service workshop.

Brakes
We urgently advise you to have all work at the braking system only effected in a service workshop.

The hydraulically-operated foot brake which simultaneously acts on all 4 wheels is additionally equipped with the **Ate T 50/12 booster brake**, which is installed under the brake fluid container. Access is gained by removing a cover at the inner panel of the body, at the front, on the left, beside the driver's seat.

The booster brake Ate T 50/12 is a vacuum-assisted, hydraulic braking mechanism which exploits the pressure difference between the vacuum produced in the exhaust manifold of the engine and the atmospheric pressure and uses it as a source of energy. It reinforces the braking pressure produced in the master brake cylinder when the brake pedal is depressed and transmits this reinforced pressure to the wheel brake cylinders. This means that it relieves the driver by taking over part of the braking power. **Should the vacuum fail, then you will still be able to brake the car, but you will have to apply stronger pressure on the pedal.**

The filter element of the booster should be replaced by a new one every 10,000 miles (16,000 km), especially if you have been driving much in dusty areas. After the outer circlip has been removed, the filter disc and element can be taken out. The booster brake should be checked for leaks at all hose and screw connections every 30,000 miles (48,000 km); it is advisable to have this done in a service workshop only. The vacuum line should also be checked for leaks at the engine intake manifold and at the check valve. The vacuum line must not be contracted or clogged. If the braking system is being bled, the booster brake should also be bled at the two special bleeding screws.

The **brake fluid tank** of the master brake cylinder should always be at least ¾ full. If you notice that there is a high loss of brake fluid, then there is a leak in the brake system. Check all the lines, connections and cylinders for leaks. When filling up, only use ATE Blue Original brake fluid or Lockheed brake fluid. Caution, brake fluid corrodes, damages the paintwork and should never be allowed to come into contact with the brake linings.

The rubber parts of the braking system should never be cleaned with gasoline.

When checking the brakes before starting to drive, a certain resistance must make itself felt at the brake pedal after normal pedal travel. If this is not the case, see page 53.

How to bleed the braking system: Special tools needed to do this: 1 hose for bleeding brakes, 1 glass container.

1. The brake fluid tank should be constantly refilled while the brakes are being bled (see point 6).
2. Pull off cap at a front wheel brake cylinder and connect hose to the nipple which is now exposed.
3. Push the wrench over the bleeding hose and apply to screw for bleeding brakes.
4. Insert the other end of the hose in the glass container which should be filled with brake fluid until the hose nozzle lies under the surface of the fluid.
5. Loosen the screw for bleeding brakes by a few turns but do not unscrew completely.
6. Depress the brake pedal energetically, allowing it to return slowly to its original position, and repeat until no air bubbles appear in the glass container any more. Caution! The level of the fluid in the container should not sink right down to the bottom, otherwise air will be pumped back into the line.
7. When depressing the brake pedal for the last time, hold or clamp it in pushed down position until the screw for bleeding brakes has been completely retightened. Only then should you allow the brake pedal to return to its initial position.
8. Pull the hose out of the nipple and replace the cap.
9. Repeat this procedure at the other wheels and at the booster brake.
10. Fill up main tank and close it.

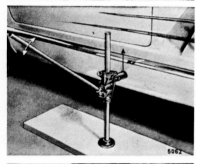

Adjusting the brakes

Foot brake: this is effected automatically and does not require any outside interference.

If the brake drums have been removed, the brake shoes must be pushed completely towards the inside over the automatic adjustment device before the drums are pulled on again. Then check whether the shoes have a full clearance within the readjusting device by lightly lifting the brake shoes (with a large screwdriver). After the drums and wheels have been mounted again, **the brake pedal should be vigorously actuated several times before starting to drive,** to ensure that the brake shoes are correctly adjusted.

Hand brake: Turn the adjusting nut at the hand brake lever to the right. Adjust so that it is still possible to easily revolve the rear wheels when the hand brake is released. The hand brake should start being effective when the hand brake lever is pulled out to the 3rd or 4th notch.

Final check: When the brakes are released and the car coasting, it should come to a standstill without any jolts. The brake drums should not have noticeably warmed up if they are felt after a drive of several miles during which the brakes were not applied.

Wheels

Greasing the front wheel bearings

Remove the rim embellisher with the flattened end of the wheel nut wrench and pull off the hub cap which is now exposed (special tool). Fill the hub cap with grease and force the grease onto the ball bearings by pressing the cap on. Replace hub cap and rembellisher.

The rear wheel bearings are greased by a grease packing which need only be renewed if any repairs are made at the rear axle.

Changing a wheel

The spare wheel, wheel nut wrench, jack and lifting pin are in the luggage compartment. The flattened end of the wheel nut wrench is used to take the rembellisher off. Before changing the wheel, the hand brake should be engaged. If possible, you should only change a wheel when the car is parked on a level piece of ground and not strongly inclined to one side. On grades, place blocks under the wheels to prevent the car from rolling downwards. Remove the rembellisher, and loosen, but do not unscrew the wheel nuts. Fit the jack into the special support of which there is one each in the center of the right and left side of the car, and jack up the car until the wheel can be easily revolved. Remove the wheel nuts and pull wheel off. Mount the new wheel as follows, using the tire lever which is included in the tool kit:

Push the tire lever through two upper wheel mounting holes and fit into the brake drum above the corresponding screws; hold your foot against it, lift the wheel with the tire lever and mount it.

Screw on all the wheel nuts but do not tighten yet. Lower the jack, and finish tightening the wheel nuts in crosswise order. Correct the tire pressure (see p. 41) and have damaged tires replaced.

Balancing the wheels

The uneven distribution of material and weight in a rotating object — wheel and tire — is known as imbalance. Excessive imbalance at the wheels may lead to steering difficulties and cause the coachwork to vibrate and the wheels to jump when driving at speeds of over 50 m. p. h. (80 km/h) even on smooth roads. Another undesirable result is that the wear on the tires is very uneven.

It is necessary to balance the wheel after a tire has been repaired or a new tire mounted. Tire wear may also gradually produce imbalance in the wheels. For this reason the running wheels should be re-balanced every 2500 miles (4000 km).

We urgently advise you to have the wheels balanced in one of our service workshops. Should circumstances compel you to call at another workshop, then the following instructions should be exactly followed: in order to avoid damaging the differential gear, the wheels should only be balanced on the front, and not on the rear axle, if this work is done at the car itself, i. e. the rear wheels should be mounted on the front axle in order to be balanced. The static method of balancing wheels generally used until now is inadequate for maximum speeds — the wheels should be balanced **dynamically.** To compensate the imbalance, **special counter-balancing weights, which may only be fastened at the special slots on both sides of the wheel flanges** and not just anywhere along the rim should be used. Normal counter-balancing weights should not be fitted between the wheel flange and the tire since there is no guarantee that they will not loosen themselves at high speeds.

In most cases, it will be found that the spot, where the counter-balancing weight should be fitted according to the information yielded by the balancing machine, does not correspond with these special slots. The counter-balancing weight which has been arrived at on the balancing machine must then be divided among 2 of the special weights so as to ensure that when these are fitted in two slots which are at a right angle to each other they produce the required compensating effect. It is advisable to use the polar diagram overleaf to subdivide the weight correctly.

After the position and amount of the counter-balancing weight have been determined with the information supplied by the balancing machine, the angle between the counter-balancing weight and the balancing slot which is located behind it in clockwise direction is measured. This is best done with the quadrant which is supplied in the car; this should be applied to the rim slots which enclose the counter-balancing weight in such a manner that the beginning (0°) will come to lie on the slot behind the weight in clockwise direction and the end (90°) on the slot in front of the weight.

156

Now the polar diagram printed below is used. The curved lines represent the amount of the counter-balancing weight (in g) while the angles (from 0° to 90°) are marked by the straight lines. You should now follow the curved line which corresponds to the weight in question (e. g. 80 g) starting from 0° to the point of intersection with the straight line of the angle of the resultant (e. g. 30°). From this point of intersection, follow

1. the horizontal line to the left and read off the weight for the slot on the scale below 0° (e. g. 70 g);
2. the vertical line downwards and read off the weight for the slot on the 90° scale (e. g. 40 g).

The weights thus arrived at should now be fastened at the 0° slot (70 g) and at the 90° slot (40 g) in accordance with the position of the quadrant. To affix the weights, the tire must be pressed off the wheel flange with commercial pliers; the end of the steel spring must be inserted in the slot and locked.

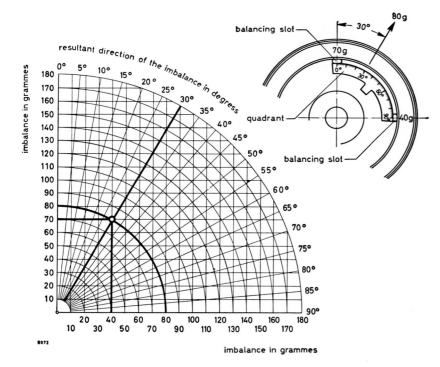

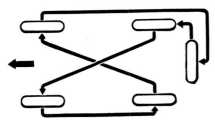

Interchanging the wheels

In order to ensure that the tires are evenly worn and to prolong their life, we urgently advise you to have the wheels interchanged every 2500 miles (4000 km) in accordance with the opposite diagram.

Tires

The high speed of Type 300 SL makes it necessary to apply a very high standard to tires, which must be extremely strong; only certain specially developed types of tire meet these requirements. Remember that even tires which have an excellent reputation and which are intended for the normal speed range of 95–100 m. p. h. (150–160 km/h), can be destroyed within a few minutes at speeds of 110–118 m. p. h. (180–190 km/h). Be sure to consult our service stations when you have to buy new tires; our personnel will be able to tell you which makes of brands have been found suitable by us as a result of conscientious tests. If you cannot consult a service station at the time, then you should buy the same type of tire as was previously used; be careful to ask not only for the same size and brand, but also for the same type designation.

Since the 300 SL can be used both as a very fast touring car and as a sports car in races, it is necessary to fit different types of tires to get the best results in each case. Depending on the wishes of the buyer, we therefore deliver the 300 SL with special touring or with super sports tires.

For normal driving. Tire size 6.70–15, type "touring special".
Design and make as specified by us.

This type of tire has the following advantages:

1. Exceptionally smooth and pleasant driving on rough roads;
2. excellent cornering qualities, particularly on slippery roads;
3. no screeching of tires, not even in sharp bends;
4. the tires will not get stuck in ruts and streetcar tracks!
5. very low tire wear.
6. With the specified tire pressure **average speeds of 112 m. p. h. (180 km/h) and a top speed up to 125 m. p. h. (200 km/h)** can be safely maintained. The resistance of the tire is therefore greater than required for reasonably careful driving on normal roads. However, the speed limits mentioned above – which are indicated on the speedometer by a red field – should not be exceeded.

Because of its above-mentioned advantages we recommend type "touring special" for all purposes, except sports events.

Tire pressure (measured when tires are cold) for type "touring special".

Front wheels: 40 psi (2.8 kg/cm²); rear wheels: 45 psi (3.2 kg/cm²).

For sporting events. Tire size 6.70/6.50–15, type **"super sport"**.
Design and make as specified by us.

This type of tire allows you to exploit the capacity of the car to the full by driving in racing style without any reservations. Of course, the contact of the tire on poor roads is then somewhat hard. If these tires are used on normal roads, the tire pressure can be lowered and the springing properties improved. It will, however, not be possible to achieve the smooth quality of the "special touring tire".

Tire pressure (measured when tires are cold) for the "super sport" type

For races, and all occasions when the car's full capacity is used	For fast driving on first-class roads and top speeds up to 135 m. p. h. (220 km/h), average speed of 125 m. p. h. (200 km/h) on the highway	For smooth driving and top speeds up to 110 m. p. h. (175 km/h), average speeds up to 100 m. p. h. (160 km/h)
Front wheels 43 p. s. i. (3 kg/cm²) Rear wheels 50 p. s. i. (3,5 kg/cm²)	31 p. s. i. (2,2 kg/cm²) at the front 34 p. s. i. (2,4 kg/cm²) at the rear	28 p. s. i. (2 kg/cm²) at the front 31 p. s. i. (2,2 kg/cm²) at the rear

Permissible pressure increase through warming up: 7 p. s. i. (0. 5 kg/cm²).
If this figure is exceeded, the tire pressure must be suitably increased in view of the conditions under which the car is running.
Before starting on a longer drive, but at least once a week, the tire pressure must be checked with the precision pressure gage which forms part of the car's equipment. Remember that the tire pressure gages at filling stations are frequently unreliable!
If the tire pressure falls by more than 2.8 p. s. i. (0.2 kg/cm²) within a week, then there is a leak at the valve or inner tube, which must be attended to as soon as possible. Usually, nails which penetrate inside do not immediately lead to complete deflation, but only to slow disinflation. During a longer drive, the damage inflicted to the tube by the foreign body constantly gets worse until, at last, the air suddenly escapes.
The deformation of the tire along the ground is larger when the tire pressure is too low than when it is correct. Even the inexperienced driver will soon notice the difference if he looks at the tires carefully. It is a very good idea to glance at the tires before every drive.

Changing the tires

First remove the valve support which is screwed on to every tire by turning the rubber valve to the left. Only a tire lever – never a sharp-edged tool – should be used to pull off the tire from the rim; do not apply any force, since the car is fitted with light-metal rims. When you fit a new inner tube, you should make sure that the size of the new tube corresponds to that of the outer cover. Insert the tube, which should be slightly inflated first, into the outer cover in such a way that the tire valve and the red point on the outer cover – which marks the point where it is lightest – lie next to each other. After it has been fitted on, inflate the tire to 57 p. s. i. (4 kg/cm²). Check the seat of the bead. Press the valve support onto the rubber valve and turn to the right so that its support base comes to lie along the rim shoulder. Inflate to the correct pressure (see above). After the inner tube has been renewed, the wheel must be re-balanced (see p. 39).

Tire wear

Sharp cornering, abrupt braking, fast getaways all result in greatly increased tire wear; on the other hand, tire wear does not rise unduly, if you drive straight ahead only at very high speeds on a highway.
In the summer, tire wear is inevitably higher than in winter since rubber is less abrasion-proof in a warm than in a cold condition.
Rough road surfaces result in greater tire wear than smooth ones.

Premature and uneven tire wear can be due to the following causes:
1. The tire pressure is too low. In that case, the tread will also be much more strongly worn along the sides than at the center.
2. Incorrect front axle toe-in. This is the case if the tires wear out prematurely but evenly along the edges. In exceptional cases, zig-zagging patches will appear in a horizontal direction.
3. Imbalance. See page 39 for balancing the wheels.
4. Defective shock absorbers.
5. Uneven pulling of the brakes.
6. Faulty camber of the front wheels or possibly a rim or half-shaft were bent by running against an obstacle.
   Points 3–6 can only be exactly checked and dealt with in a service workshop.

Care of tires. Due to the high speeds of the 300 SL Roadster, the tires require careful maintenance. The tires should be checked as often as possible for foreign bodies, which must be removed immediately; then check the tread and side walls of the tires for damage. This should always be done after having covered long distances on very bad roads, on gravel roads or if you should have got onto the sidewalk.
Worn tires **should not be re-treaded** on account of the high max. speeds.
Use only the special commercial tire paints available to brighten up the color of the tires.
Check the rims. Dented, bent or rusty rims lead to damaged beads. The rims should be de-rusted once a year.

Electric system

Battery: 12 volts, 56 Ah. It is located behind the passenger's seat under top cover compartment; it is fitted with a cover which can be removed after the retainer screws have been loosened.

Keep the outside of the battery clean and dry. The electrolyte must come up to 0.4–0.6 in. (10–15 mm) above the upper edge of the plate. Fill up with distilled water only. We warn you against using special electrolytes as they can shorten the service life of the battery. The acid density (when the temperature of the acid amounts to 68° F (20° C) of a regularly serviced battery reveals whether it is well-charged or not; you should, therefore, check the charging with a hydrometer.

Battery charged:	acid density 1.285 = 32° Bé	} If the density is too low,
Battery half-charged:	acid density 1.20 ≈ 24° Bé	} recharge from an outside
Battery not charged:	acid density 1.12 ≈ 16° Bé	} source of current.

Terminals should be washed in hot soda lye. (Caution! no lye should get into the battery). Rinse with cold water, and grease the terminals with acidproof grease.

Fuses: These are located in a small box at the front, on the right, at the dashboard (as seen in driving direction). The lead to the spark plugs does not pass through a fuse.
Note: The following consumers are switched off when the ignition key is pulled out:
Cigar lighter, windshield wiper system, signal horns, fuel gage, white control lamp for the knob "Start", defrosting equipment for stationary car, blinkers, auxiliary fuel pump, brake lights and bright beam blinking system.

List of fuses from left to right (seen facing the fuse box):

No.	Fuse element DIN 72 581	Lead	Consumers
1	8	30	Socket; electric clock
2	8	30	Clearance lights, light for interior compartment, light for glove compartment, (radio)[1]
3	25	54	Windshield wiper system, cigarette lighter, signal horns and horn relay
4	8	54	Fuel gage, control light for knob "Start", defrosting equipment[1] for stationary car right and left with control light. Idling shut-off solenoid at the throttle housing
5	8	54	Blinkers with control light, auxiliary fuel pump
6	8	54	Brake lights, bright beam blinking system
7	8	58	Back-up light, identification plate light, tail light right, parking light right
8	8	58	Instrument panel light, fog headlights, tail light left, parking light left
9	8	56 a	Bright beam control light, bright beam right
10	8	56 a	Bright beam left
11	8	56 b	Low beam right
12	8	56 b	Low beam left

[1] Only supplied upon special request.

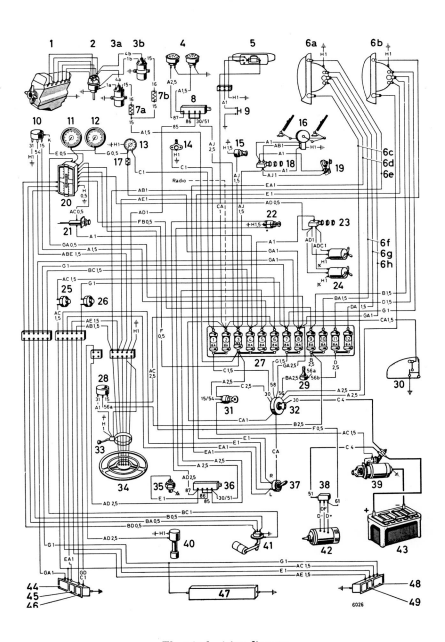

1 Engine
2 Distributor
3a 1. Ignition coil
3b 2. Ignition coil
4 Horns
5 Light for interior compartment
6a Light assembly, left [1]
6b Light assembly, right [1]
6c Cable for fog light
6d Cable for clearance lights
6e Cable for blinkers
6f Cable for bright beam light
6g Cable for low beam light
6h Cable for parking light
7a Series resistance for 1st ignition coil
7b Series resistance for 2nd ignition coil
8 Horn relay
9 Door contact switch
10 Blinker light transmitter
11 Tachometer
12 Speedometer
13 Clock
14 Socket
15 Cigarette lighter
16 Windshield wipers
17 Dimming resistance for instrument panel lighting
18 2-stage pull switch for windshield wipers
19 Switch for automatic wiper switch mechanism
20 Combi-instrument
21 Starting device
22 Pull switch for auxiliary fuel pump
23 2-stage pull switch for heater blower motors
24 Heater blower motor
25 Brake light switch
26 Back-up light switch
27 Fuses
28 Bright beam blinker transmitter
29 Low beam switch
30 Light for glove compartment
31 Ignition and starter motor switch
32 Rotary light switch
33 Bright beam blinker switch
34 Signal ring and blinker lights switch
35 Hydraulically-operated switch for auxiliary fuel pump

36 Relay for automatic auxiliary pump switching mechanism
37 Clearance lights change-over switch
38 Generator regulator
39 Starter motor 12 v
40 Auxiliary fuel pump
41 Fuel gauge
42 Generator 12 v
43 Battery 12 v
44 Tail light, brake light, clearance light – left
45 Blinker light – left
46 Back-up light
47 Identification plate light
48 Tail light, brake light, clearance light – right
49 Blinker light – right
50 Fuse
51 Relay
52 Cable connection

Colors of the leads

A = black	F = light blue
B = white	
C = red	G = gray
D = yellow	H = brown
E = green	J = lilac

Code for leads

Letter = color
Number = cross-section

Electrical wiring diagram

[1] Arrangement of electric bulbs see page 46.

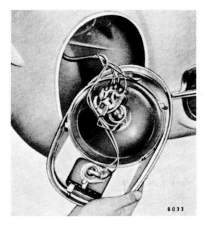

Lamp housing

The headlight and other lights are mounted in a single housing which forms an integral part of each front fender. It is only necessary to dismount this lamp housing if a bulb has to be renewed: unscrew the lens head screw at the lamp housing, below, remove the ornamental ring, after which the retaining screw can be loosened and the lamp housing lifted out of the fender. The bulbs can then be changed in the usual manner. Caution! Do not handle a bulb with damp or oily fingers, otherwise the moisture will vaporize later, settle on the reflector and dull the light which is projected to a considerable extent. Do not clean dirty bulbs with gasoline, but with alcohol. After inserting the bulb, wipe with tissue paper or some similar material.

Arrangement of the bulbs from the top downwards:

a) in the European design:

blinker light	15 watts
high-and low-beam light,	
two-filament bulb	35/35 watts
parking light	5 watts
clearance light	2 watts
fog headlight	35 watts

b) in the USA design:

Seal Beam unit	50/40 watts
fog headlight	35 watts
blinker light	15 watts
parking light	5 watts
clearance light	2 watts

Checking the headlight aiming: Place the normally loaded car on level ground at a distance of 16 ft. (5 m) from a perpendicular wall:

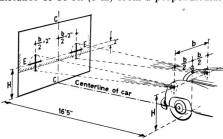

I. **Measure at the headlight lenses:**
1. Height of the central point from the ground = (H) ins. (cm)
2. Horizontal distance from each other = (b) ins. (cm)
3. Horizontal distance of each headlight from the center of the car; must in each case be half of b $\left(\frac{b}{2}\right)$.

II. **Mark on the wall:**
1. A vertical line at a right angle to the longitudinal axis of the center of the car (C–C).

2. Two setting crosses (E) in the following position:
   a) height from the ground = H ins. (cm),
   b) each cross at a horizontal distance of $\frac{b}{2}$ + 2 ins. (5 cm) from the center line.

III. **Switch on the low-beam light:**
The bright-dark limit (low-beam light) must lie 2 ins. (5 cm) under the center of the headlight (E) when the car stands at a distance of 16 ft. (5 m) from the wall. Should this not be the case, then the low-beam light can be horizontally adjusted after the ornamental ring has been removed (see above) by turning the **upper** setscrew. While a headlight is being adjusted, the other headlight and the remaining lights must be covered up.

IV. **Switch on the high-beam light:**
The spots of light projected on the wall by the headlights must correspond with the setting crosses (E). Should this not be so, then the high-beam light can be adjusted sideways by turning at the side setscrew (ornamental ring removed).

V. If the high-beam light has been readjusted laterally, then the horizontal adjustment of the low-beam light (section III) must be finally checked.

Tail light unit

The following lights are located on each side at the rear of the car in a single housing and arranged as follows from the outside inwards:

In the outer section behind the red pane:
right at the edge: two-filament bulb 5/20 watts for tail and brake light, beside it: 2 watts bulb for clearance light,

In the central section behind the orange-colored pane:
15 watts bulb for blinker light,

In the inner section behind the glass-colored pane:
only mounted in the left housing: 15 watts bulb for the back-up light.

Cooling system:

Cleaning the cooling system:

If the temperature of the cooling water gradually rises above the normal level, then the cooling system is dirty. In that case, it must be degreased, descaled, and cleaned.

Caution! Superpressure cooling system, to open, see p. 14.

a) **Degreasing:** Throw in about 2 lbs. (1 kg) of soda or about 1 lb. (0.5 kg) of P 3 at the filler cap of the water tank. Drive one day with this additive. Drain the solution at the two drain cocks – at the radiator below, on the left, and at the engine, on the left, below. Thoroughly flush the cooling system with fresh water while the engine is idling.

b) **Descaling:** Have the descaling carried out in a service workshop only. It is best to use a hydrochrome treatment since it is then possible to control the cleaning process exactly with the testing stripes supplied by the manufacturers. Closely follow the instructions given for the hydrochrome treatment:
Pour in about 0.4/0.5 imp./US pint (¼ ltr.) of hydrochrome solution into the cooling system which should be filled with untreated water, while the engine is running. Briefly dip a testing stripe through the filling opening into the cooling water after a longer drive, or, at the latest, after a day. Refer to the color scale which is supplied by the manufacturers with the testing instructions and the testing stripe to find out which pH-value corresponds to the shade on the testing stripe which has been used. If this amounts to more than 6, the cooling water should be drained, the cooling system throughly flushed again and the procedure repeated. The cleaning process is completed as soon as the pH-value remains under 6 after a longer drive. Drain off the cooling water again, thoroughly flush the cooling system and treat the cooling water which is then filled in according to the instructions (see page 14).

c) **Cleaning:** In order to thoroughly clean the radiator ribs and expel all foreign bodies, compressed air should be blown or water flushed through the radiator from the engine side. The rubber hose connection between the radiator and the pipeline should be checked for leaks and replaced if it is cracked or worn.

Dismantle the **thermostat** and clean it thoroughly.

Every 10,000 miles (16,000 km), the oil level in the water pump should be checked at the oil level control screw of the **water pump** (at the side of the bearing housing about 0.17 in. (4.5 mm) under the center of the shaft). The oil level should also be checked if the water pump was dismounted or if a replacement pump is being installed. If the oil level does not come up to the control screw, then the same hypoid oil must be filled in at the filler screw (top) as is used for the steering gear housing. At the same time, make sure that the ventilation bore in the filler screw is not clogged.

Garaging and storing the car

The garage should be airy and dry and adequately ventilated at regular intervals.

Caution! Never allow the engine to run in a closed garage, as there is a danger of poisoning.

If the car is to be stored for a longer period of time, then it must be thoroughly cleaned both outside and inside and the chassis greased with a grease gun. Check the painted parts of the body for damage, and patch up, if necessary. Apply some special protective paste to all chrome-plated parts. Check the chassis for damage to the paintwork and patch up with chassis paint. Grease all unpainted parts including the springs and spring suspension with anti-corrosive vaseline or anti-corrosive paste.

As far as the engine is concerned, the crankcase, combustion chambers, injection system, cooling system and the unpainted outside parts – the sides of the pulley, injection pump, etc. – must be given proper care before the car is stored. To do so, drain engine lube oil and replace by filling up with the normal amount of "anti-corrosive oil for engines", SAE 10 [1]; add 5% of the same "anti-corrosive oil for engines" SAE 10 to the fuel in the tank as well as to the oil in the cam space of the injection pump. Add about 6 cu. ins. (100 c.c.) (0.5%) of anti-corrosive oil which is soluble in water – see p. 14 – to the cooling water. Drive until the engine has warmed up (the cooling water temperature should amount to at least 140° F [60° C]) and then proceed to park the car as planned.

To protect the combustion chambers, unscrew the spark plugs and spray about 0.6 cu.in. (10 c.c.) of "anti-corrosive oil for engines" SAE 10 through each spark plug bore. Screw the plugs on and crank the engine with the starter motor for 1 second only. The thick high-tension cables should have been pulled out of the ignition coils previously.

Finally, the unpainted parts of the engine should be sprayed with "anti-corrosive oil for engines" SAE 10; before spraying, cover or dismount the V-belt.

The cooling water should only be drained if frosty weather is likely to occur and if no anti-freeze has been added to it. For draining, see p. 22.

If possible, the battery should be dismounted and stored in a spot where there is no danger of frost. We urge you to have the battery checked at intervals of 4–6 weeks to find out whether it is well-charged or not. If nec. the battery should be carefully re-charged.

The tires should be kept at the specified pressure. If the car is going to be stored for a longer space of time, jack it up to relieve the tires. To do so, place supports at the ends of the cross members at the rear, and at the cross members of the front axle. Do not place blocks at any other frame tubes or at the rear axle housing under any circumstances. Keep tires which have been relieved in this way inflated to a pressure of about 7–14 p.s.i. (0.5–1.0 kg/cm²).

When you take the car out of storage, check the level of the cooling water and replenish if necessary. Crank the engine with the starter motor for about 10 seconds without switching on the ignition (to do so, pull the thick high-tension cables out of the ignition coils). Then unscrew the spark plugs, clean them with gasoline and replace them.

The engine can still be run for a short while with the "anti-corrosive oil for engines"; however, this should be drained off as quickly as possible and you should then fill up with one of the normal HD-oils which have been approved by us and which are of the correct viscosity.

If you intend to store the car for longer than 6 months, you should get in touch with one of our service workshops for advice concerning additional precautions which should be taken.

[1] Our service stations will tell you which "anti-corrosive oils for engines" SAE 10 can be recommended.

Hints for emergency repairs

If you regularly service your car yourself in accordance with the maintenance instructions or, as is advisable, have this work done by our service organization, it is very unlikely indeed that your engine will not fire or that you will have to cope with any more serious trouble on the road than a tire defect.

The injection system will only function satisfactorily if it is constantly kept free of impurities. If it proves necessary to do any work at the injection system, it is, therefore, essential to prevent dirt of any kind from penetrating into the lines or connections. Should you, nevertheless, have trouble with your car, then we hope that the following hints will help you find out what is wrong and successfully deal with it. To open the engine hood, see p. 10.

The tool kit, the jack and lifting pin, the wheel nut wrench as well as the spare wheel which form part of the car's standard equipment are housed in the luggage compartment where they can easily be found.

If the car has to be towed away, the towing rope should only be fastened at the front at the bracket of the fender mounting. When driving, the rope between the two vehicles must always be stretched. The driver of the first vehicle must therefore see to it that the rope gets stretched when he starts to drive by carefully engaging the clutch; on the way, the driver of the car which is being towed away should make sure that the rope remains stretched by shrewd and prompt braking – in particular, when driving downhill.

The starter motor fails to turn over

To find out what is wrong, switch on the high-beam light first and then the starter motor. If

1. the lamps suddenly go out, then there is a poor contact at one of the two battery poles or at one of the two cable connections of the starter motor. Thoroughly clean the poles and terminals so that they are quite bright;

2. the lamps go out slowly, then the battery is insufficiently charged. Have the battery charged from an outside source of current;

3. the lamps go on burning with unimpaired brightness, then there is a defect in the starter motor itself and this can only be dealt with in a service station.

The engine does not fire although the starter motor turns over

Possible causes:

I. Mistakes on the part of the driver:
   A. No fuel in the tank. The fuel gage only indicates when the ignition is switched on; it does not indicate the last 1/1¹/₃ imp./US. gallon (5 ltrs.) any more.
      If you have driven until the fuel tank is empty, you should fill up the main filter with fuel through the filler screw.
   B. The "Start" knob has not been pulled out when the engine is cold.
   C. The auxiliary fuel pump has not been switched on when the engine is warm.
   A. Defects in the ignition system

II. Defects in the vehicle:
   Use a leather glove or a dry cloth when carrying out the following check-ups; as there is a danger that a short-circuit may occur, do not use any metal tools, but a dry piece of wood. The cable at the battery should not be loosened unless you have found out what is causing the trouble and are dealing with it.

   Check as follows: pull off the socket from a plug and unscrew the spark plug socket from the cable. Caution, take hold of the high-tension ignition cable at least 1–1.5 in. (30–40 mm) from the end. A second person should then crank the starter motor while the ignition is switched on and the clutch disengaged. At the same time, the end of the ignition cable should be kept at a distance of about 0.25–0.30 in. (7–8 mm) from the grounding cylinder block. The spark should easily jump over the gap from

161

the cable end to the cyinder block. If it fails to do so, there is a defect; in that case check

1. whether a) the lead cables to the ignition coils (terminal 15),
   b) the high-tension cables (thick) and the low-tension cables (thin) between the ignition coils and the distributor,
   c) the cables to the spark plugs

   are broken and whether they still have a good contact at the ends. Also check the spark plugs (see p. 35) to see if they are clean and have the correct electrode gap.

2. whether current reaches the ignition coils: to do so, unscrew the lead cables to the ignition coils at terminal 15. Press the loose cable end against the brass pin bushing of the hand lamp socket and hold its middle contact against the cylinder head. If the hand lamp lights up, the supply of current is satisfactory. If the lamp does not light up, either a cable is broken or the ignition lock is defective. Emergency solution: lay an emergency cable from terminal 51 (thick lead) of the generator regulator to terminal 15 of the ignition coils. This means, however, that when the engine is not running, current is constantly taken from the battery, and, for this reason, the emergency cable must always be removed when the engine is not in operation. Call at a service station and have the trouble dealt with by an expert;

3. whether the ignition coils are in order: to do so, consecutively disconnect the thin cables, which lead from the ignition coils to the condensers, terminals 1 a and 1 b of the distributor, at the distributor, press the loose cable end at the brass pin bushing of the socket of the hand lamp and hold its middle contact against the cylinder head. If the lamp does not light up and the supply of current was found to be in order when checking as described under point 2, then there is a defect in the ignition coil involved (broken wire or short-circuit in the coil); this can only be dealt with in a service workshop.

   If the lamp does light up, then connect the cables to the distributor again and check:

4. whether the distributor is in order; see p. 34.

   If the final test shows that the distributor is in a good condition and if you have not yet found the cause of the trouble, then check again:

5. whether a spark jumps over to the grounding cylinder block from an ignition cable – the socket of the spark plug should be unscrewed – when the engine is being cranked by the starter motor. Should this not be the case, then the high-tension winding of one of the ignition coils is defective and should be replaced.

B. Faulty fuel system. Possible causes:

1. Dirty fuel pre-filter. To clean, see p. 32.
2. Dirty main fuel filter: replace element, see p. 33.
3. Leaks in the pipe connections.

When it is cold, the engine fires reluctantly or stops firing after a short while:

Possible cause: the cold start gate valve sticks: make the cold start gate valve function smoothly or renew the spring, if nec. (possibly the thermostat braket is bent).

When it is hot, the engine fires reluctantly although the auxiliary fuel pump is switched on:

1. Defective auxiliary fuel pump: renew the drive motor of the pump or the pump itself, as the case may be. Check the electrical parts of the pump.
2. The check valve in the fuel line sticks: clean it.
3. Defective thermostat at the injection pump: renew thermostat.
4. The overflow valve at the injection pump sticks because dirt has got in: dismount the valve, disassemble it and clean it.

Points 3–4 can only be dealt with in a service workshop.

The engine runs irregularly when idling and in the partial-load range: Possible causes:

1. Clogged air nozzles in the throttle housing: clean the air nozzles. Location of the nozzles, see p. 36.

2. Fuel line to the fuel feed pump leaks: fit a new gasket or replace the flexible line as the case may be.
3. The overflow valve sticks: clean it.
4. Defective fuel feed pump: replace it.
5. The pressure pin in the spring-loaded stop for the partial-load valve sticks: renew spring-loaded stop. However, do not tighten the nut too much, as the pressure pin may stick otherwise.
6. There is a leak in the vacuum connection or in the vacuum line: check the vacuum.
7. There is a leak in the governor diaphragm: replace injection pump.

Points 3–7 can only be dealt with in a service workshop.

The engine "rasps" when idling

As a result of changing over to another fuel, it may prove necessary to change the idling nozzle which has been installed in the plant. Select an idling nozzle which ensures that the "rasping" is reduced to a minimum. Location of the nozzle, see p. 36.
If at all possible, the idling nozzle should only be changed in a service workshop.

The engine does not idle smoothly

The release spring does not completely close the throttle. If nec., shorten the release spring. This can only be done in a service workshop.
In new cars, the idling range of the engine tends to shift upwards after some time, since the frictional resistance in the engine falls. In that case, the idling range must be reset with the idling air throttle screw, see p. 36; this can only be effected in a service workshop.

The engine has a high fuel consumption (the exhaust emits black smoke)

Possible causes:

1. Starting device sticks: check it and the release spring.
2. An injection nozzle leaks: check the injection nozzles, and renew them, if nec.
3. The cold start thermostat is defective, the cold start gate valve does not switch itself off: install a new thermostat.
4. A vacuum line or he governor diaphragm leaks: this can only be checked and dealt with in a service workshop.

The engine runs irregularly in all ranges. Possible causes:

1. An injection line is broken: install a new line.
2. An injection nozzle functions irregularly: have injection nozzles checked in a service workshop.
3. Defective pressure valve in the injection pump: install a new injection pump.
4. Control rod sticks: install a new injection pump. After the cover has been unscrewed, the control rod can be checked for smooth functioning.
5. Fuel overflow valve at the injection pump sticks: clean it.

Points 2–5 can only be dealt with in a service workshop.

Engine stalls at high revolution speeds (output falls). Possible causes:

1. Dirty check valve in the fuel line: clean check valve.
   This can only be done in a service workshop.
2. Overflow valve at the injection pump sticks: dismount valve, disassemble it and clean it.
3. Inexact ignition timing: check the ignition timing – with a scintillation stroboscope, see p. 35.
4. Spark plugs do not function properly: clean them and check the electrode gap, see p. 35.

The red charging current lamp lights up while driving.

If the red charging control lamp lights up while driving, that is to say, in the medium and higher engine speed ranges, then there is a defect in the electrical system. Stop the car and check immediately! Possible causes:

1. **Defect in the generator;** this should be dealt with as quickly as possible, since if the generator fails, the battery will not be charged any more.

2. **V-belt loose or defective**: to readjust, see p. 32.
3. The **cable** from the charging current control lamp to the generator or from the charging current control lamp to the battery has a grounding.

The oil pressure suddenly falls. Possible causes:

1. **Too little oil.** Lack of oil can make itself noticed by the oil pressure falling when the car is cornering, whereas it still remains at the normal level as long as you are driving straight ahead: the oil level in the oil container must reach up to the 1st mark of the oil dipstick at least.
2. **The oil pressure relief valve at the engine is dirty or leaks:** Dismount the oil pressure relief valve, disassemble and clean it.
3. **The line between the engine housing and the oil filter leaks.** Tighten the connecting screws.
   If points 1–3 are in order:
4. **Check the oil pressure gage itself:** Loosen the connecting line at the filter. If oil then oozes out at the connection while the engine is running, then only the oil pressure gage itself or the line to the oil pressure gage is defective and should be replaced. Otherwise there is a defect at the engine which can only be dealt with in a service workshop.

The cooling water boils. Possible causes:

1. **Too little cooling water in the radiator. Caution! Superpressure cooling system.** The permissible cooling water temperature amounts to 239° F (115° C). **For this reason only open when the cooling water temperature is below 194° F (90° C).** First turn to 1st notch and allow the excess pressure to blow off, then go on turning and remove the cap. To close, turn until you reach the stop (2nd notch). Replenish slowly while the engine is running.
   Check the hose connections above and below between the radiator and the engine, and, if a heating unit is installed, at the right and left between the engine and the heater unit, for tight seat and tighten.
2. **The radiator may be covered up to much.**
3. **The tension of the V-belt for the fan blade and the water pump is insufficient**, see page 32, or the V-belt is torn.
4. **The radiator filler cap does not fit properly**, so that no superpressure can form. The cooling water already boils at 212° F (100° C) in that case.
5. **Defective radiator thermostat**; install a new one.
6. **The cooling water line is clogged.**
7. **Defective water pump.**
8. **Excessively retarded ignition**; in that case, the output also suffers.
9. **Defective cylinder head gaskets.**
   Points 5–9 can only be dealt with in a service workshop.

The clutch slips.

If you notice that the engine speed rises when you step on the gas pedal and that the car fails to accelerate, then the clutch is slipping. If it is absolutely unavoidable, you may still slowly drive on to the nearest repair shop, but you should make sure that the clutch does not slip when you depress the accelerator pedal. This can usually be done by engaging a lower gear. Possible causes are:
1. The clutch pedal does not have the prescribed free travel. See p. 36 to readjust.
2. The clutch has got fouled by oil.
3. A defect at the clutch facing or at the clutch itself; have it dealt with in a repair workshop.

Brakes

When checking the brakes before starting to drive, marked resistance must be felt at the brake pedal after a normal amount of travel. Should this not be so, you may have to deal with the following defects:

1. It is possible to completely depress the brake pedal when you actuate it either **quickly** or slowly. Possible causes:

a) A wheel brake cylinder or a brake line leaks. Before starting to drive, eliminate the leak by tightening the connections or call at a service workshop.
b) Defective master brake cylinder. This does not make itself noticed by an external leak. The master brake cylinder can only be reconditioned in a service workshop.

2. **The brake pedal can be almost completely depressed while an elastic resistance can be felt.**
   In that case, there is air in the brake line. Bleed as described on page 37 and if nec., fill up the brake fluid container with brake fluid.

When driving.

1. **If it is possible to push down the brake pedal completely during a longer drive down-hill:** briefly release it and actuate it twice in rapid succession, whereby resistance must make itself felt again. If the brakes still do not grip, you should bring the car to a standstill with the hand brake and, if nec., by shifting back to a lower gear.
   Check for 1 a or 1 b. Have the braking system checked in a service workshop as soon as possible.
2. **Inadequate braking power.** Possible causes:
   a) Defective brake linings: have them checked in a service workshop.
   b) Not enough vacuum in the ATE-T-50/12 booster brake as a result of a leak in the lines, in the booster brake itself, or, on the engine side, in the intake pipe or at the throttle: check all pipe connections and if nec. install new ones; if need be, have the booster brake checked in a service workshop.
3. **Retarded reaction of the brakes.** Possible causes:
   Slow increase in the vacuum in the booster brake cylinder: check the hose of the vacuum line; if it has been crushed, install a new one.
4. **Slow releasing of the brakes.** Possible causes:
   a) The pedal linkage sticks.
   b) The piston in the ATE-T-50/12 booster brake does not function smoothly; have the booster brake checked in a service workshop.
5. **Poor gradation.** Possible causes:
   a) The linkage, including the pedal, does not function smoothly; make it function smoothly; grease.
   b) The piston in the booster brake does not move smoothly; have the booster brake checked in a service workshop.
6. **Rattling brakes.** Possible causes:
   a) Brake drums are out of true (motion can be felt in the pedal): have them refinished.
   b) Burned brake linings (the brakes tend to move in jerks): exchange the linings, refinish the drums.
7. **Skewing or vibrating of the pedal when the brakes are being actuated or released.** Possible cause:
   The piston in the booster brake does not move smoothly; have the booster brake checked.
8. **The brakes do not disengage although the hand cable and pedal have been completely released.**
   Remedy:
   a) Draw off brake drums, check the shoes to see if they function smoothly and have the full clearance.
   b) Check whether the relief port in the master brake cylinder is unobstructed when the brake pedal is in initial position. To do so, remove the filler screw of the brake fluid container and depress the brake pedal: if the port is unobstructed, brake fluid gushes out when the brake pedal is actuated; should this not be the case, have the adjustment of the brake pedal checked in a service workshop.
   c) Check whether the hand brake cables move smoothly.

Defects in the electrical system

All the fuses are located in a small box on the right at the dashboard (see p. 43). Possible causes for the failure of an electrical instrument are:

1. A fuse has a bad contact: turn it, polish the contacts until they are bright, if nec.. bend the contact spring.

2. A defective fuse; it has either blown or the fuse wire has no contact in the cartridge; you cannot find this out from the outside. As replacements, use only fuses which have been soldered, welded or whose metal parts are in **one** piece.

3. Defective contact at a connection: tighten the connecting terminals.

4. Grounding in a lead: check the harness for worn spots.

5. The instrument involved is defective: it is best to have a service workshop deal with points 3 to 5.

Specifications

Engine

Type .... M 198 I

Mode of operation
four-stroke gasoline injection

No. of cylinders 6

Bore/Stroke .... 3.34/3.46 ins. (85/88 mm)

Total piston displacement
182.8 cu ins. (2996 cm³)

Compression ration .... 8.55 : 1

Output: 240 gross HP/6100 r.p.m. acc. to SAE

R. p. m. at 62 m. p. h. (100 km/h):

2520	2650	2820	3020	3190
3.25 : 1	3.42 : 1	3 64 : 1	3.89 : 1	4.11 : 1

Max. engine speed
6,400, in the gear 6000 r. p. m.

Oil capacity (tank, filter and lines), max./min. (dry sump)

for normal driving:
max. 19¹/₃/23¹/₄ imp./US pints (11 lit.)
min. 14/17 imp./US pints (8 lit.)

for sporting events:
max. 26¹/₃/31⅜ imp./US pints (15 lit.)
min. 19¹/₃/23¹/₄ imp./US pints (11 lit.)

Cooling . Water circulation through pump, thermostat with short-circuit lead, fan

Capacity of cooling system
without DB heating
4/4⁴/₅ imp./US gals. (18.25 lit.)
with DB-heating
4²/₅/5¹/₃ imp./US gals. (20.0 lit.)

Valve clearance when the engine is cold
Intake valve ...... 0.003 in. (0.08 mm)
Exhaust valve ..... 0.008 in. (0.20 mm)

Firing order
Cylinder 1 nearest radiator 1–5–3–6–2–4

Spark plugs .... see p. 35

Ignition timing control .... automatically. by centrifugal force

Factory ignition timing, stamped in at the engine .... see p. 35

Distributor .. Bosch ZV/PCS 6 R 1 Tmk.

Ignition coil (2 pieces) Bosch TK 12 A 10/1

Starter motor .. Bosch EGD 1.0/12/AR 5

Generator . Bosch LJ/GJJ 150/12–1600 R 4

Injection pump Bosch PES 6 KL 70/320 R 3

Injection nozzles . Bosch DC 10 A 30 R 6/4

Spraying pressure
570–680 p. s. i. (40–48 kg/cm²)

Feeding end................. 60° AUDC

Fuel feed pump ... Bosch FP/KLA 22 K 2

Auxiliary fuel pump...... Daimler-Benz

Oil cooling ...... Oil-air heat exchanger

Vital car statistics

Transmission .... DB-four-gear transmission, fully synchronized
Steering DB ball-type central gearshift self-adjusting recirculating steering system with steering shock absorber
Front wheel camber ....about 0°20′ to 0°45′ unloaded
King-pin inclination, related to the camber .... 2°15′ to 2°40′
Front wheel toe-in ....about 0.08–0.15 in. (2–4 mm) unloaded
Caster of front wheels .... about 5° unloaded
Camber of rear wheels .... about –3° to –4°, loaded

Rear-axle ratio	Driving speed dependent upon number of permissible max. engine revolutions				Driving speed, obtainable on level roads	Climbing ability			
	1st g. n = 6,000 app. mph	2nd g. n = 6,000 app. mph	3rd g. n = 6,000 app. mph	4th g. n = 6,400[1] app. mph	4th gear n = 6,400[1] app. mph	1st gear 1 in	2nd gear 1 in	3rd gear 1 in	4th gear 1 in
(4.11 : 1)[4]	34.8	59.6	85.0	128.0	128.0[2] 128.0[3,1]	1.1	2.40	4.0	6.6
3.89 : 1 (series USA	36.6	62.7	90.0	133.5	133.5[2] 133.5[3,1]	1.25	2.56	4.30	7.40
3.64 : 1 (series)	39.7	67.0	96.2	142.9	139.7[2] 142.9[3]	1.36	2.85	4.70	8.30
(3.42 : 1)[4]	42.2	71.4	101.8	150.2	140.9[2] 150.2[3]	1.49	3.12	5.20	9.0
(3.25 : 1)[4]	44.1	75.0	107.4	155.3	142.9[2] 142.9[3]	1.58	3.30	5.60	9.40

[1] The max. permissible engine speed of 6,400 r.p.m. must not be exceeded.
[2] Standard model with wrap around windshield and closed top.
[3] With racing windshield, co-driver seat cover and removed bumpers.
[4] Special request.

Rims .... Drop-base rims 5¹/₂ K × 15, tire pressure at the front } see p. 41
Tire size .... see p. 41, tire pressure at the rear }

Overall length .... 178 ins. (4570 mm)
Overall width ..... 70¹⁵/₃₂ ins. (1790 mm)
Overall height, unloaded about 51¹/₄″ (1300 mm)
Wheelbase .... 94¹/₂ ins. (2400 mm)
Track, front .... 55¹/₂ ins. (1398 mm)
Track, rear.......... 57 ins. (1448 mm)
Ground clearance, when car is occupied ...... about 5¹/₈ ins. (130 mm)
Dia. of turning circle about 37′9″ (11.5 m)
Top speed timed with stop watch approx. 128 to 155 m.p.h. depending on the equipment[1] of the vehicle.

[1] Depending on rear axle ratio, windshield, co-driver seat cover.

Engine lube oil consumption
about 176.5/147 m.p.imp./US pint (0.20 l/100 km)

Fuel consumption, depending on the way the car is driven 23 54/19.60 – 14.87/12.38 m.p.imp./US gal. (12–19 l/100 km)

Fuel consumption acc. to DIN 70030 22.6/18.6 miles per Imp/US gal., measured at 68 mph.

Fuel tank capacity about 22/26 imp./US gals. (100 ltrs.)

Battery .... 12 v 56 Ah

Weights

Chassis .... 2130 lbs. (970 kg)
Car weight, ready to drive (dry weight acc. to DIN 70020) depending on equipment .... 2930 lbs. (1330 kg)

Max. permissible weight 3440 lbs. (1560 kg)
Payload .... 510 lbs. (230 kg)
Permissible axle load, front .... 1565 lbs. (710 kg)
Permissible axle load, rear .... 1875 lbs. (850 kg)

Subject to modifications